and *On the Waterfront*, revealing in the process previously unknown dimensions of those works.

This book is not a final assessment of Kazan and his work, nor is it meant to be a biography. Based on interviews with Kazan and on the author's extensive knowledge of the films, plays, and novels, the book provides a long-needed overview of the work of a major cultural figure—and probably the most complete study possible for several years to come.

Thomas H. Pauly is Associate Professor of English at the University of Delaware.

AMERICAN CIVILIZATION
A series edited by Allen F. Davis

Photo Courtesy of Elia Kazan.

An American Odyssey

Elia Kazan
and American Culture

Thomas H. Pauly

Temple University Press

Temple University Press, Philadelphia 19122
© 1983 by Temple University. All rights reserved
Published 1983
Printed in the United States of America

Library of Congress Cataloging In Publication Data

Pauly, Thomas H.
  An American odyssey.
  Bibliography: p.
  Includes index.
  1. Kazan, Elia. 2. Moving-picture producers and
directors—United States—Biography. 3. Theatrical
producers and directors—United States—Biography.
4. Authors, American—20th century—Biography.
I. Title.
PN1998.A3K356 1983   791.43'0233'0924   83-399
ISBN 0-87722-296-7

Contents

Contents

Acknowledgments

I am indebted to many people for helping me to complete this study. First I would like to thank the staffs of the various libraries and research facilities that I visited: the Film and Copyright Divisions of the Library of Congress, the Theatre Division of the New York Public Library at Lincoln Center, the Wisconsin Center for Theatre Research at the University of Wisconsin and at the Archives Division of the Wisconsin State Historical Society, the Study Center and Stills Collection at the Museum of Modern Art, the theatre and film collection of the Philadelphia Free Library, and the manuscript archives of the Firestone Library at Princeton University, the Edward L. Doheny Memorial Library at the University of Southern California, and the Humanities Research Center and Hoblitzelle Theatre Arts Library at the University of Texas, along with the script collections and legal department of the Twentieth Century–Fox Studio.

I am grateful to Elia Kazan, Harold Clurman, Paul Osborne, and Audrey Wood for talking with me and to Richard Murphy, Budd Schulberg, and Walter Bernstein for corresponding with me on matters pertinent to Kazan's career. I would also like to thank Aubrey Solomon and Israel Katz for providing valuable background information for this study. Elia Kazan, Tennessee Williams, Arthur Miller, Elaine Steinbeck, Mrs. Alfredo Valente, Eileen Darby, the Humanities Research Center, and the Theatre Division of the New York Public Library were kind to grant me permission to use quotations and photos. The University of Delaware was generous in granting me funds that helped to bring this work to completion.

Acknowledgments

I want to express my gratitude to the three secretaries who helped me at various stages of this project's development—Alison Chandler, Betty Sherman, and Deborah Lyle.

I am especially indebted to the staff of Temple University Press, particularly Ken Arnold for his abiding trust in this project and Zachary Simpson whose sensitive editing enriched the finished product. Finally, words cannot express my gratitude to James Curtis for his support and helpful advice.

An
American
Odyssey

Introduction

After working in the theatre and on films, first as an actor and then as a distinguished director, Elia Kazan turned novelist. His first work, *America America*, which depicts the ordeal of a young Greek immigrating to the United States, was an extended reflection upon apects of his own struggle for success. Near the end of the story, Kazan's main character, Stavros, finds himself without the permit that will allow him to pass through customs. Driven to the brink of madness by this final setback, Stavros begins an anguished dance that draws the attention of a group of wealthy Americans. Meanwhile his fellow immigrant, Hohaness, who is deathly ill but holds a permit, slips over the side of the boat, sacrificing himself so that Stavros can enter Ellis Island.

These two characters, whose friendship spans this story of broken allegiances, exhibit contrasting attitudes that have been Kazan's obsessions. Hohaness is an impractical idealist propelled by his dream of a life free from suffering. Passionately believing that America will be the fulfillment of his hopes, he is destroyed by the ordeal of getting there and, in the process, saved from the disillusioning reality just ahead. Stavros, on the other hand, is a fighter who reaches out to people who might help him. Like Hohaness, he is a sensitive and passionate seeker for a better life, but the diverse characters he encounters consistently alter his understanding of himself and the ways of the world. With each he leaves behind an irrecoverable portion of his innocence, but, in compensation, he gains the assistance and knowledge that assure his eventual success. In their persistent quest

America America: A fateful alliance of idealism and determination. (The Museum of Modern Art/Film Stills Archives, New York.)

for the meaning of America, Kazan's plays and films were products of a similar idealism and determination—along with an equal measure of practicality and adaptability. To lack the latter qualities, as Hohaness did, was to fall by the wayside.

Kazan's drive again and again struck friends and acquaintances as frightening. "He was never a man at peace," Lee J. Cobb once observed. "Kazan, like Bonaparte [the lead character of Odets's *Golden Boy,* whom Kazan once played], was always trying to get somewhere and it seemed to many of us in the Group he would do *anything, really anything* to get there."[1] This was the Kazan who was the resourceful, hard driving pragmatist. This Kazan shrewdly assessed the difficulties confronting him and located the path through them. He was a survivor prepared to do that which was necessary to gain his objective. This was the man whose own ideas and his own advancement were to be of paramount concern, the one who in identifying with the common crowd, was intent that his be the face that was noticed.

Equally important, though less often noticed, was Kazan's sensitivity and vulnerability—qualities as crucial to the characterization of

Joe Bonaparte as they were to Hohaness and Stavros. From adolescence Kazan would be a dreamer fervently yearning for an America that would accept and respect his kind. Although he arrived in the United States when he was only three, he was to spend most of his life fighting to overcome his acute sense of alienation. Consequently he identified with the downtrodden, the rejected, and the exploited. He understood their needs, their feelings, their aspirations. By pleading their cause he discovered an outlet for his enormous energy and overcame his anonymity. Like Stavros's dance, Kazan's acting and directing transformed very intense personal feelings into arresting examples of social injustice. This sublimation gave Kazan professional purpose.

In the course of his Broadway work, Kazan was responsible for the original productions of *All My Sons, A Streetcar Named Desire, Death of a Salesman, Cat on a Hot Tin Roof,* and *J. B.* His list of films includes *Gentleman's Agreement, A Streetcar Named Desire, Viva Zapata!, On the Waterfront, East of Eden,* and *Splendor in the Grass.* Behind the critical acclaim and commercial success of these achievements lay an abiding commitment to drama critical of unhealthy American social conditions. Throughout his career, Kazan took on plays and films that ran the risk of offending his audiences. In a distinctly bold, abrasive manner, Kazan called attention to situations of alienation and oppression and challenged entrenched taboos. This demanded skillful styling and a shrewd assessment of prevailing tastes. To expose defects within the existing social order was to court objection, but to do so with sensitivity, imagination, and flair drew audiences. With his selections, Kazan proved himself to be a remarkably accomplished judge of his material and viewer expectations. For more than twenty years, he crafted riveting depictions of troubling social conditions. As a director of social problem dramas, he was without equal.

In view of this achievement, the dearth of scholarship on Kazan's career is most surprising. While there are numerous books on John Ford, Alfred Hitchcock, and Frank Capra and major studies of directors such as Henry King, Frank Boetticher, and Michael Curtiz, existing critical discussion of Kazan's work has been confined to a few unpublished dissertations and random articles. Kazan himself is partially responsible for this. For the past fifteen years, between novels, Kazan has been working on his autobiography and has adamantly refused anyone access to his large collection of scrapbooks, preparation notes, and personal letters. Until Kazan has had his own say, any biographer intrudes upon hostile territory. For this reason, my study has confined itself to Kazan's professional career and generally known facts of his personal life.

The cloud of controversy and ill will surrounding his career has also discouraged scholarship. Kazan's theatrical apprenticeship overlapped the turbulent upheaval of the Depression years and the emergence of a muscular drive for social reform. Consequently, his initial affiliation with the Group Theatre and its aspiration of bringing social consciousness to Broadway led, in turn, to active participation in the heady experiments of the left-wing theatre movement and to eventual membership in the Communist Party. Some twenty years later, after he had gained prominence on Broadway and in Hollywood, this past returned to haunt him. In 1952, he was summoned before the House Committee on Un-American Activities investigating Hollywood and pressed to account for his Communist past. With a testimony that he defended with a full page ad in the *New York Times,* Kazan carefully explained his rejection of Communism, voiced his support of the Committee's efforts, and volunteered names of former Communist associates. For this move, friends, associates, and critics branded Kazan a turncoat, a ruthless promoter of his own career, and traitor to his theatrical heritage.

In discouraging critical interest in his work and contributing to the frequent condemnation of it, this lingering distaste for Kazan's HUAC stand has prompted an even more unfortunate refusal to consider how this political about face might have affected his professional undertakings—other than the usual assumption that it enabled him to continue working. Given Kazan's preoccupation with contemporary American social problems, the sort of concern voiced in Kazan's testimony would inevitably have influenced his choice of material and his handling of it. Moreover, to the extent that the fruits of these decisions then met with commercial success or failure, they shed light upon the changing nature of America's social problems and the public response to them. For example, *Waiting for Lefty*, a cornerstone of Kazan's early career and left-wing allegiance, and *On the Waterfront*, a hard-

6

won achievement arising from the aftermath of his infamous testimony, both deal with worker exploitation by union leadership and culminate in the outspoken response of an enraged individual, but the differences in these responses and their impact upon the union membership are equally striking. In other words, the alteration in the cultural climate from the thirties to the fifties, affected Kazan's directing as much as his politics. By the same token, Kazan's undertakings were equally sensitive to changing working conditions in Hollywood and on Broadway.

Nonetheless, whatever Kazan's work reveals about American social history and the evolution of its entertainment industry, the dominant concern of this study is to follow the chronological progression of his career, to explore the factors that shaped it, and, above all, to assess his artistic achievement. "A play should hit you where you live," Kazan once commented, "but not just because it screams. It has to have something to say, but say it in terms of human beings struggling with each other, fighting. A good play has power to move you, frighten you, terrify you."[2] Kazan's work, with its aggressive appeal for audience attention and concern, has often been faulted as an exhibition of raw emotion and disregard for subtlety. Yet his charged encounters complement his material. For Kazan, violence, pain, and injury were the inevitable result of a blockage and breakdown in healthy social intercourse. Kazan also realized that to get audiences to watch what they do not want to see might call for eye-opening tactics. Kazan's pursuit of this sort of engagement was nonetheless premised upon a concerted effort to make the behavior and interaction as convincing as possible. Whatever social commentary his dramas ventured, they first had to satisfy his demand that they present human beings locked in absorbing struggles.

This approach inclined him to see large problems in terms of actual, concrete situations and the sequence of events in terms of credible motivation. Kazan was a master of realism. He presented audiences with conditions that often lay beyond the range of their experience but were presented so graphically and so skillfully that they appeared accurate and convincing—real. For all his sensitivity to the visual effects this involved and his command of the technological resources at his disposal, his artistry was always greatest in that which underlay appearances—the compelling psychology of his character's demeanor and conduct.

Kazan has insisted: "My first obligation is to the script."[3] This obligation entailed enormous care in the selection of his scripts and in the preparation of his approach which always included a searching investigation into the operative psychology of both his characters and his colleagues. Kazan has been acclaimed repeatedly for the superb performances he evoked from actors and actresses. He was also unique in getting prominent authors like Tennessee Williams, John Steinbeck, Budd Schulberg, and Arthur Miller to prepare filmscripts for him. One of the reasons this close collaboration with writers and performers was to yield such impressive results was that he brought to it such perceptive, carefully formulated understanding of how each role should be played. He invested an exceptional amount of time in getting to know the people with whom he was working; Kazan was an adept mediator and shrewd judge of talent. For Kazan, an understanding of motivation was crucial to his directorial control, and his handling of every scene was premised upon it.

At the heart of this approach was always Kazan's understanding of himself. "He does not direct," Arthur Miller once remarked, "he creates a center point, and then goes to each actor and creates the desire to move toward it. And they all meet, but for different reasons and seem to have arrived there by themselves."[4] That "center point," as Miller realized, was the core meaning Kazan saw in the drama, and over the course of his career, that meaning increasingly evidenced very personal obsessions. In this respect, Kazan's directing efforts benefitted from his Group Theatre training in the Stanislavsky method by which the performer draws upon his own experience in order to grasp the essence of the character he is portraying. Kazan's many years of psychoanalysis had an even stronger effect upon the role of his personality in his work. From his search into the confusion, compulsion, and repression behind his own behavior, Kazan developed a heightened sensitivity to the intrusion of these elements not only upon the behavior of characters in his dramas, but upon his own work. Thus Kazan's psychoanalytic quest for self-understanding evolved into a reckoning with the longing for self-expression implicit in his directing. His consequential decision to turn novelist represented a decision to display the creativity which was only implicit in his plays and films and thus often missed or misunderstood.

As products of this special sensitivity, Kazan's protagonists would again and again be tough but damaged pariahs, misunderstood victims of social injustice who are troubled by the unsustainable identities thrust upon them. Reluctantly but unavoidably they must face the truth of suppressed lies and false complacencies. Because such admissions sorely tax their willpower and usually their self-understanding, they are naturally confused and defensive. Their words turn against them and aggravate their distress. Perhaps the single most telling mark of Kazan's direction was his ability to dramatize this corrosive effect of thought and emotion. He was hardly the first director to explore the intrusion of subjective impulses upon behavior, but he broke new ground in communicating an agonized cleavage between conscious and unconscious responses.

Over the course of his career, Kazan's attitude toward these pre-occupations changed as did the expectations of his audience—the former being closely cued to the latter. During the Depression, Kazan and the country at large were intent upon effectiveness and solutions. Distress translated itself into determination and action. Thus Kazan's enter-prising fight for recognition culminated in his acclaimed portrayals of Agate and Eddie Fuseli, two characters whose intense drive and insistent demands were the direct result of frustrated longings for respect and power. For these characters, like the man playing them and the audiences impressed by them, self-consciousness was a debility, a vulnerability to be forged into steely resolution.

During the Second World War, the outbreak of which was preceded by the demise of the Group Theatre, Kazan was able to fulfill his longstanding wish to become a director. With a record of success that corroborated his remarkable talent, Kazan found himself in a position of being able to pick assignments, yet troubled by a mounting uneasiness that his work had carried him afield of the Group's dedication to theatrical excellence and heightened social consciousness. This blend of optimism and anxiety helped to attune Kazan to the spirit of the times. Just as America began the searching reappraisal of postwar adjustment, Kazan started seeing a psychiatrist (and con-tinued to do so for more than twenty years). His dramatic presentations dwelled increasingly upon the workings of the mind and more of his effort went into giving them a convincing presentation. "Psychology into behavior," as he jotted in his notebook for *Streetcar*, became the premise of his stage preparations.[5] His films, on the other hand, culti- vated documentary realism, but with increasing emphasis upon emo- tional distress and mental confusion. His distinctive brand of realism gradually evolved beyond a vivid depiction of the concrete, familiar, everyday world and sought accommodation for the mind's response to it. The formerly anguished victim of unjust circumstances turned into a person crippled by the attitudes they instilled. Social oppression be- came a mental condition. Thus Blanche DuBois, Stanley Kowalski, and Willy Loman are all debilitated by the values they have inter- nalized. At its best, it was a drama of complex characters whose peculiar behavior and twisted motives Kazan was to portray convinc- ingly and with exceptional sensitivity.

By the outbreak of the Korean War, Kazan was a director of the first rank in Hollywood and on Broadway and a leader in the resurgence of hard-hitting social drama. Two years later, his career was on the line. Rising affluence and the growing threat of Communism suddenly turned America against the self-criticism the postwar years had unleashed. Kazan found himself in the nerve-wracking position of having to clear himself before HUAC's inquisition and to win back an audience that was losing interest in the sort of drama with which he had become identified. As his work took on a McCarthyesque flavor of paranoia, his succession of triumphs gave way to a string of failures. Beleaguered by these setbacks and the ill-will generated by his testi- mony, he agonized over his renewed alienation and grew defensive. Then, with a combination of two plays and two films—*Tea and Sym- pathy* and *Cat on a Hot Tin Roof, On the Waterfront* and *East of Eden*—each of which featured a male protagonist suffering from rejec- tion for well-intentioned, misjudged waywardness, Kazan staged a spectacular comeback and reaffirmed the abiding appeal of his bruising psychological struggles.

Now in a position where he was finally free to do as he pleased, Kazan grew increasingly unsure, directionless, and discontented. His stage work deteriorated into a consolidation of his position. His films ran the gamut of material but with an emergent nostalgia for the past and

10

the bygone fights that had once given him purpose. His styling grew mannered and was decried by critics as frenzied and hysterical. Finally, he threw up his career and in a series of fictionalized probings of his identity, vented the yearning for self-expression at the heart of his directing.

Voicing a standard criticism of Kazan's career, Robin Bean has observed, "Kazan will probably never be critically accepted as a Great *Film-maker* because he is too intensely personal in his work, and when you work entirely from within yourself you are bound to antagonize various elements, particularly the film purists!"[6] Kazan himself does not deny this criticism. "I am not, it seems to me, a very comprehensive personality," he once told a French interviewer. "I am not very catholic. I do not have very diverse tastes. I cannot make films of very different kinds, and, even, in a sense, I always make the same story (a little changed), again, and again, and again, the same." He then hastened to add, "Yet I develop, anyway I think so, I change, but as if the same thing were changing, the same current hollowing out its way, in proportion to different progressions."[7] What some have considered a weakness was, in fact, his source of strength. In the area of social problem drama, he was unmatched. Within the limits of his range, he produced remarkable variations. Again and again, his presentations evidenced innovative turns and unique shadings. In this respect, he was both a creator and a master. Until the climate of change finally eroded traditional standards of authority and social values and thereby muddied the premise of his artistry, Kazan was brilliant in attracting audiences to a harsh, upsetting view of life.

ONE

Heritage of the Outsider

Alienation characterized Kazan's formative years. He was the oddity, the misfit, the unwanted foreigner. Cursed with self-consciousness, he was reluctant to do anything that might call attention to himself and precipitate the rejection he feared. For years, he passed unnoticed, forgettable. Yet inside there smouldered an intense desire to make his presence felt. "Growing up," an early interviewer of Kazan noted, "he was an outsider who wanted in."[1] The few willing to look beyond his manifest ordinariness discovered a fierce ambition and boundless capacity for hard work. This opened doors and gradually gained him acceptance. Finally, as an actor, he won recognition in roles which exploited his former limitations.

Kazan's heritage was that of a persecuted minority. His parents were Anatolian Greeks. At the time of his birth they were living in the suburbs of Istanbul. This meant that, in the age-old struggle between the Greeks and the Turks, they were part of a small colony stranded in enemy territory. Because Greeks were rigidly excluded from all positions of power and at the mercy of the Turks in all their dealings, the livelihood of Kazan's parents hung perilously upon the measure of favor they were able to win. As Kazan has said, his family "survived by their wits [and] lived under constant threat."[2] The irresolvable uncertainties of this situation naturally made immigration a longed-for alternative. Soon after Kazan's birth in 1909, his father attempted to relocate to Berlin, but it was not until 1913, when Kazan's uncle put up the money for the expensive voyage and gave his father a job in his oriental carpet business, that the whole family arrived in the United States.

The first six years of Kazan's life in America were spent in various New York city ghettos. These years were to leave an indelible imprint upon the way Kazan talked, dressed, and carried himself, but, to the extent that Kazan was a product of his environment, New York's Lower East Side had almost the same effect as middle-class New Rochelle, where the family moved when his father's business temporarily prospered. In both places, he was the unwanted alien. "I did not play with any children until I was eleven years old," Kazan has said. "I don't remember any single 'outside' person in my life until I was eleven."[3] Only when Kazan had ranged far beyond the ghetto would he allow himself to identify with it. Interviewers repeatedly associating Kazan's rumpled clothing and effusive profanity with his slum background often miss his wily conversion of a liability into an asset. First as an actor playing sinister gangsters and then as an exceptionally engaging director, he shrewdly exploited Americans' feelings of fear and respect for the resourceful achiever who overcomes his ghetto origin while still bearing its imprint.

Kazan grew up in a large, tightly knit family. The security and interaction it naturally afforded was intensified by the strange, radically different environments the family encountered in its various relocations. Like most immigrants, the Kazans made the family circle their emotional base. Outside the home, one dutifully conformed, to the best of his ability, to the role expected of him. Only when safely removed from those responsibilities could one allow his basic feelings and needs to show. Yet Kazan found that home actually did little to allay his insecurity, in large measure because of the sharp contrast in his parents' expectations. Since his father shouldered the burden of providing for the family, he was anxious that his sons have schooling that would bring good jobs. He measured education strictly in terms of its prospective financial returns. To the eyes of the sensitive young Kazan, his father appeared a stern advocate of propriety and hard work, who insisted that his wishes be obeyed. He was a grand inquisitor forever pushing him to distinguish the "usey-less" from the "usey-ful." "My father aimed me straight at something called 'commercial course,' Kazan has said. 'Learn something usey-ful,' he would say. Then add, 'For God's sake.'"[4] He was also a failure, broken financially and emotionally during the early years of the Depression. His fervent belief in the reward for enterprise and in America as the land of opportunity, set against the grim record of his own experience, made him an obvious victim of a defective social system. Though Kazan's comments on his father are usually attended by a mixture of fear, hatred, and pity, there can be little doubt that his real feelings were a good deal less one-sided. His antagonism was grounded in respect and, for all his determination to follow a very different course, he was to be his father's son. He would later display the same obsession with practicality and achievement he always associated with his father. It is hardly coincidental that Kazan's best plays and films tend to feature a love-hate relationship between father and son—*All My Sons, Death of a Salesman, Cat on a Hot Tin Roof, East of Eden, Dark at the Top of the Stairs,* and *Splendor in the Grass.* Other works, such as *Boomerang, Panic in the Streets, On the Waterfront* and *Man on a Tightrope,* offer a similar theme of a stern older man of experience and a wayward young associate whose drive for independence is crossed with a latent admiration and affection.

Kazan's mother, on the other hand, came from a more prosperous, more cultured background than her husband and was therefore quick to defend the value of an education that offered less tangible benefits. In a manner that sharply contrasted with her husband's outspoken emphasis upon duty and responsibility, she quietly cultivated her son's feelings. She furnished compassion and encouraged him to pursue his intellectual interests. She cajoled and mollified her husband so that Kazan would be allowed time for his compulsive reading. Confined as she was to the house and the family circle, she directed his attention outward to the possibilities America offered and heightened his awareness of the limitations of their tightly enclosed world. She also helped him to effect this difficult transition by demonstrating an approach his later career would mirror. As Kazan was to describe Eddie's mother in his strongly autobiographical novel, *The Arrangement*:

She gave me my first mask of compliance. It was from her that I learned to put a smoke screen of indifference around the objec-

15

tives I wanted most, play it cool, escape all attention to myself and so not bring attention to the prize I desperately wanted. It was from her that I learned that the only way I could get the thing I wanted was to go after *it* tenaciously, yes, single-mindedly, yes, but in silence and secrecy. I learned from her how to live in the territory occupied by the enemy, gain my victory while I seemed to be bowing to his hegemony.[5]

Respecting his parents, admiring their strengths yet uncomfortably aware of their limitations, Kazan found his life at home filled with choices and decisions he preferred to avoid. Amidst these conflicting pressures school came to offer Kazan something neither parent envisioned. It was an escape, an imperfect refuge from harsh responsibilities. In later years Kazan would recall spending his youth "reading 'Tom Swift'; all books, everything."[6] When Kazan graduated from high school, his father pressed him to go into the family business or to a trade school, while his mother urged him to attend a college, believing that this would extend his exposure to America and enrich his understanding of it. Because Kazan was less opposed to his mother's advice, the path that had carried him from Istanbul to the New York ghettos to middle-class New Rochelle now led to affluent Williams College which he attended from 1926 to 1930. But the young Kazan derived little satisfaction from his apparent progress. Since his father refused to finance a "usey-less" education, Kazan had to earn his way with long hours of work as a waiter and dishwasher. Removed for the first time from the protective shelter of his family, he grew even more acutely alienated. His only friends were fellow misfits whom he would later characterize as "freaks, the Negroes, the Jews, Greeks and outsiders."[7] He continued to immerse himself in his books, which led rather naturally to a concentration in English literature in which he graduated with honors.

Not until his senior year, when he took a course from Professor A. H. Licklider, did Kazan develop an interest in the theatre. For this course, Kazan wrote a paper entitled "The Common Element in the Drama," which went on to win the Graves Prize. This discussion of audience reaction and drama's emotional impact is a revealing document of his early theatrical orientation. He finds two "problems" inherent in all theatre since primitive rituals. The first is the need for the creators of a presentation "to please the audience" and the second is to "shape their dramas so as to clearly express what is in their mind to their audience." He sees drama as the art of the people because its appeal is grounded in elemental emotions. In order to succeed it must remain constantly in touch with its primitive origins and fulfill the audience's wish to abandon itself to its feelings. "The modern definition for the stage drama," he concludes, "is that of Lucas, 'A Banquet for the Emotions.'"[8] Kazan constructs a high-minded discourse to argue that *ideas* are secondary to that emotional communication on which his future efforts would concentrate. Not until the cautious undergraduate had had some first-hand experience with the theatre would it seem to him an important vehicle for social commentary.

An even more powerful influence upon Kazan's professional future was his encounter with Russian films, particularly Eisenstein's *Potemkin*. These inspired Kazan to consider the possibility of a career in moviemaking. Unsure of a practical way of implementing this pipedream and resolved to avoid his father's business, he hit upon the idea of accompanying his roommate to the Yale Drama School with the intention of preparing for a career in films. Thus he wrote in his application for admission: "Would you advise me to work in your school if I intended to seek employment in motion pictures? I have heard that several of your pupils are holding positions in that branch of the theatre. . . . I am utterly without experience of the practical or production aspect of either stage or motion pictures."[9] In his recommendation, Professor Licklider argued that Kazan's potential more than compensated for this lack of experience. He described the young Williams undergraduate as a "quiet, unobtrusive young man, apparently of independent opinions and unusual personal character" who had shown "originality, immense industry, and the keenest interest."[10]

The "immense industry" that Licklider noted earned Kazan his famous nickname "Gadge." He was a curious mechanism in constant motion. Kazan's later reluctance to comment on the term's origin hasn't diminished its aptness. Those who knew him best would often notice that this side of Kazan's character contained a facet that was not as engaging as the tag suggests. Alan Baxter, Kazan's roommate at Williams, who coined the nickname, would always remember the frightening intensity of Kazan's driving determination. As Boris Aronson would later observe, "Gadget darted around like a man with a bomb in his belly. You never stayed near him that you weren't aware something was about to happen."[11]

Licklider's cautious recommendation was good enough to get the would-be filmmaker into the Yale Drama School, which he entered the fall of 1930. Over the next two years Kazan took standard courses in directing, voice, and diction (Yale offered no courses in acting), and Professor George Pierce Baker's playwriting seminar, which influenced Kazan much less than it did O'Neill. Meanwhile, he wrote six plays and appeared in approximately ten student productions. Because he had come to Yale with an announced intention of gaining "technical training" that would enable him "to do production and directorial work in motion pictures,"[12] Kazan made a concerted effort to learn as much as he could about costuming, scenery, lighting, and production.

During the two years he spent there, 1930 to 1932, Kazan grew increasingly aware of the contrast between Yale's gothic repose and the developing Depression largely because so many of his fellow classmates did. At Yale, for the first time, Kazan found himself among people who did not readily ascribe to the optimistic tenets of the dominant culture. There he encountered wealthy students who openly questioned their heritage. Others, who came from impoverished backgrounds and did not hide them, were not accorded second-class citizenship or ostracized. Though Yale produced few close friendships, Kazan was drawn to his classmates' push for a revitalized theatre. The frequently voiced denunciation of current offerings as mindless promotion of American life and its beneficiaries was for some a cry for change and for others a plea on behalf of their excluded experience, but above all, it was a shared belief. During his second year, Kazan appeared in an experimental production of *Merry-Go-Round*, which criticized the close ties of the underworld with police and city government and could almost be said to have provided Kazan's class with its orientation. The enthusiasm it generated, reinforced by a Provincetown Playhouse opening, inspired its student authors, Albert Maltz and George Sklar, with hopes of a Broadway run, but their failure to gain financial backing drove them to the left-wing Theatre Union, where their radical creations were to become featured offerings. Another classmate, Michael Gordon, who also worked on *Merry-Go-Round*, accompanied them to the Theatre Union and later crossed paths with Kazan at Group Theatre and Frontier Films. The close association between Kazan and Baxter that extended from Williams to Yale and involved them in *Merry-Go-Round* now carried them both to Group Theatre. The common educational experience of these men brought with it a shared commitment to drama that would be innovative in both form and social consciousness. They believed that the desperate needs spawned by the Depression necessitated that plays address themselves to pressing issues and sound the call for new solutions. Instead of a collection of individuals happily or unhappily pursuing their destiny, society now seemed an elaborate conspiracy predetermining the fate of those at the lower end of the scale. Consequently Kazan and these classmates all launched their careers with budding left-wing troupes searching for alternatives to prevailing Broadway fare that shied away from this harsh reality.

Kazan, like several students in his class, decided to skip his final year of classwork and forego his degree. He was weary of the six years he had now spent tending tables and washing dishes. He was also anxious to make some practical application of what he had learned, to do something useful. Given Kazan's ambition and filmmaking aspirations, the most logical step at this point should have led from Yale to Hollywood. By 1932, Broadway had ninety fewer shows per season than it offered in 1927, and theatres were only managing to stay lit an average of 19.6 weeks a year.[13] By 1934, 80 percent of all stage employees were estimated to be unemployed.[14] The faltering economy was just one side of this dire state of affairs. The handsome profits Broadway ran up during the 1920s were further reduced by the introduction of talking pictures. Sound gave films' ghostly images a reality that brought stage and screen into more direct competition with one another. Few trying to earn their way amidst this decline could miss Hollywood's surging prosperity. Many of the theatres that folded during the early years of the Depression promptly reopened as movie houses. Meanwhile, droves of stage people with talent were defecting to the West Coast.

But Kazan decided to head for New York instead. However much

19

this decision reflected his Yale exposure to a theatre of reform, its principle determinants were the fellow student he was planning to marry and a young instructor he had befriended. Molly Day Thacher was the granddaughter of a former Yale president. Her WASP background and polished, well-groomed manner belied her fervent commitment to the theatre. Over the course of her life, she was to be a hardworking drama critic, a perceptive play reader, and a talented playwright. As part of the vital support she was to give Kazan and his career during the difficult years following his departure from Yale, she strongly encouraged his leftist allegiances, often initiating his contacts. In the course of his concentration upon the technical aspects of theatrical production, Kazan had worked closely with Philip Barber, a young assistant professor who maintained an active association with the newly formed Group Theatre, offering technical assistance and serving on the executive committee. With Kazan he discussed the advantages of joining this innovative offshoot of the Theatre Guild. When Kazan showed interest, Barber arranged an introduction and interview.

At the time of Kazan's arrival, the Group Theatre was a year-old collection of twenty-eight players under the leadership of Harold Clurman, Lee Strasberg, and Cheryl Crawford. In the eyes of its founders, the Group's dedication to disciplined schooling and close interaction of the members, patterned after the example of the Moscow Art Theatre, was aimed at bringing the theatre more into touch with life outside its doors. The Group's aspiration to the highest level of artistic expression was coupled with a concern for social responsibility. The Group was not a self-contained community of professionals, striving to achieve its own standards of excellence. On the contrary, the very name of the organization was understood to represent a move away from the individualism that so dominated Broadway theatre of the previous decade. The commitment of the players to the interests of the Group and an on-going program of plays was designed to involve the audience more in the staged presentation. It was a practical exercise in theatrical intercourse that sought to reach beyond the narrow circle of regular playgoers and their approval and to communicate a point with relevance for American society as a whole. In his original application for funding from the Theatre Guild, Harold Clurman wrote:

20

We believe that men cannot live without giving themselves completely to some force outside themselves and that this must have
a concrete object and form which can absorb the activities of
men in their daily lives. The generations before us seemed to
have been strenuously individualistic without believing very
steadily in any particular good for their individuals. We, on the
contrary, feel that the individualism of self-assertion which made
of the ego the sole and final reality of life is self destructive, and
we believe that the individual can realize himself only by seeking
his spiritual kindred and by making of their common aspirations
and problems the object of his active devotion. We believe that
the individual can achieve his fullest stature only through the
identification of his own good with the good of his group, a
group which he himself must help to create.[15]

Applause and entertainment were the hollow goals of an age preoccupied with superficialities. Group Theatre, on the other hand, sought
a higher ideal of social interaction and communion.

If the Group had not accomplished its hoped-for revolution of
Broadway when Kazan arrived, it had managed to demonstrate that it
was a unique company with solid talent and a promising future. This
was a young company that could give Kazan valuable training and
practical experience. Here was an accommodating society of fellow
misfits with whom he might be able to overcome the reserve and guilt
engendered by his homelife and schooling. But for his first year with
the Group, he was to remain a second-class citizen, an unwanted outsider. The introduction that Barber had arranged with the Group's three
directors was disastrous. "They gave me an interview," Kazan remembered "and sat around me like three dogs around a lambchop, grilling
me."[16] Afterwards they told him they had no place for him. Refusing to
accept rejection and consequential failure, Kazan maneuvered an additional meeting with Clurman and was finally invited to attend the
Group's summer outing as a paying apprentice at $20 a week. Through-
out the summer of 1932 Kazan's self-conscious reserve, his lack of
social grace, and his awe for his associates prevented him from par-
ticipating in the interaction the situation stimulated. He managed to
learn just enough to realize how much this remarkable company had to

offer but was unable to convince them that he had something valuable to contribute. "You may have talent for something," Cheryl Crawford told him at the end, "but it certainly isn't acting. I'm afraid you'll have to go."[17]

Even though Kazan was now forced into working for his father and accepting the job he had for years avoided, he was resolved to make a place for himself in the Group. For him, as for so many other people throughout the country, this was to be a trying period of hanging on and getting by. The Group may not need him, Kazan reasoned, but that did not mean that it could not use him. So he volunteered to perform any task or errand which presented itself. Already Kazan's

Group leaders Lee Strasberg, Harold Clurman, and Cheryl Crawford: "They gave me an interview and sat around me like three dogs around a lamb chop." Then they told Kazan they could not use him. (Photo by Alfredo Valente; reproduced by permission of Mrs. Alfredo Valente and the Billy Rose Theatre Collection, The New York Public Library at Lincoln Center, Astor, Lennox and Tilden Foundations.)

22

actions were shaping the words he would have the main character of his second novel speak: "I lived on enthusiasm or, to nail it down, approval. I just had to have it."[18] Willingly, even eagerly, he typed plays and helped with programs, costumes, scenery. Besides assuming responsibility for all the petty chores connected with upcoming productions, he became the company's press agent, broadcasting every bit of news the papers might print and then carefully filing each notice in the company scrapbooks.[19] Commenting on the determination Kazan channeled into these chores, Kazan himself has said, "I looked like a hungry wolf; I was thin, my eyes were close together and I wouldn't look at anybody."[20] Such enterprising initiative and fierce loyalty did not go unnoticed amidst the trying 1932–33 season in which John Howard Lawson's *Success Story* and Dawn Powell's *Big Night* were box-office washouts. Thus, when spring of 1933 brought the Group necessary funding for its summer outing, Kazan received an invitation to participate as a nonpaying apprentice.

These summer gatherings were so closely connected to the Group's operation that they were integral to its identity. They were workshops in techniques and objectives, and their diverse exercises and discussions ranged considerably afield of the upcoming production. The development of the Group's theatrical talents received as much attention as the play being prepared. Essentially the summer camp was a concerted implementation of Constantin Stanislavsky's techniques of actor training.

Harold Clurman's twofold division of Stanislavsky's system into "work on the self" and "work on the part"[21] affords a useful way of defining the camp's major concerns. On one hand, actors practiced a spectrum of exercises to broaden the range of their skills. These consisted partly of experimentation with "affective memory": an actor was urged to recall a past experience in order to evoke the emotion associated with the dramatized action, or to play the so-called "Magic If," in which he speculated on how he would have responded were he in his character's situation ("How would I have felt were I in King Lear's position?"). Group members also devised various "improvisations." In these a performer might be given three different words—such as "sleep," "knife," and "rage"—and then be expected to shape them into a brief scenario. In a play or skit where there was dialogue, the actor might be pressed to play the situation in his own words or to render it as though he were speaking a foreign language. Or he might pantomime a familiar routine, such as brushing his teeth. Or he might invent a short skit to go with a piece of music. These had the advantage of training the actor to rely more on the devices of gesture, expression, and stance, and less upon memorized dialogue and props to communicate the point of the action. As their ultimate goal, these exercises sought to turn all the actor's movements, even his very presence, into a more realistic, more imaginative demonstration of thought and feeling. Group players appeared more convincing not only because they were better trained but also because they brought more of themselves to the roles they were playing.

These improvisations were also part of an overall design. As such, they were accompanied by a close analysis of the interrelated roles and the themes in the plays under consideration. As Kazan himself would later explain: "I think improvisation is a technique whereby, freeing yourself of the lines temporarily, you can find behavior that is truer and more original and more meaningful and expressive of what's happening. But improvisation without objectives is useless. Improvisation hinges on the word *want*. Once you set *that*, you can move. On the basis of that psychological impetus you can improve in every other way."[22] According to this logic, each play was viewed as having a "core" or "superobjective" that was reducible to a short explicit statement. Each role, as it related to this center, was similarly definable. Once this skeleton had been identified and the intended style of the production had been determined, decisions could be made regarding how particular scenes related to theme and characterization. Although this was essentially the responsibility of the director, it was presumed that the actors would assist in defining these points. These would then be made the objectives of training and rehearsal. This approach was used on all Group plays from *The House of Connelly*, its original offering in 1931, and it later served as the basis for the careful notebooks Kazan was to prepare for each production he directed. From preparation to performance, the Group sought to bring more mind and emotion to bear upon its offerings.

Kazan's second summer outing went well enough for him to win an appointment as assistant stage manager for *Men in White*, which was planned as the opener for the Group's 1933–34 season. This minor position assured Kazan of continued affiliation with the Group, but since he had also hoped that it would be accompanied with an acting role, he greeted the news with a burst of tears. As a compromise he was granted the makeshift part of an intern who pushes a stretcher on the stage, says "Hello, sweetheart" to a passing nurse, and slips into the wings.

Men in White finally brought Kazan membership in the Group when he was allowed to take the place of the regular stage manager, who decided to head for England. This play marked a turning point for the Group as well. Although the play's conflict between doctors' personal lives and their professional obligations seems trite today, Sidney Kingsley's dramatization was judged sufficiently exciting and original to be awarded the Pulitzer Prize for best play of the 1933–34 season and went on to run for almost a year. For the first time Group members were freed from the need to make harsh financial sacrifices: their capital was assured for their next production.

But along with money and recognition came the nagging sense that the Group had betrayed its founding mission. Instead of raising the social consciousness of Broadway audiences, it had merely demonstrated that the modern hospital possessed dramatic potential. To its dismay, the Group discovered other groups were upstaging it in dramatizing the pressing social issues of the moment. The rude polemical skits mounted by the Workers Laboratory Theater in the early days of the Depression had reached impressive fruition with *Peace on Earth*, written by Kazan's classmates Maltz and Sklar and presented by the newly formed Theatre Union during the same season as *Men in White*. In its review of *Men in White*, the recently founded, left-wing *New Theatre* proclaimed that the play "hasn't the guts of real drama" because "there is no bitterness against the social system . . . no protest." By contrast, the authors of *Peace on Earth* drew praise for having "plunged into the social-political whirlpool and hav[ing] emerged to say something vitally important."[23] The disturbing challenge posed by the Theatre Union would become even more painfully evident the following spring when it came out with an equally powerful *Stevedore*, while the Group foundered with *Gentlewoman*, a play which pleased no one.

The barrage of left-wing criticism directed at *Gentlewoman* so disturbed its author John Henry Lawson that he rushed off to report on the Scottsboro trial while other Group members were left in New York fretting over how best to cope with their distressed social consciences. Harold Clurman's often repeated insistence that a play need not deal with explicit problems in order to have social significance was rapidly losing support. Debate over how the Group should address itself to the deepening Depression was intensifying and drawing members toward radical alternatives. Of these none was more alluring than the blazing flame of the Communist-supported Workers Laboratory Theater (WLT). Its motto, "Theatre is a Weapon," defined its mission: its theatrical entertainment was specifically intended to make statements about current political and economic issues and to spur audiences to effective action. The various playlets and skits fashioned by the WLT, along with their accompaniment of Vaudevillean dances, songs, and recitations, were devised to attract disgruntled workers to union gatherings and to spotlight the abuses they proposed to correct. As the end to the Depression seemed remote and worker restiveness intensified, membership in WLT skyrocketed. This was followed by a proliferation of theatrical groups in New York and around the country with titles attesting to a militant alliance of worker and theatre.

Kazan was among those Group members swept up by this mounting push for reform and, like them, he gravitated toward various WLT units—The Shock Troupe, The Theater Collective, and the Theater of Action. Inspired by the political aspirations of these groups, he eagerly participated in their drive for theatrical innovation. The typical agit props that were the initial backbone of the WLT's repertoire were rude creations utilizing stylized slogans, newspaper headlines, and mass chants to make political statements—they were agitation and propaganda. Characterization was reduced to caricature. Plot, in the sense of developed action linking scene with scene, was virtually abandoned in favor of charged confrontations between examples of corrupt capitalism and their helpless victims. Injustice was paraded and reform demanded. The all important message was stressed in the rhythmic, almost ritualistic pacing that was to be a hallmark. Props and scenery were minimal, often dispensed with entirely, so that the show could be easily adapted to diverse performance sites. This was drama cued to the ongoing Depression, insistently dispensing with embellishment in order to emphasize basic issues and elemental reforms.

When Kazan first saw *The Sell-Out*, which won the 1933 competition by the League of Workers Theater, he is reported to have remarked, "This is the first time I've seen real theatre!"[24] Like so many of his fellow Group members, he was sincerely impressed by the daring and forcefulness with which the play had struck out at shoddy political handling of worker programs. Nonetheless, effective as this kind of drama was in its attack upon social abuse, Kazan could also see that it had distinct limitations. The lack of subtlety that gave the presentation power quickly rendered it trite. Moreover, in overstressing violations of human rights, these dramas failed to explore their ramifications and to persuade general audiences of the need for their action in the called-for reform. The situation was made to appear urgent without being involving. Kazan could see how the simplicity and forcefulness of these presentations might benefit enormously from heightened realism. First, focus of the drama might be shifted from generalized conditions to actual events. The effect of situational truth could then be buttressed by the behavior of the participants. The more believable their bearing and conduct, the more the audience would be inclined to sympathize with their plight and their response.

Leadership of the WLT was sufficiently sensitive to these limitations and possible improvements that by 1934, it decreed that future offerings should aim for increased realism.[25] Existing policies were amended, announcements of changes were issued, and groups were formed to implement these objectives. For Kazan, these developments transformed an initial attraction into a professional opportunity. Kazan was originally impressed by the WLT's agit prop dramas because they were using the theatre to promote the social reforms he had grown to believe were imperative. As much as he wanted to work on behalf of a cause that subsumed long standing discontents, he needed to feel that he had something valuable to contribute and to harvest professional benefits in return. He could see ways in which the WLT's move toward realism might be well served by his Group training. He also understood how the differing objectives of the Group and the WLT might be

Kazan playing Clancy in *Waiting for Lefty*: As an outraged voice from the audience, Kazan expressed social injustice and gained his first professional recognition. (Photo by Alfredo Valente; reproduced by permission of Mrs. Alfredo Valente and the Billy Rose Theatre Collection, The New York Public Library at Lincoln Center, Astor, Lennox and Tilden Foundations.)

served by more exchange. Above all, he realized that WLT furnished a testing ground for his developing skills that was not open to him within the Group.

Such logic explains why Kazan's initial involvement in left-wing activities was attended by a fling at playwriting. During 1933, he was to write two strike plays which were never produced,[26] their only value being their demonstration of how much his view of the theatre was taking on the political aggressiveness of the WLT. However, a third play, written in collaboration with Art Smith, was judged impressive enough to be published in the Summer 1934 issue of *New Masses*. It also sheds helpful light on how Kazan's developing left-wing involvements overlapped his Group training and advanced his pursuit of professional recognition.

Dimitroff consists of eleven brief scenes dramatizing the recent trial and conviction of two prominent German Communists, Ernest Thaelmann, the party head, and Ernest Togler. These two men were accused by the Nazi government of a conspiracy to burn down the Reichstag in 1933, which Hitler himself had perpetrated. In calling attention to Hitler's harsh treatment of Communists, the play denounces Nazi perversion of justice. While the playwrights aimed at exposing Germany's tyrannical social oppression, Kazan and Smith saw this problem as not confined to Germany alone. In an introductory note, they stated: "The hero of the production should be group pressure. The production of the play should be an account of how the pressure of the world proletariat forced the release of the class war prisoners."[27] In other words, the play is grounded in standard agit prop obsessions and employs some of its more distinctive techniques. In rather conventional fashion, *Dimitroff*'s rapid scene shifts and staccato dialogue exchanges emphasize the disparity between the reality of the event and public understanding of it. Likewise, the only unifying thread is an insistence upon the corruption of justice and a snowballing outrage that culminates in a final call for action. Nonetheless, *Dimitroff* contains elements that departed from conventional agit prop styling. Doctored though the events are to stress the underlying issues, they nonetheless are based upon actual, documented occurrences and real people. The play's concentration upon interrogation scenes converts ritualistic chanting into familiar dialogue and charged exchanges. *Dimitroff*'s

29

restriction of its stage action to a specific locus marks a noticeable retreat from the abstraction and surrealism so characteristic of agit prop fare.

Dimitroff also appears to have been premised upon the Group's improvisational technique. Scenes depend heavily upon their immediate intensity to hold the audience's attention. A premium is placed on the actors' ability to wring variety from the accumulated confrontations. The WLT's Sunday night programs, for which *Dimitroff* was written and first performed, always included a sampling of brief skits and mime acts. For such occasions Group members would polish up some of the more successful productions of their workshop exercises. One mime for which Kazan became distinguished was that of a surgeon performing an operation on Hitler in which he removed a host of bizarre objects only to discover his patient had no heart. The routine was obviously inspired by the Group's current production of *Men in White*, but it also evidences a reaction to Hitler that could be called the "core" of *Dimitroff*. Whether Kazan actually performed this routine as a prelude to *Dimitroff* is not clear, but, had he done so, it would have been a complement of play and exercise, purpose and performance, usually missed by audiences and players unfamiliar with the Group's approach to theatre.

Dimitroff gained attention and respect for Kazan and Smith in left-wing theatre circles. It also elevated their status within the Group. Up to this point, Crawford, Strasberg, and Clurman had maintained absolute control over the Group's operations. But the troupe's growing restiveness and recent string of failures, made some new delegation of authority imperative. Amidst the ferment of left-wing theatre circles, the leadership's dictatorial policies were driving too much energy away from the Group. Also, the Group was again laboring with a problem that was to haunt them throughout their entire existence: that of coming up with a play that would both challenge the talents of the Group and offer a reasonable prospect of success. As a stopgap measure, the triumvirate established four divisions of activity and delegated responsibility for each to selected members of the Group. Three of these sections, under the individual directorship of Sanford Meisner, Bob Lewis, and Morris Carnovsky, were charged with preparing productions of specific plays.

The fourth section, headed by Kazan and Smith, was charged with finding new playwrights and coming up with new plays. In this assignment, Kazan and Smith were not to function as mere literary agents. Their appointment came with a handful of actors that were used to develop a proposed script into a playable result. "The procedure is," as the *New York Times* reported in May 1934, "for the hopeful playwright to present a sheer scenario to the performers, discuss it with them and assist them in brief scenic inventions. If the result is dialogue or actual dramatic construction of any dimensions, an immediate record will be made and a continued effort to produce a full play along these lines."[28] Clearly this approach represented a creative implementation of the improvisational techniques held in such high esteem by the Group. It also went well beyond the usual process of separating good plays from bad ones. This fusion of directors, actors, and playwrights sought to identify weaknesses in a proposed play and suggest improvements which the playwright might develop. In such an exchange, scenes moved off the page and gave everyone a chance to see how they were developing. This was schooling for those involved, with prospective benefits for the entire company.

That Kazan and Smith should have received their charge the very month that *Dimitroff* was performed suggests that this workshop approach may have been used in the development of their play. Still, this appointment would mean little if *Dimitroff* was the major fruit. However, the playwright with whom Kazan and Smith were reported to be working most closely was Clifford Odets.

Though neither Kazan nor Smith participated in the actual writing, Odets's *Waiting for Lefty* bears enough resemblance to *Dimitroff* to suggest that this important play developed from a similar line of thinking. During the fall of 1934, Odets, who was then an actor within the Group, harboring an intense desire to become a playwright, was drawn to a taxi strike of the previous spring that had been reported in the pages of *New Masses*. In this actual event, Odets detected the same dramatic potential Kazan and Smith perceived in the trial of Thaelmann and Togler. In his concentration of this strike's development into a single angry meeting pitting disgruntled workers against corrupt union leadership, Odets likewise fashioned his creation along agit prop lines. The play spotlights a glaring social problem and recruits the

31

Kazan as Agate sounding the call for a strike at the conclusion of *Waiting for Lefty:* An outspoken defiance remarkably at odds with the self-conscious reserve of the young Kazan offstage. (Photo by Alfredo Valente; reproduced by permission of Mrs. Alfredo Valente and the Billy Rose Theatre Collection, The New York Public Library at Lincoln Center, Astor, Lennox and Tilden Foundations.)

audience to support reform. The staccato-like progression of abbreviated scenes accelerates normal dramatic tempo and impels the audience toward the play's concluding call for a strike. Of course, *Waiting for Lefty* went beyond theatre in support of a cause; it was moving drama. More significant that Odets's innovative casting of the audience as union membership trying to decide upon an appropriate course of action is his coupling of the strike scenes with vignettes illustrating the human side of the workers' situation. After watching corrupt union heads maneuver to thwart the proposed strike, the viewer is shown the personal pressure impelling the workers to take action. Each of the workers is a victim of circumstances that force him to drive a cab and deprive him of the sort of life he rightfully deserves; the familiar Depression problem of unemployment is shown to be a product of widespread social injustice against which the proposed strike holds out the prospect of constructive reform. Thus, the concluding participation of the audience in the drivers' cry for "strike" proclaims a shared refusal to accept conditions which deprive *all* enterprising citizens of the respect they deserve.

The effectiveness of these background scenes hinges upon their suggestion of pervasive social injustice and the resourcefulness of the actors in keeping the effects vivid and diversified. In challenging the performers to make full use of their improvisational skills, *Waiting for Lefty* added a dimension of realism to agit prop drama that went beyond its depiction of an event that actually occurred. Along with its tense union meeting, it presented the audience with believable situations and familiar emotions; to the extent that the audience could identify with the suffering these characters experienced, it was impelled to support their cause. *Waiting for Lefty* was a powerful vehicle for the imaginative realism sought in the Group's training efforts that also advanced the cause of reform sought by agit prop drama.

Odets finished *Waiting for Lefty* in December 1934, at an opportune moment for both the Group and Kazan. When *Gold Eagle Guy* proved the disaster everyone feared, the only project in the Group's plans was a January performance of *Waiting for Lefty* for a New Theatre Sunday program. Suddenly the company faced the hard question of whether to cut the season short or to hurry another offering into production. The excitement touched off by the initial performance of

Lefty resurrected new hope that better days lay ahead. The spontaneous fervor with which audiences joined the final call for strike affirmed the uniqueness of Odets's creation and left the Group performers with an unforgettable memory. The Group was still alive and the power of Odets's pen was finally acknowledged. Odets's full length *Awake and Sing* was now deemed worthy of Broadway and rushed into production. Its successful debut spurred the Group to give *Waiting for Lefty* a Broadway opening of its own, with the result that within the space of two months the Group had two successful productions. Suddenly the Group had fulfilled its stated mission and won the approval of Broadway audiences.

This tidal wave of good fortune carried Kazan along with it. *Waiting for Lefty* was to provide a small but critical role that allowed him to steal the show. Today Kazan is still remembered for his explosive portrayal of Agate, the worker who sounds the concluding call for a strike. Plum that this part was, it did not just fall into Kazan's lap. He first had to demonstrate that he was capable of the power it demanded. In the original New Theatre production of *Lefty*, Kazan was a strongly felt presence, but as Clancy he did not even appear on stage. When Fatt, the corrupt union president calls upon Clayton to convince his fellow taxi drivers of the futility of their proposed strike, Kazan as a voice from the audience denounced him as Fatt's pawn and gave authority to his words by revealing that he was Clayton's brother. The effect was stunning—Fatt's final defeat became only a matter of time. So successful was Kazan in setting up this downfall that he eventually won himself the right to bring it about. Presumably Kazan would have remained in his original role had the hectic course of developments not necessitated changes. When the Group's success with *Awake and Sing* generated enough confidence and funding for the Broadway opening of *Waiting for Lefty*, it left gaps in *Lefty*'s original cast. Because Edward Bromberg, the original Agate, was tied up playing Uncle Morty in *Awake and Sing*, Kazan was tapped to play Agate with all the fire of his Clancy.

In presenting a much needed outlet for Kazan's unique talent, *Waiting for Lefty* vindicated Kazan's two year struggle to overcome the Group's bleak evaluation of his acting talent. The conviction and defiance that Kazan displayed as Clancy ("the voice") and Agate was remarkably at odds with the reserve people usually noticed in the young Kazan. Yet these dispositions were not as opposed as they appeared. The ingrained hurt of rejection and compensating regimen of hard work had built up in Kazan a reservoir of anguish and anger which came spilling out in playing these characters. In these outbursts against injustice, Kazan discovered a voice that communicated his feelings and he was able to overcome the awkward self-consciousness that betrayed his earlier attempts at acting. This is not to say that Kazan's performance was a spontaneous outpouring of raw emotion. On the contrary, it was the product of careful preparation, a disciplined implementation of his training. As he was later to say, "I worked like a maniac . . . much harder than actors work today. I thought of the roles most psychologically. . . . But I was a very limited actor, I was intense, an intensity that came from all the pent-up anger in me."[29]

For Kazan, the past three years had been a rambunctious schooling in theatrical effectiveness. Amidst the disputes over objectives and methods, one obvious lesson emerged—the benefits to be gained from increased realism. From his active participation in the left-wing theatrical movement and its drive to spur social change, Kazan was to discover that its objectives and the Group's quest for more convincing characterizations did not have to be at cross purposes. Given the right mixture, presenting a believable picture of current life might legitimize a call for reform. *Waiting for Lefty* proved the point and furnished an example of social realism that Kazan was to emulate in his subsequent undertakings.

TWO

Strength and Sensitivity

During his apprenticeship, Kazan was learning how to heighten realism by reaching into himself and converting personal sensitivity into professional strength. From the Group's Stanislavsky method he had learned how to create a more believable character by sensitizing himself to the rationale governing the character's conduct and by associating the character's reactions with ones from the ken of his own experience. By approaching Odets's Clancy and Agate in this fashion, Kazan tapped a reservoir of suppressed feeling and came up with convincing depictions quite different from his normal manner. The vividly realized characters that were to distinguish Kazan's future directing efforts would be grounded in a similar sublimation of personal obsessions. For Kazan the theatre would always be introspection in pursuit of an audience. First as an actor and later as a director, Kazan would consistently relate to his characters, understand the particular cast of their behavior, and endow them with credibility by reference to his own wants and longings for approval.

A newspaper article on Kazan occasioned by his appearance in *Waiting for Lefty* noted his hope that his career would one day read as having led "from stage manager, to actor, to director."[1] Thus, amidst his first professional acclaim and without any directing experience, Kazan sensed that his future lay in shaping the drama rather than performing it. (Appropriately in the two roles which first brought him distinction, Kazan played a member of the audience who beheld the unfolding drama from its perspective and reacted in such a way as to give direction to its response.) For all its prescience, Kazan's confession gave little indication of just how he planned to engineer this difficult change of profession. Because the Group's leadership exercised uncompromising control over its productions, Kazan could see that he would have to turn elsewhere for the practical experience he needed. His most likely prospect by far lay in his close association with the WLT. Over the two years following *Waiting for Lefty*, a happy marriage was to exist between Kazan's eagerness to capitalize on his recognition as an actor and his wish to become a director, between his dedication to social reform and his drive to get ahead, between his idealism and his practicality. However, the setbacks incurred by the Group and his left-wing affiliations, coupled with their competing priorities, eventually sundered Kazan's balanced allegiances.

Kazan's involvement with the WLT gradually narrowed to a close association with a subordinate unit called the Shock Troupe. Originally formed back in 1933, this group became the backbone of the Theatre of Action, which was established early in 1935 for the express purpose of capitalizing upon the possibilities opened up by *Waiting for Lefty*. The *Daily Worker*'s announcement in February 1935 that the WLT had been renamed the Theater of Action explained that the Shock Troupe had been set up "on a full professional basis for the indoor presentation of realistic plays."[2] Its first offering was to be *The Young Go First* by Peter Martin and was to be co-directed by Alfred Saxe, a mainstay of the old WLT, along with Elia Kazan.

Kazan was awarded this assignment because his two year association with the WLT and his prominence in the Group's most recent success particularly qualified him to help the Shock Troupe fulfill its founding purpose. The original idea for *The Young Go First* sprang from Arthur Vogel's experience in the recently formed Civilian Conservation Corps, which impressed him as a boot camp preparation for war rather than invigorating, outdoor work for the unemployed young. Even though it had already been shepherded through several drafts by different Troupe members, the script was still very rough when Kazan received it. He immediately sought to tighten the work scenes and sharpen their meaning by involving the actors in a series of improvisations.[3] Through this implementation of the Group techniques presumed upon by *Dimitroff* and *Waiting for Lefty*, Kazan managed to endow *The Young Go First* with a very similar form and flavor. The result was another collection of scenes of abuse and degradation building to a final call for unified resistance. Focusing upon that same group consciousness discussed in his introduction to *Dimitroff*, Kazan planned his presentation to reflect a growing worker solidarity. Thus he staged the climactic outburst of defiance so that it came as the performers formed a large huddle.[4]

Despite Kazan's contribution, the production fell short of the high expectations attending it. The company's conviction that the time for political theatre was at hand was shaken by the play's run of only forty-eight performances. The final curtain killed much of the spirit in which this ambitious project was undertaken. Practically the only thing giving direction to the few who decided to remain with the Shock Troupe was their determination to pay off the outstanding bills. When a more modest venture was proposed for the following spring, Kazan and Saxe were again asked to co-direct. Michael Blankfort's one act play, *The Crime*, depicted a recent meat packers' strike in terms of its effect upon individual workers. The theme of corrupt leadership and the placement of characters in the audience to spur involvement echoed *Waiting for Lefty* strongly enough to make the result now seem mannered. After two Sunday performances, the Shock Troupers tossed in the towel.

Meanwhile, in the course of his work with the Theater of Action, Kazan also became associated with its film division Nykino. First he appeared as an actor in two short films, *Pie in the Sky* and "Café Universal" (which does not exist and was perhaps never assembled). Though *Pie in the Sky* was a modest undertaking that attracted little attention, it presents a revealing application of Kazan's Group training to the left-wing cause.[5] Its makers initiated the project in the fall of 1934 "to see if they couldn't do a film improvisation on what they found in the dump."[6] According to the program circulated at its premiere, *Pie in the Sky* began when Kazan gathered various discarded Christmas decorations—trees, wreaths, etc.—and incorporated them into a free-spirited rendition of a Greek Orthodox religious ceremony. New and different oddities were then introduced by the other actors as vehicles for their participation. These altered the original direction and meaning. What started out as a parody of ritualized religion took a sharp turn when the camera picked up an old sign reading WELFARE DEPT. At this

The reformed Group with Harold Clurman in charge and Kazan and Bob
Lewis his chief assistants: Having retreated from its left-wing and Hollywood
alliances, it compromised with Broadway and pursued commercial success.
(Photo by Alfredo Valente; reproduced by permission of Mrs. Alfredo Valente
and the Billy Rose Theatre Collection, The New York Public Library at
Lincoln Center, Astor, Lennox and Tilden Foundations.)

point, the actors loaded a collection of their props into the car and
returned to the city "where work was started on what is generally called
a scenario."

The completed film then represented a concerted effort to preserve the spontaneity of the original performance and to build upon its
discovered meaning. Thus it opens with a sequence, presumably shot
later, entitled "Grace and Hope." In it a minister lectures a hungry,
disheveled congregation on the solace to be gained from religion.

Meanwhile the bored Kazan and Lerner snap rubber bands and pick apart flowers as they await lunch, but when the pie is finally served, there is not enough for them. The camera then pans to a wall sign that reads: "But do not despair, dear friends, the Lord will provide." The camera next picks up the pair moving about a dump in a style obviously patterned after Charlie the Tramp. The ensuing improvisations, which couple Kazan's original religious parody with an imagined ride in a wrecked car, culminate with the two miraculously receiving another pie that also disapears before it can be eaten. The film ends with Kazan raising a clenched fist and cursing heaven. With the hungry tramps, the handout mission, and the dump serving to evoke the ongoing Depression, the activities of the performers communicate the folly of cheerful acceptance and trust in the Lord. The reference to the welfare department, linked with the parody of religious ritual, intrudes the suggestion that reliance upon the government is as foolish as trust in the Lord. Thus, the rather surrealistic styling of the presentation was shaped along the lines of agit prop's social commentary. But, in dwelling upon the comic energy and charm of the actors and not forcing them into the service of this message, *Pie in the Sky* achieved a refreshing, original result.

Two years later, Kazan served as assistant director on a much more ambitious film entitled *People of the Cumberland*. Though more ponderous, this had a more significant bearing upon Kazan's future. *People of the Cumberland* was an outgrowth of Nykino's evolution into Frontier Films. The growing emphasis upon realism, heralded by the transformation of agit prop dramas into propagandized dramatizations of actual events, persuaded Leo Hurwitz and Ralph Steiner that documentary depictions of specific, identifiable social problems were preferable to fictional commentaries like *Pie in the Sky*. These two founders of Frontier Films began making films in the belief that current newsreels were too fragmentary, too discursive, and, above all, too reluctant to plumb the social implications of their subject matter. With the foundation of Nykino, they had envisioned a "synthetic documentary film" that would "allow for more inclusive and implicative comment on our class world."[7] To their disappointment, they discovered their results to be "a conceptualized statement, a film concerned with objects and the purely external manifestation of people without their emotions

41

or motivations, a pamphlet on the screen, to which you could say 'yes' with your mind, but your emotions weren't involved."[8] Imaginative framing, cutting, and montage such as exemplified by *Pie in the Sky*, notably in the automobile sequence, exploited the film's visual potential without emotionally involving the viewer in its social message. Frontier Films was established to correct this.

Amidst this left-wing drift toward realism, the founders of Frontier could not help noticing the dazzling success of the *March of Time* series, which began appearing in 1935.[9] Louis de Rochemont's concentration upon a single topic in preference to the potpourri of the conventional newsreel, his heavy use of dramatizations and rapid cutting, along with the rousing narration of Westbrook Van Voorhis, pioneered a major breakthrough in documentary presentation. Nonetheless the longstanding commitment by organizers of Frontier Films to "the creation of a highly developed American revolutionary film that has nothing in common with Hollywood or the Hollywood production"[10] (or, by implication, *Time* magazine) made them anxious to move beyond whatever they derived from *March of Time*. Group Theatre oriented them toward the solution for which they were searching. In an article entitled "A New Approach to Film Making," Steiner and Hurwitz open with an account of the benefits they gained from a recent course on theatre direction given by Lee Strasberg. Noting the lack of available schooling for filmmakers like themselves, they itemize the special features of the Group's approach to staging plays from which they profited: a method of research for determining the basic idea of a script, the application of this finding to the production, and the stimulation of audience involvement in the presentation.[11] These techniques offered a solution to their dissatisfaction with Nykino's approach. Consequently, *Variety,* in announcing the establishment of Frontier, reported that "the organization is described as the 'Group Theatre of motion pictures.' "[12]

Kazan was appointed co-director for *People of the Cumberland* because his Group training gave him insight into what made a scene or action convincing. He was to help the film convey the authenticity of being shot on location and to get credible performances from local people. He could help with the scenario so that the depiction of ordinary situations and commonplace material would generate dramatic effect.

In its portrayal of the lives of the impoverished workers inhabiting the rural Cumberland area of Tennessee, *People of the Cumberland* promotes the cause of unionization by presenting the objectives of agit prop dramas with the persuasive realism of a documentary. Its graphic, on location depiction of these people's plight is shaped so that the problem appears upsetting *and* correctible. Close-ups of impoverished individuals, showing the failure of the promise implied in the opening montage of rolling pastoral landscape, are followed by scenes of spirited group gatherings at the Horton School and of the union's Fourth of July celebration. This progresssion from dark images of ominous isolation to bright ones of cheerful cooperation is carefully cued to the narrator's comments of "Get wise, organize" and "They're not alone anymore; they've got a union." The closing shots of water pouring over Hoover Dam, miners taking oaths, and flags waving promote the cause of unionization as a natural fruition of a healthy American spirit. For all its calculated effect of authenticity, *People of the Cumberland* exercised considerable license with its subject matter to gain audience support for its cause. The Highlander School, the union member's murder, the Fourth of July celebration, and Hoover Dam are presented in such a way that documentary shades into propaganda. In his review, Mark Van Doren worried because the makers "do not bother with evidence as a historian understands evidence." After pointing out that the Tennessee woman is not *proven* to be a Tennessee woman, he questions "whether one *must* believe the documentary film as we have it."[13] *People of the Cumberland* is a distinctly contrived portrait of its subject that cannot be understood apart from the evolving intent of its makers and the gravitation of left-wing aesthetics toward "realism." As an important first step in Kazan's career as a filmmaker, it was yet another marriage of Kazan's Group-radical allegiances. It also turned out to be a final one.

Between the spring of 1935 and the late fall of 1936, the period in which Kazan worked most actively for the Theater of Action, the Group again faced hard times. All its offerings since *Waiting for Lefty* and *Awake and Sing—Weep for the Virgins, Paradise Lost, The Case of Clyde Griffiths*—had been boxoffice flops and there was mounting feeling that, rather than products of misguided judgment or bad luck, these failures were symptomatic of a central breakdown within the

Group itself. During November and December of 1936, while the Group was fighting a losing battle to keep alive its lone attempt at a musical, *Johnny Johnson*, members became openly critical of Harold Clurman, Lee Strasberg, and Cheryl Crawford. Exactly two years after the dark, soul searching meeting that produced the decision to go ahead with *Awake and Sing*, the Group found itself locked in another fierce debate over whether to continue. With a document that Clurman would call "a landmark of our history,"[14] the Actors' Committee charged that the Group's leadership had grown aloof and insensitive to the needs and ideas of the members. On January 17, 1937, the *New York Times* announced that the Group had discontinued its activities for the season.[15] The impression left by this letter—that the company was finished—gained support when the *New York Times* carried another announcement in early April that Crawford and Strasberg had resigned from the board of directors.[16]

In dwelling on the clash of personalities and the frustrations of coming up with acceptable plays, Harold Clurman in *The Fervent Years* passes over the role that politics played in this mounting divisiveness. During this period of turmoil, rumors of the Group's drift toward Communism were so widespread, Clurman and Crawford felt compelled to issue public statements denying them.[17] In his later testimony regarding his membership in the Theater of Action and the Communist Party, Kazan was to reveal that, during the winter of 1935–36, his Communist superiors tried to get him and his fellow Group associates Bromberg, Brand, Carnovsky, Odets, and Smith "to capture the Group Theatre and make it a Communist mouthpiece." Kazan would maintain that the pressure for this coup, in conjunction with a humiliating demand that he swear strict allegiance to the Communist Party, prompted him to give up his membership.[18]

Whatever specific bones of contention may have figured in Kazan's break with the Communist Party and the Theater of Action,[19] the course of his professional development was already carrying him away from the left wing. Kazan had eagerly sought membership in the Group after Williams and Yale not simply because its founding mission gave voice to his supressed frustrations over American social injustice but also because it held the prospect of substantial benefits. In envisioning how his fierce ambition might make a valuable contribution,

Kazan's eye was shrewdly turned on the professional experience he might reap. His subsequent involvement with the WLT was essentially an extension of this thinking. He could see how his professional aspirations might be aided by the WLT's growing power and eager quest for theatrical innovation. To the extent that the Group also benefitted from this ferment, Kazan turned out to be an important intermediary. His participation in the left wing had the effect of raising his status within the Group.

By the spring of 1935, however, Kazan was beginning to question the benefits of this allegiance. The Theater of Action was running out of energy and funds; there was little likelihood that it would field more productions for him to direct. He was also being called upon to subvert the Group. Meanwhile within the Group he had become a major liaison between the members and the three heads. In serving on the Actors' Committee that presented the landmark criticisms of the leadership, he was working to promote understanding, to bring harmony, and to raise his professional worth. Even though the Group was struggling to stay alive, he remained convinced its prospects exceeded those of the Theater of Action.

Meanwhile, despite the left wing's stimulus to its creative development, the Group was moving toward a similar parting. Instead of destroying the Group as it first appeared that it might, the tempest of January 1936 actually cleared the air. From this thorough reevaluation of its purpose and operation, the Group discovered that it could not sustain its entangling left wing allegiances without destroying itself. The inherent strain of its philosophical premise and its quest for commercial success had always placed the Group in the precarious position of holding "a collective ideal in a competitive society."[20] Broadway's preoccupation with big star packages and financial success was much more in tune with the basic spirit of the competitive society from which its audience came. However objectionable they may have been, Broadway's aesthetics were securely grounded upon the economic system of the society that patronized it. Conversely, the Group's aesthetics, from its collective interaction to its critical view of American values, impelled it leftward. "From an ideal of collective acting," John Gassner has observed, "it was a short step to a more or less collective social ideal."[21] Up until 1935, there had been constant pressure from within the Group to follow this leftist bias. In large measure because the three heads, especially Clurman, fought to prevent the Group from aligning itself with any special interest, from giving up its push for Broadway success, from disregarding the allure of public recognition and acclaim, this natural drift never occurred.

Following the departure of Crawford, Strasberg and several members, Clurman gathered together a band of Group actors, including Kazan, whom he was now to characterize as "actor, friend, 'disciple,' "[22] and embarked for a six month visit to Hollywood. Having survived a threatened Communist takeover and a messy civil war, this remnant of the Group now seemed to be playing into the hands of an even more dangerous adversary. Up to this point, Hollywood had been viewed as *the* embodiment of the enemy the Group was fighting. It was frivolous, compromising, and recalcitrant. For its high salaries, people with talent were exploited. Hollywood's needs always remained the dominant consideration. What Clurman and his followers found did little to alter this bleak estimate. The picture on which they were hired to work, *Blockade*, was not made until after they were long gone. If the Group returned from Hollywood still committed to Broadway, it evidenced a new determination to be successful. By way of shaping up for its next try, the Group now took long-avoided precautions. The company was much smaller and under one head—Clurman. Gone was the old policy of distributing roles so that no one held privileged status. The Group would henceforth display its stars, and salary would be paid to only those directly involved in the current production. There was no summer workshop. The Group did not even reassemble until late August.

Its season's opener, *Golden Boy*, written by Odets while he was working in Hollywood, was almost a commentary on these modifications in the Group's former identity. Odets's dramatization of the rise and fall of Joe Bonaparte explored the cost of success—the dedication and intensity it demands, the hurt and misunderstanding it causes. At the outset of the play, Joe is a cocky young boxer who gets a chance to show his stuff when a scheduled match is jeopardized by an injury to one of the fighters. Joe's impressive showing persuades his manager that he can be turned into a meal ticket and starts Joe on the road to wealth and glory. However, this course demands that he forsake his musical talent and disregard his family's objections. In his presentation of Joe's drive for the championship, his involvement with his manager's girl friend, his alienation from his family and friends, and his final destruction, Odets turned the corrupt world of boxing into a vivid metaphor for the American way of life. The glittering opportunities of the ring were attainable only by those willing to make the sacrifice; to get to the top one had to be hard, stoic, and selfish. Odets, of course, was not the first to be attracted by the toughness demanded of the boxer, but he was one of the first to consider the possibility of his tenderness. The choice he has Joe face of becoming a boxer or a violinist, a moneymaker or an artist, was contrived, yet it provided an ideal vehicle for showing the loss in getting ahead. By making Joe first of all a man of feeling, Odets impressed upon audiences a point that was quickly to become a dramatic convention—no matter how much he may win, the boxer is a fated loser.

Golden Boy was emphatically not theatre crusading on behalf of reform. It was drama which moved away from cause in order to examine consequences. The social problem of *Golden Boy*, unlike that of *Waiting for Lefty*, is a general condition, a given, which brings the characters into conflict. This was social realism that presumed social injustice in order to plumb the depths of character that had always been the Group's dominant concern.

Golden Boy was to present Kazan with a role that would mark the zenith of his acting career. As Eddie Fuseli, he played a ruthless, uncompromising gangster who takes a personal interest in Joe and assumes control of his career. He educates Joe to the spoils, alerts him to the dangers, and arranges for him to get a shot at the champ. He is the perfect foil to Joe. In contrast to Joe's initial doubt, hesitation and concern for others, he is cold and implacable, rigidly suppressing whatever feeling he possesses. He prefigures the man Joe becomes. His mounting demands for control of Joe measures the gradual breakdown of differences between them. In the end, as though confirming his Mephistophelian function, Eddie completely owns Joe. Yet despite their initial differences, Eddie and Joe have much in common. Eddie feels more than he allows himself to show. Eddie loves Eddie above all, but he truly cares for Joe, in whom he sees a younger version of himself. His paternal concern for Joe carries with it an ingrained belief

Kazan as Eddie Fuseli in *Golden Boy:* Showing the emotional discipline needed to be a winner. *Left to right:* Joe Bonaparte (Luther Adler), Eddie Fuseli (Kazan), Moody (Roman Bohnen), and Lorna (Frances Farmer). (Photo by Alfredo Valente; reproduced by permission of Mrs. Alfredo Valente and the Billy Rose Theatre Collection, The New York Public Library at Lincoln Center, Astor, Lennox and Tilden Foundations.)

that in order to succeed, Joe must learn to be a disciplined man of iron like him.

Eddie Fuseli was an extension of another gangster, Kewpie, in Odets's *Paradise Lost*, which Kazan had played two years earlier. Not only was the playwright aware of Kazan's earlier performance when he created Fuseli, but Kazan's approach to this new and more demanding role subsumed his previous preparations. Harold Clurman had Kazan prepare for Kewpie with an improvisation in which he was to imagine himself pitching a baseball to a friend at a playground. Clurman then secretly told the catcher to pretend that he was hit with the ball. When Kazan rushed up to express his sorrow and offer to take him home, the injured catcher was instructed to say that he could not allow that because his family did not want him to go around with a person of poor background. This exercise, according to Clurman, was designed to get Kazan to realize that Kewpie was not all that bad. This unjust treatment during his youth caused him to develop the "twisted kind of hurt feeling" that has turned him into a social outcast.[23]

As Kazan played him, Kewpie's tough demeanor was a mask for a wounded sensibility. His manifest lack of feeling was a defense

Kazan as Joe Bonaparte in the road show of *Golden Boy*: A fighter as vulnerable as he was tough. *Left to right:* Lorna (Betty Furness), Joe (Kazan), Moody (Roman Bohnen), Roxy (Bob Lewis). (Photo by Alfredo Valente; reproduced by permission of Mrs. Alfredo Valente and the Billy Rose Theatre Collection, The New York Public Library at Lincoln Center, Astor, Lennox and Tilden Foundations.)

mechanism for an inherent vulnerability. Eddie Fuseli's behavior was
the product of a similar mentality. In order to communicate its paradoxical complexity, Clurman and Kazan worked out some more specific actions. At the end of Act III, scene 1 of *Golden Boy*, Joe
evidences a distress over the consequences of his boxing career that
upsets Eddie. After reminding Joe of all his support, Eddie tells him,
"Don't think so much—it could make you very sick." While delivering
this line, Kazan gave Luther Adler a pinch. As Eddie adds "You owe
me a lot—I don't like you to forget," Kazan followed his gesture of
affection with a smart slap.[24] Eddie is, of course, threatening Joe to
make him box, but he is also expressing himself and giving Joe an
important lesson in behavior: Joe must learn to be hard and overcome
any feeling for others which might impair his effectiveness. Like Kewpie, Eddie is an example of what poverty and rejection does to the
social impulse.

Whereas Agate won Kazan attention, Eddie brought him recognition as an accomplished actor, the earlier part being almost an orientation of Kazan's acting skills, which gained fullest expression in the
later one. Brooks Atkinson would describe his performance as one of
"the most effective characterizations in the cast."[25] In playing Eddie
as convincingly as he did, Kazan was to draw heavily upon that selfish
determination so evident in his own professional ambitions. Like his
Kewpie, his Eddie was no mere villain; his behavior comprehended
the cost involved. Significantly Kazan's portrayal of Eddie earned him
the role of Joe Bonaparte in the road show of *Golden Boy* where he
demonstrated that he indeed possessed those qualities Eddie strove to
suppress. Kazan's Joe was a fighter with all the sensitivity Odets
imagined. He was as vulnerable as he was tough. For Kazan, *Golden
Boy* was to possess a resonance that extended beyond the acclaim and
opportunity it brought him. Although Karl Malden and Lee J. Cobb
were playing only minor roles in *Golden Boy*, these two actors would
figure prominently in some of Kazan's greatest achievements—
notably *A Streetcar Named Desire, Death of a Salesman,* and *On the
Waterfront,* perhaps Kazan's most personal undertaking, which was to
feature another boxer's agonizing battle between the suppression of his
feelings and a compelling need to express them.

One important consequence of the Group's various changes was an opportunity for new directors. The departure of Strasberg and Crawford compelled Clurman to delegate some of his responsiblities and one of his first moves was to make Kazan a key administrative assistant. This acknowledged Kazan's long record of service to the Group and opened the prospect of even greater power. What Kazan had learned from Clurman about directing had been studiously practiced in workshop exercises and then fruitfully applied in his work for the Theater of Action and Frontier Films. Consequently no one was surprised when Kazan was appointed to direct two Robert Ardrey plays, *Casey Jones* (1938) and *Thunder Rock* (1939).

Though both plays proved to be commercial failures, Kazan's directing was generally commended. Following *Golden Boy* as they did, *Casey Jones* and *Thunder Rock* were more important for what they signified than for what they achieved: the Group was backing away from its strong social commentary of a few years earlier. Unlike *The Crime* and *People of the Cumberland*, which Kazan had directed two years before, *Casey Jones* contained no call for reform. Certainly Ardrey had ignored an obvious opportunity by concentrating on Casey's enforced retirement and not attacking a heartless industrial system for failing to provide better for one of its most devoted employees. Quick as the left-wing press was to call attention to such backsliding, Kazan welcomed these assignments because they pushed him hard to extend the range of his directing style. Staging Casey's final trip, on which he imagines the warning signal that forces his retirement, carried Kazan on a theatrical journey toward fantasy and surrealism. *Thunder Rock* likewise presented Kazan with the difficult task of staging products of the chief character's imagination. In coping as well as he did with the special demands of these scenes, Kazan demonstrated that his Group training was not the straightjacket it might have seemed. The Group's dedication to stage realism did not militate against flights of imagination. *Pie in the Sky* had certainly shown that fantasy had a place within realism and social criticism. If Ardrey's dramas failed to draw audiences, they helped Kazan gain versatility.

Meanwhile Kazan continued with his acting. From 1938 to 1941, this occupied the bulk of his time. It was almost as though Kazan were pressing to see just how far his acting talent might carry him. Much of Kazan's initial failure at acting had stemmed from his self-conscious

51

awareness that he sorely lacked the impressive good looks expected of actors. Kazan once said that when he told his father that he wanted to be an actor, "he wouldn't believe it. He said 'Go look in the mirror.' "[26] Even after Kazan had become a distinguished director, Murray Schumach identified this self-consciousness about his unattractiveness as one of Kazan's two most striking features.[27] The Group taught Kazan to disregard this liability and concentrate his energies upon making his stage presence striking and convincing. This he had proven he could do, but, in order to extend his initial success into a durable career, he realized that he would have to demonstrate greater skill and versatility. During the years following his portrayal of Eddie Fuseli, he found that there was now a market for his acting talents. Broadway and Hollywood were after him. But where would this lead? Because he portrayed such a striking Eddie Fuseli, would he be doomed to play mindless variations? Would he ever be able to maneuver from the strong supporting role to the lead? These were the questions that ran through Kazan's mind in his ensuing stage appearances. The disappointments of *Casey Jones* and *Thunder Rock* had not altered his belief that his future lay in directing but, for the time being, he was prepared to see what doors his acting might open.

As Eli Lieber in *The Gentle People*, Kazan passed up another gangster role in order to play a young Jew whose frustrating love affair demanded that he openly expose the hesitant sensitivity and soft-spoken vulnerability that his Eddie Fuseli and Joe Bonaparte both fought to suppress. For his efforts, Kazan won high marks. He was even more impressive playing the lead, Steve Takis, in Odets's *Night Music*. His blend of the driving emotional intensity so distinctive of his Agate, Kewpie, and Fuseli with the innocence, warmth, and vulnerability of his Eli moved Brooks Atkinson to write: "In Elia Kazan it [*Night Music*] presents one of the most exciting actors in America. . . . Although Elia Kazan has long been recognized as an excellent actor, he plunged into 'Night Music' with extraordinary resourcefulness-acting like an artist released from all bondage, with drive, range, and imagination."[28]

Unfortunately both plays fared poorly and closed quickly. The failure of *Night Music* sealed the fate of the Group. Rather than languish in his disappointment, Kazan ambitiously moved to promote his own career. But, try as he might, he was unable to shore up the subsequent erosion of his promise. In landing the role of Ficzur in Molnar's *Liliom* just six weeks after the closing of *Night Music*, Kazan played a low-life thief who bore superficial resemblances to Kewpie and Fuseli, but Ficzur's cardsharp displays of misdirection and his backhand mockery of his superiors exceeded Kazan's range and brought unfavorable reviews. Moving next to Hollywood, Kazan wound up in two more lackluster recastings of his earlier success. *City for Conquest* was an obvious variation upon *Golden Boy* and, as Googi, Kazan had a gangster role obviously modeled upon Eddie Fuseli. For variation, Kazan offset his expected display of hardened resolve with outbursts of spirited affection. Among friends, Kazan's Googi was a boistrous Eli, a cheerful Takis, but his drive to get ahead and to avenge his victimized friends finally transformed him into a cold ruthless Fuseli. The dedicated, compassionate musician he played in *Blues in the Night* was little more than an inflation of Googi's better side. Finally, he returned to Broadway in *Five Alarm Waltz* in a lead role patterned upon William Saroyan and conceived as a variation upon Steve Takis. The play closed in eight performances and, worse, Kazan's acting received scathing reviews.

Abruptly Kazan decided to give up acting. Embarrassed as he was by his recent efforts, he was much too tenacious to let a few setbacks defeat him. This decision was more a hard-headed evaluation of his prospects. All the work of the past three years was leading nowhere. Despite his attempts at diversity, he was rapidly getting into roles that travestied his achievements. The strong conviction he was often supposed to project was being undermined by his frustration with poorly realized characters. Moreover, like his fellow Group members, he was discovering that this background and training did not automatically open doors. The shift of taste that forced the Group to alter its fare and precipitated its dissolution also raised questions about how effective the Group performers would be with the more fanciful material then being featured. This problem was particularly acute for less proven players like Kazan. Elaborating on this decision to quit acting, Kazan once told Maurice Zolotow:

Kazan as Googi in *City for Conquest*: Determined and ruthless. (The Museum of Modern Art/Film Stills Archive, New York.)

Kazan as Eli Lieber in *The Gentle People*: Shy and sensitive. (Photo by Alfredo Valente; reproduced by permission of Mrs. Alfredo Valente and the Billy Rose Theatre Collection, The New York Public Library at Lincoln Center, Astor, Lennox and Tilden Foundations.)

You're so damn exposed. I was always a self-conscious person anyway. I didn't go into acting because I was an exhibitionist. . . . They were type-casting me anyway. I did Eddie Fuseli the gangster in *Golden Boy*, so well that all I could get were jobs as gangsters, or as Saroyan, and nobody was writing too many Saroyan parts. The hell with that. I figured directing was a more significant job. Also more steady.[29]

Hindsight enabled Kazan to present this decision to concentrate upon directing as being much simpler and more obvious than it actually was. At the time, he had not directed a play in two years and none of his assignments had been able to attract audiences. Kazan had little reason to believe he would have any better luck with directing than he had recently had with acting. All he had was a determined faith—and a decade of expert training in what made theatre alive and meaningful. This, the next few years were to confirm, would make all the difference.

THREE

The Conquest of Broadway

By 1941 the Group was dead and, like it or not, its members were on their own. Having gained prominence by their response to Depression conditions, the Group was unable to survive America's drift toward war. The telltale signs that theatrical tastes had moved away from dramas agitating on behalf of social reform were evident by the later 1930s. In trying to stay abreast of this shift,[1] the Group shied away from specific social criticisms and achieved one of its few successes with William Saroyan's *My Heart's in the Highlands*. Following Pearl Harbor, there was no mistaking this shift. Wartime audiences displayed a marked preference for fantasies, comedies, and musicals. In order to stay alive, serious drama adopted some of these elements. The threat of foreign aggressors and the need for unified retaliation squelched attacks upon domestic injustice and the residual left-wing movement was quickly channeled into the war effort. To emerge a successful director in these conditions, Kazan had to range beyond his Group training. During the difficult months ahead, he had to capitalize on whatever opportunities came his way. He had to forget his Group allegiances and concentrate upon showing that his talents could be adapted to changing times. Still he could not turn his back on the past ten years without leaving behind a crucial element of his identity.

Writing to Kazan in the aftermath of the Group's demise and reflecting upon challenges facing him, Harold Clurman gave his former charge some helpful advice. "Finding your way in a world without guarantees, without (American) safe securities," he wrote,

57

it doesn't matter if you are ambitious (and succeed or fail) in
making a theatre, or that you are in a theatre at all, or that you
knock 'em dead in Hollywood or raise peas in a garden, or are
despondent or triumphant . . . it matters that you keep your integrity of life, your sense of life; life itself will provide the particular problems and place for your life to work on and from
working on it with whatever life you have you will carry out the
"mission" of life that is within you to perform to "contribute."[2]

In urging Kazan to hold onto his integrity, Clurman obviously hoped
that the aspiring director would not jettison his Group heritage and
allow fickle audience preferences to determine his course. Kazan was
not to forget Clurman's advice. Although Kazan's immediate concern
was to prove himself a capable director, once he gained experience
and respect, he would return to the drama of social criticism that the
war years scotched, though with that same ambitious calculation of
how his reputation might be served.

Of the Group members who remained to the end, Kazan was the
quickest to achieve an independent professional livelihood. In less
than a year he had rebounded from his disastrous performances in
Five Alarm Waltz with his direction of the surprisingly successful *Café
Crown,* which *Theatre Arts* described with unwitting irony as an account of "the efforts of a retired actor to make a come-back as a
director."[3] This sharp turnabout was no mere stroke of fortune. Like
most of Kazan's intitial assignments, it came from an enterprising
pursuit of opportunity and nimble jockeying. Well before he appeared
in *Five Alarm Waltz*, Kazan was hard at work on alternatives to acting.
With the Group's business manager, Kermit Bloomgarden, he had
purchased rights to a play by Edwin Gilbert, which passed through a
series of aborted production plans and was finally sold to Warners as
the basis for *Blues in the Night*, netting Kazan a fat profit and the
acting role of Nickie.[4] While working on *Blues in the Night* on behalf
of a new repertoire company (Dollar Top), which also failed to get off
the drawing board, Kazan secured an option on a play entitled *Café
Crown* by screenwriter Hy S. Kraft. When *Café Crown* was later taken
over by Carly Wharton and Martin Gabel, these producers honored
Kazan's initial commitment to the play and made him director.

Integral to Kazan's appointment was his ability to resolve the thorny issue of casting. He was instrumental in securing Sam Jaffe, who had been in *The Gentle People*, and Morris Carnovsky, a fellow Group member who volunteered to take a leave of absence from the long running *My Sister Eileen*. As a slight comedy based on a famous cafe associated with New York's Yiddish Theatre, *Café Crown* was expected to run only two weeks, but it generated enough interest to play for more than three months. By carefully orchestrating the affectionate antagonisms in the featured relationship between a once-prominent actor down on his luck and a wily prosperous waiter and coupling it with an appropriate array of stage antics, Kazan got the play to exceed its presumed potential and vindicated his original interest.

Kazan's achievement with *Café Crown* opened two doors, one leading nowhere and the other to a production that was to win a Pulitzer Prize. While *Café Crown* was still playing, Kazan was offered the job of directing *The Strings, My Lord, Are False*, which depicted the emotional problems of a group of English townspeople gathered together by a Nazi air raid. The production was plagued with frustration from the outset of rehearsals. The distraught producers almost fired Kazan just prior to opening night. But the play was not to be saved and closed after only fifteen performances. Kazan's second assignment, *The Skin of Our Teeth*, which was agreed upon well before the opening *of Strings,* was equally fraught with risk. Thornton Wilder, whose *Our Town* had been the most celebrated play of the 1937–38 season, had written a new play. It humorously depicted the unremitting afflictions of Mr. and Mrs. Antrobus, whose battle to survive and hold their family together extends from prehistoric time up to the impending war. Wilder's freewheeling mockery of verisimilitude sought to show that most current middle-class worries are centuries old and laughable in the very seriousness accorded them. The finished result was so zany and so bizarre that it had been rejected by numerous producers. Finally, late in January 1942, it was picked up by Michael Myerberg, whose only distinction came from serving as business manager for the All American Youth Orchestra and arranging for its director, Leopold Stokowski, to supervise the music for Walt Disney's *Fantasia*. Kazan's name was included in the earliest production discussion because Robert Ardrey, who had been one of Wilder's favorite students at the University of Chicago, had praised Kazan to his mentor for his handling of his two plays.[5] If Wilder's peculiar play defied characterization, Kazan's work with the allegorical fantasy of *Thunder Rock* and the comedy of *Café Crown* were strong qualifications. So also was his willingness to work for rockbottom salary, since Myerberg had minimal funding.

Skin of Our Teeth was a director's nightmare. Joseph Wood Krutch was to judge the play "more imaginative, less merely neurotic" than the famous experimental plays of the German and Russian playwrights.[6] The script called for a complex array of machinery including overhead projectors, trap doors, and scenery that collapsed and rose. The large thirty-five member cast included roles for a baby dinosaur and a mammoth. Much more troublesome, though, was the problem of getting viewers to understand and enjoy the way Wilder had brought the ice age to modern suburbia and had destroyed the distance between the audience and the stage action. His fantasy invited theatregoers both to delight in the outspoken complaints of the Antrobus maid, Sabina, that she doesn't understand a single word in the play and to appreciate the timely meaning of man's struggles to survive, confused and exasperated, "by the skin of his teeth."

The most formidable of all these difficulties, as it turned out, was dealing with Tallulah Bankhead, who was playing Sabina. By the fifth day of rehearsal, relations between her and Kazan were already strained. Then on the final day, war broke out. "There," Kazan once told an interviewer, "Tallulah got her first look at the scenery. She didn't like it, for hours on end she didn't like it. We tried to run through the play, using the scenery, but it took until three in the morning just to finish the first act. What a night. Myerberg was sick, stretched out on a cot in the aisle, Tallulah was screeching, Florence Eldridge was nursing hurt feelings, Florence Reed was being very much above all this sort of thing, Freddie March and the rest of the cast were trying to work and me—I was scared to death." What made this ordeal so particularly trying was the fact that Myerberg was depending on a successful out-of-town run to recoup his investment and to generate the additional financing he needed for the Broadway opening. That is to say, the production itself was surviving by the skin of its teeth.

"When we finally quit for the night," Kazan went on to explain, "Tallulah and I bandied a few thousand words. It was a real brawl; my voice is as loud as hers and I know almost as many words. As she left, I got off a parting shot and the stagehands applauded. This may have started the legend that I won a victory. But I never did really beat her down."[7] As his remarks suggest, Kazan was not intent upon besting Bankhead so much as affirming the integrity and authority that went with his position. "Every fighter has one fight that makes or breaks him," Kazan later said of the incident to Murray Schumach. "That was my fight."[8]

Kazan gained the respect of everyone in the company and Bankhead made the show. Given the recalcitrant, wayward eccentricity which makes Sabina such a striking character, one is tempted to suspect that this feud may have actually contributed to the power of Bankhead's performance. Over the years following this episode, Kazan developed the practice of instigating clashes such as this for the purpose of getting his performers to give him the effects he wanted. In any event, Kazan presented Myerberg with a success that exceeded his wildest dreams. The New York critics resoundingly affirmed the raves garnered by the out-of-town run. Controversy continued to surround the play as many chose to follow in Tallulah's footsteps and storm to the exits, but it was of the kind that drew crowds. In addition to the Pulitzer Prize, *The Skin of Our Teeth* won Kazan the New York Drama Critics' Award for best director of the year and went on to run for more than a year.

Kazan followed *The Skin of Our Teeth* with *Harriet*, which was not so highly acclaimed as a play but did even better at the box office. Helen Hayes's success at playing famous ladies of history, most notably in *Mary of Scotland* and *Victoria Regina*, had sent her searching for another such figure to play. This she found in Harriet Beecher Stowe. After researching Stowe for several years, she and her producer, Gilbert Miller, commissioned Florence Ryerson and Colin Clements to draft the play, which was then tested in an experimental production at Syracuse University. Once Hayes was convinced that the play's potential measured up to her talents, Kazan was asked to direct it.

Harriet, like *The Skin of Our Teeth*, presented Kazan with a combination of humor and message, though here the balance was more neatly defined, more conventional. In portraying Stowe's evolution from familial devotion to an espousal of a national cause, this drama was directly addressed to its wartime audience and fashioned to provide

61

Helen Hayes with the bravura performance she turned in. "The present part," Miller told a reporter at the time, "is such that it gives her the opportunity to exercise every talent. The role is a difficult one, calling for the display of every emotion, from the lightest to the heaviest."[9] Thus Kazan became responsible for steering the star away from pitfalls and surrounding her with carefully diversified effects that would buttress her centrality.

Jacobowsky and the Colonel by Franz Werfel was a third variation on this emerging pattern of timely dark-edged comedy. This play, which grew out of the complications and confusion of the Austrian playwright's escape from Nazi Germany, bore the mark of several different pens. Clifford Odets had been recruited to adapt it to American tastes and then replaced by S. N. Behrman, whose comic touch brightened the somber mood of Werfel's original. In his notes, which he would systematically prepare for each one of his projects, Kazan characterized the finished product as "'A Modern Legend'—'a legend is fanstastic, its essence is romance. Its comicality, though abundant, is wise; its figures, though human and essentially comic, are still both representative and universal.'"[10] The play's featured exchange between two Polish expatriates struggling to escape Nazi-occupied France is reminiscent of the actor-waiter relationship in *Café Crown*, although their contrasting sets of values held much more personal significance for the young director. The colonel is an old-world aristocrat who lives by a code of formal manners and extravagant behavior that ill equip him to fend for himself. Jacobowsky, on the other hand, is a Jewish refugee intent upon survival—self-effacing but practical, resourceful, and quick-witted. The comedy resulting from the clash of their responses is constantly checked by the seriousness of their situation; beneath the surface merriment lies a serious debate over the meaning of life and how best to preserve it. In the end, disagreement leads to a deeper appreciation of each other, thereby enabling them to escape. As Kazan was to describe their situation: "Each has his virtues, but for each his virtue will not be sufficient for survival; so the play becomes the story of how, out of these two relics of the old, something new is born."[11] The progression from hostility to respect, attended as it was by a comic atmosphere with poignant overtones, posed a formidable challenge for Kazan. He was so dissatisfied with his initial results that he redid all his directing plans.[12] Though several critics still found the production to be uneven, Kazan sufficiently sparked the production that it enjoyed a healthy run of 417 performances. This was neither the first time nor the last time that Kazan was to rely upon clever theatrics and slick performances to stage a difficult play. In an autobiographical sketch written three years later, Kazan proudly noted: "His work, it was agreed, helped make the play a success."[13]

These productions, along with the musical *One Touch of Venus*, which was to enjoy the longest run of all, and a diversionary revue for the Department of Agriculture, *It's Up to You*, amounted to an enviable record of achievement. Of the six different plays he had staged by the end of the 1944–45 season, four had been major hits and only one a clear failure. At one point during the war, Kazan had three productions running concurrently. After years of struggling to convince producers of his ability, Kazan was a director in demand. He was now approached for far more productions than he could ever handle. He was offered what insiders considered to be the best. He was in a position to choose. He was also being wooed by Hollywood. Though he had so far directed only a single low-budget film, his record of achievement was strong enough that several studios were extending him long-term contracts. Finally he agreed to the one offered by Twentieth Century–Fox, which called for him to direct a movie a year for the next five years and left him free to take on whatever Broadway assignments he chose and even to direct for another studio if he wanted.

While I have chosen to postpone discussion of the reasons for this decision and the resulting films until the next chapter, it is important to realize the profound effect this contract had on the nature of Kazan's Broadway work. Kazan now had an impressive annual income and one which was guaranteed for years to come. With these assurances, commercial success became a less critical consideration. Though he was now in the enviable position of being able to let the momentum of his previous accomplishments determine his course, Kazan was too restless, too ambitious, too eager for a different kind of reputation to do so. Whatever satisfaction he drew from the strong audience appeal of his recent efforts was countermanded by an uncomfortable realization that his work had not expressed anything meaningful to himself or anything pertinent to the times in which he was living. Looking back on his situation at this time, Kazan was to say, "To me *Jacobowsky and the Colonel, Dunnigan's Daughter, Harriet, The Skin of Our Teeth* were just technical jobs."[14] Indeed they were, and, as such, they were necessary to prove he possessed the skills of an accomplished director. But they were not a source of pride to him.

Fox's contract freed Kazan to take on more satisfying material. Having demonstrated that he could draw audiences, he found himself challenged to prove that he continue to do so with more venturesome, more personal selections. Having triumphed over the Group's roller coaster plunges from boom to bust, he was left with a nagging uneasiness that his comedies and musicals were considerably afield of the Group's high ideals, which remained his definition of theatrical achievement.

Kazan was also discovering that the fierce push for recognition that carried him to preeminence at thirty-five had a dangerous potential for destroying him unless he came up with a more challenging outlet, something against which to battle, something that communicated the suppressed tensions which drove him. Already there were ominous clouds developing in his personal life. Within months of signing the Fox contract that acknowledged his achievement and guaranteed his future, Kazan, like the successful protagonist of his later novel *The Arrangement*, became embroiled in a dangerously disruptive affair. Though Kazan had had and was to have many extramarital liaisons, this one was exceptional in its threat to his marriage. In the end, Kazan decided that his commitment to his wife and children was too strong. In part this was an emotional decision consistent with the reverence and centrality accorded the family in so many of Kazan's plays and films. In part it was the product of that shrewd evaluation which entered into his assignment choices. Not only was Molly the mother of his two children (and two more which came in the aftermath of this decision), she was one of his best advisers. She had persuaded him of the advantages of the left-wing movement at the outset of his career and had repeatedly counseled him on the direction his professional efforts should take. In the years ahead, her enthusiasm would strongly influence his decisions to direct *A Streetcar Named Desire, Boomerang,* and *Tea and Sympathy.* Nonetheless, by far the most significant outcome of this temporary break was the terms of reconciliation. As a condition of their reunion, Molly insisted that Kazan agree to see a psychiatrist.

In the absence of information about these sessions, which Kazan continued on a regular basis for the duration of his career, one can only speculate as to their bearing upon his directing. However, following his submission to psychoanalysis, Kazan began handling darker, riskier material and started gravitating toward deeply troubled characters whose behavior ranged beyond their own understanding and control. Moreover, Kazan's decision to handle the plays in which they appear evidences a strong personal commitment notably lacking in his earlier assignments, often spurring him to speak out on these plays' merits. From this reorientation and reevaluation would come both *All My Sons* and *A Streetcar Named Desire*.

On a professional level, these turns in Kazan's personal life were reinforced by his new assessment of the prevailing social climate. The light-hearted fare so popular during the war had been sanitized of criticism of domestic conditions and designed to offer a comfortable diversion. Now with war's end in sight, Kazan was confident that the impending readjustment would produce major changes in the dramas people would prefer. Describing the "audience tomorrow" he saw in the soldiers he met on a U.S.O. trip to the Pacific in the spring of 1945, Kazan wrote: "We, along with the men and women who run the radio, the newspapers, the magazines, make the spiritual climate of our country. Too often we have followed the law of the least common denominator, only to discover too late that we had misjudged and underestimated. . . . Coming back, I feel that the audience is ahead of us. We, the makers of entertainment, are faced with a job. We must try, in our field, to be as honest and grown as these kids. It is not a matter of chance any longer. . . . They're a lot tougher, more honest, and a lot more progressive."[15]* To Kazan, the return to peacetime

---

*In an article two years earlier Kazan had written, "I am not calling for a barrage of war plays. But surely civilian morale is important and surely it is not merely a matter of escapism. It is my opinion that the theatre could and still can contribute much more to the real tone and spirit of our people than it has . . . and where the theatre could on the one hand inspire and teach, it has allowed itself to become debased." *New York Herald Tribune*, Sept. 12, 1943, v, 1.

augured a return of the serious social drama the war had squelched. Already the government and the populace were discussing the difficulties of a return to peace, and both sensed that the battles would be far from over once the guns were silent. Whatever its strains, the war had provided a clear definition of the enemy and priorities that would be sadly missed. The spirit of patriotism and cooperation infusing the war years from Pearl Harbor to V-J Day was about to be replaced with a searching evaluation of the costs of the effort and the validity of the hopes that sustained it. Thus amidst the bright glow of victory, films and plays suddenly took on a darker cast that complemented the searching introspection to come out of Kazan's own success.

At the war's end, Broadway harkened to the plight of the returning veteran. His reintegration into civilian life became an occasion for reevaluating the past and confronting a problem-ridden present. Starting with *Deep Are the Roots*, which opened a little over a month after V-J Day and overlapped his account of the "audience tomorrow," Kazan began to veer away from the bland material of his previous directing assignments and embarked on a series of darkening dramas assessing the war's aftermath. For his first production venture since 1940, Kermit Bloomgarden, who had been the Group's former business Manager, had come up with a play that cautiously resurrected criticism of existing social conditions within America as a calculated departure from wartime propaganda. The play's authors, Arnaud d'Usseau and James Gow, first gained Broadway acclaim during the war with *Tomorrow the World*, which analyzed the problem of adjustment caused by the adoption of a Nazi-indoctrinated child into an American family. Though set in America, the play was a devastating indictment of the Nazi mentality. By making white treatment of blacks the ideological focus, *Deep Are the Roots* sought a peacetime equivalent of *Tomorrow*'s wartime concerns. "We decided," the authors explained in an article entitled "Manufacturing a Problem Play," written for the play's opening, "that whatever idea we picked it would have to deal with a post-war theme. . . . We then asked ourselves what urgent problem— other than the war—was troubling Americans most." This approach led them to the conclusion that racial prejudice would be one of the most pressing issues. "What makes many decent Americans," they

Deep Are the Roots: A jolting return to problems on the home front. *Left to right:* Alice Langdon (Carol Goodner), Howard Merrick (Lloyd Gough), Brett Charles (Gordon Heath), Genevra (Barbara Bel Geddes), Ellsworth Langdon (Charles Waldron). (Photo by Alfredo Valente; reproduced by permission of Mrs. Alfredo Valente and the Billy Rose Theatre Collection, The New York Public Library at Lincoln Center, Astor, Lennox and Tilden Foundations.)

asked, "consciously or unconsciously embrace those notions of race superiority that Hitler found so profitable?"[16] The horrifying photographs of the survivors of Auschwitz, Buchenwald, and Dachau raised implications too troubling to be ignored. Once Americans recovered from the initial shock of these pictures, they would begin to realize they were responsible for a situation, less graphically repugnant but no less ugly and unjust. Were the German concentration camps not grim lessons in what happens when a populace willfully disregards prejudice and its consequences?

The transition of these playwrights from the wrongs of a wartime enemy to complementary ones on the home front, facile as it may have been, still heralded an important change. Now deprived of a clear, identifiable enemy, the moral indignation generated by the nation's war effort was turning back upon itself and growing self-conscious. The previous sense of purpose and conviction was being replaced by guilt, anxiety, and above all, a troubled introspection. As an initial expression of this new mood, *Deep Are the Roots* situated its "problem" in the consciousness of its characters and explored the resulting confusion.

The play takes its direction from the discharge of a southern black who has spent the war teaching soldiers to "believe they were fighting for a better world for themselves." Eager to pass on to his fellow blacks back home the many fruits of his experience, Brett returns with the intent of becoming a teacher. Willing as the whites are to commend him for all that he has accomplished, they oppose the potential change he intrudes. They do not believe that the equality of wartime should extend to peacetime conditions.

Brett turns out to be less a character than an exemplar of all that a black might become, given sufficient opportunity, and a theatrical device for exposing deficiencies in white attitudes towards blacks. The Langdon family, on which the play concentrates, is a tightly knit circle that presumably shares the same outlook. In fact, its members have little in common outside of their background and family name, and sharp differences in their temperaments are linked to conflicting attitudes toward blacks. As a mirror of the existing social climate, they constitute an unrealized potential for divisiveness which the ensuing course of events precipitates. The father, Senator Ellsworth Langdon, is a perverse reactionary intent upon keeping blacks subordinate and submissive. His daughter Alice wants the lot of blacks to be improved, but with herself serving as the architect of reform. Genevra is held up as an ideal who freely accepts Brett as an equal and even displays a willingness to marry him. The amount of sympathy enlisted for her practically measures the guilt in the contemporary white response to the racial issue. Yet her view too is finally shown to be flawed and inadequate. *Deep Are the Roots* is the "problem" play its authors called it not only because it calls attention to a festering social condition and sounds a call for reform, but also because, unlike its thirties' counter-part, it advanced no statement about the direction it should take.

Period piece that it was, *Deep Are the Roots* enjoyed a very suc-cessful run while two competing treatments of the same issue, *Strange Fruit* and *Jeb*, lagged far behind. In his direction, Kazan shaped *Deep Are the Roots* into a drama of confrontation—a jolting encounter with a current issue whose power derived from the human conflict it caused. But despite the intensity of their antagonisms, the characters remained familiar stereotypes and the play relied on contrivances such as the misplaced watch, which Brett is accused of stealing, to provide the occasions for conflict. *Deep Are the Roots* contained ingredients to be found in Kazan's best work, but its dramatization of racial prejudice in terms of conventional outlooks made it less venturesome than it initially appeared.

Kazan's next two assignments were crushing failures and hard lessons in the danger of allowing his ambitious projections to cloud his judgment. *Dunnigan's Daughter* was an attempt by S. N. Behrman to apply *Jacobowsky's* mixture of tragicomedy to a depiction of the downfall of a corrupt and ruthless American industrialist. The flawed result was rejected for production by the Playwrights' Company, which Behrman had founded along with four equally gifted playwrights. Refusing to accept this appraisal of his work, Behrman pushed for a release from his original agreement and arranged for a production to be handled by the Theatre Guild, which produced *Jacobowsky*.[17] When Kazan was invited to be director and to affiliate himself with this rearrangement of the Broadway establishment, he quickly accepted. The agonizing out-of-town run hammered home a painful realization that modifications could not remedy *Dunnigan*'s problems. As the bad reviews piled up, Kazan replaced all of the principal members of the cast except the lead, adding June Havoc, Luther Adler, and the then unknown Richard Widmark. Major revisions were made in the script. To iron out these changes, a stop in Boston was added which pushed the scheduled opening back two weeks. But all for naught. The play folded after thirty-eight performances.

The result vindicated the preliminary estimates of the Playwrights' Company and compounded its problems. Another one of its founders

Maxwell Anderson, subsequently came forth with a new play that seemed equally lacking in promise. Anderson was so annoyed by the Company's reluctance to back his work that he tendered his resignation.[18] With the defections of Behrman and Anderson threatening to carry other members with them, the Playwrights' Company teetered perilously on the brink of collapse. As a stopgap measure, it offered to go ahead with the play despite its reservations if additional support could be enlisted. Again Kazan jumped at the opening created by this breach, though his participation in *Truckline Café* was to be as producer, with his former mentor Harold Clurman serving as director and co-producer.

Although Kazan was obviously cultivating an alliance with another Broadway giant, he also saw *Truckline Café* as an example of the "new drama" he thought returning veterans would favor. Among the diverse characters who come to Anderson's café, the dominant concern is the effect the war has had on the relationships between husbands and wives. The troubled situations of the two main couples illustrate how enforced separations aggravated discontent and spawned adulterous affairs, thereby eroding the prospect of happy reunions and intruding the likelihood of tragedy.

However, the production was a disaster. The reviews, almost without exception, were scathing. Clurman, Kazan, and Anderson were so distressed by these estimates that they financed ads in New York's major newspapers charging that the critics were a calloused, narrow union with a stranglehold over the fate of any production.[19] The result was a lively debate over the integrity of the critical establishment, which had the unfortunate effect of diverting attention from the formidable obstacles currently facing serious drama. Over the war years there had been a 100 percent increase in the expense of mounting an average play. The enormous loss now attendant upon an outright failure was not only causing a sharp reduction in the number of productions, it was also restricting the plays producers were willing to back. Recommendations by critics were a growing determinant of whether a play would recoup its investment, but in the case of hardhitting social plays, mere approval was not enough to keep a production alive.[20] Actually, serious social drama was not as endangered as Kazan, Clurman, and Anderson suggested. While most dramatizations of the plight of the returning veteran—*This Too Shall Pass, Skydrift, Sound of Hunting,* and *On Whitman Avenue,* along with *Strange Fruit, Jeb,* and *Home of the Brave,* lost money, *Deep Are the Roots* had enjoyed a long, profitable run. More accurately, the shifting concerns that fueled Kazan's optimism about the future for serious theatre produced enormous uncertainty as to what might attract audiences. Kazan's experience with Behrman and Anderson, the Theatre Guild and the Playwrights' Company, convinced him that the establishment probably would not come up with the "new drama" for which he had been calling. Perhaps better results could be gained by breaking with the proven and turning to young unknowns. Perhaps their work would accord better with these changes.

In October, 1946, Clurman and Kazan announced that they had joined Walter Fried to establish "a new permanent production association."[21] Like Bloomgarden, Fried had once been a business manager for the Group and had just finished serving as general manager on *Truckline Café.* Without proposing to revive their old company, this alliance of three Group alumni was hoping to extend its achievements. Their rallying point was a new play, currently entitled "Sign of the Archer," by the relatively unknown Arthur Miller, who had only one play to his credit, and that a failure. It was to be a test case for their charges about *Truckline.* As a *Variety* review reported, it was "a stagecraft campaign for restoration of principles that were shunted aside in the years of the great conflict."[22] With Kazan now serving as director and without entangling controls, the organizers, convinced they had come up with a superior offering, were anxious to see how the results would be received.

Clurman and Kazan were attracted to Miller's play because its commentary upon postwar problems reminded them of Odets's best work. With the family of the play displaying current, widely shared anxieties, the characters had well-crafted, individualized identities and participated in a complex interrelationship. Miller portrayed how wounds incurred during the war made it impossible for the Keller family to adjust to peace. Haunted by the possible return of a son lost in action during an air force mission, none was able to resume a normal life. This problem was aggravated by accusations that Keller's company produced defective airplane engines during the war. An ear-

71

lier trial exonerated Keller, but sent his partner Deever to prison. The play opens with the visit of Deever's daughter Ann, who was engaged to the lost son, and intrudes the possibility that the longstanding attraction between her and Keller's other son Chris will produce an alternative marriage. For this to happen, however, everyone must admit that Larry is actually dead. In thus compelling the family to take a stand on this sensitive point, Ann unwittingly forces a reevaluation of the defective engines. Both she and Chris learn what his mother has long suspected—that Joe knowingly allowed the engines to be shipped and then shifted the responsibility onto his partner. Thus the whole drama moves inexorably toward painful revelations about the corrosive effect of the war upon previously held ideals—Keller's handling of the defective engines was a betrayal of Deever and Larry's last flight was a suicidal expiation for this injustice. These destroy the spiritual integrity of the family that everyone, particularly Joe, has fought to uphold.

Kazan's hectic schedule left him less than two months to prepare his approach, and a large portion of this was necessarily eaten up by production arrangements. Yet since more than the play itself was at stake, Kazan wanted it to be as strong as possible. He spent three weeks working closely with Miller establishing the play's "core" and defining how each character related to it. They agreed that the play showed that "man was accountable for his actions not only to his family but to society as a whole."[23] (Was this not a Kazan preoccupation in the aftermath of his own family reunion?) As they traced each character's development in relation to this theme, they discovered points in the script where the presentation could be improved. Most of these were minor deletions and additions that would enliven the tempo, intensify the exchange, or highlight an important point. For example, a passage was eliminated in which Jim Bayliss expresses a desire to get away to a jungle where he might be able to pick up emeralds, a superfluous point here but one that would be essential to the characterization of Ben in *Death of a Salesman*. Of these changes, probably the most significant is the reduction in Chris's outspoken pronouncements; rather than a suppression of possibly offensive views, this was done to make him less a mouthpiece of social criticism, a quality which critics were still to find objectionable in his characterization.[24]

The changes made in the long first two acts were little more than commonplace production procedure. The short third act, however, was revised radically. These modifications altered profoundly the audience's final impression of the characters and the drama's meaning. Miller, of course, made these, but Kazan so obviously influenced them that they constitute a telling gauge of his directing approach and its departure from the effects he sought in *Deep Are the Roots*.

As initially written, the last act confrontations were bruising clashes of will. The characters openly challenge one another in order to make the force of their conviction felt. Their drive for vindication and justice renders them insensitive to the impact of their conduct. Fearful that the revelation of his sickness as feigned might lead to another trial, Joe insists upon holding to his lie and pressures Kate into agreeing that she will back him up. Joe then fantasizes Larry's return, thereby supporting Kate's vain belief by way of repayment. Next Ann comes to tell Kate that she is going away with Chris. Angered by the injustice done her father and by Kate's hostile insistence that Chris will not leave with her, she presents Larry's letter to Chris and demands that he read it. Persistently maintaining his father's innocence up to the revelations of this letter, Chris immediately turns on Joe, decries his immorality, and proclaims his intention of turning him over to the police. Joe's quiet response of going to get his coat and committing suicide leaves unclear whether his decision was motivated by Chris's denunciation or by an annihilating sense of guilt.[25]

The revised third act, on the other hand, altered this interaction so that each of the characters displays an acute sensitivity to the damage he or she might inflict. Instead of pushing for necessary solutions, each shies away from the truth that insists upon being acknowledged. Each also senses a measure of guilt. Worrying about his or her own deficiencies, the potential assailant proves reluctant to act and the person formerly assaulted is now left free to realize his or her own fault. Angry resolution is replaced by a circumspect compassion and a discomforting enlargement in self-understanding. With this modified depiction of justice being served by a dawning realization of sustained losses, Miller fashioned a resolution with a devastating psychological impact that set his drama apart from Odets's work. Audience sympathy, which could have been diminished by cruel accusations, now comes freely—most of all for Joe. By building up Joe's expressed

All My Sons: Forced optimism and cheer undermined by anxiety. *Left to right*: Chris Keller (Arthur Kennedy), George Deever (Karl Malden), Kate Keller (Beth Merrill), and Joe Keller (Ed Begley). (Photo by Fred Fehl; reproduced by permission of Hoblitzelle Theatre Arts Library, Humanities Research Center, The University of Texas at Austin.)

devotion to his family and linking it to a final terrible error, Miller endowed his lead character with tragic stature. Kate announces the theme of this revision—"There's something bigger than the family." The response Miller penned for Joe, "if there's something bigger . . . I'll put a bullet through my head," sets up the play's devastating conclusion. The one remaining revision was to change the play's title to *All My Sons*.

In his tongue-in-cheek review, Robert Garland opened: "Harold Clurman and Elia Kazan, who took part in the production of *Truckline Café*, have decided to give us theatre reporters a second chance to make good with them. Even if we still remain 'unqualified, either by training or taste,' to pass judgment on the Broadway drama, they last night joined forces with Walter Fried and Herbert Harris in the initial metropolitan exposure of 'All My Sons,' and invited us to come and see it."[26] Certainly the same thoughts were running through the mind of Brooks Atkinson, but he set his response in a very different key. "Fortunately," he wrote, "'All My Sons' is produced and directed by people who value it and who have given it a taut and pulsing performance with actors of sharp and knowing intelligence. It is always gratifying to see old hands succeed in the theatre. But there is something uncommonly exhilarating in the spectacle of a new writer bringing unusual gifts to the theatre under the sponsorship of a director with taste and enthusiasm. In the present instance, the director is Elia Kazan."[27] Though not all the reviewers agreed with this glowing estimate, the play rallied enough support to win the critics' award for play of the year and went on to enjoy a strong profitable run.

As in the past, Kazan demonstrated that there was an audience for serious drama presented in the right spirit. With a sensitivity to Miller's potential and a well-crafted production that communicated the play's brooding atmosphere of psychological distress, Kazan showed that *All My Sons* was such a work. Its subtle depiction of contrived displays of confidence, good cheer, and optimism being undermined by doubt and anxiety was to break new ground.

Kazan wanted to forget the feud touched off by *Truckline Café* and get on with the business of presenting worthwhile plays. But again there were extenuating considerations and more controversy. During the course of its run, *All My Sons* acquired a reputation for being a

Communist-inspired attack upon the American way of life. In its suggestion that Americans may have exploited the war for profit, a play like *All My Sons* seemed to cast suspicion upon the war effort and to tarnish the national image. Consequently, pressure was put on the government and plans for a tour of the play at military bases abroad were scrapped.[28]

In his qualified recommendation of the play, Joseph Wood Krutch had noted that "Mr. Miller seems rather unnecessarily careful to express explicitly his warm respect for all the leftist pieties" and then hastened to add that "the play is a play about personal guilt and personal atonement,"[29] as both Miller and Kazan intended it to be. However, to less sensitive viewers more concerned about threats to national security than about moving drama, the social criticism in *All My Sons* represented a danger that called for suppression. This reaction upset Brooks Atkinson and altered his outlook on the *Truckline* controversy. With obvious passion, he wrote in defense of the play:

> If a man of genuine talent cannot write a play about a family of Americans and base it on a situation that resembles something already discussed in public, there is not much point in doing anything in the American theatre more serious than "John Loves Mary." . . . Either a playwright has or has not the freedom to choose his own subjects without first making sure that it does not tread on touchy toes. The only alternative to this freedom is a censor. . . . And since there are a lot of very grave problems unsolved in the world, we may as well quit looking for political mares' nests in the best new play of the season. Hunting for bogey-men is the occupational disease of neurotics, which puts it on the level of American Communism.[30]

All My Sons was an impressive achievement and an important precursor of things to come. Just as Kazan had perceived the dramatic power in the unacknowledged deterioration of the Keller family's moral fiber, so he recognized the drawbacks to Miller's use of Chris as a mouthpiece for social criticism. He seemed to sense that outspoken condemnation of American life was inappropriate to the political and social environment of the postwar era. The passionate conviction of the thirties was a thing of the past. The social problems of the postwar era necessitated a different dramatization. As the widespread mood of doubt and uncertainty was intensified by a growing sense of danger, the most meaningful drama was to be that which subjected ingrained beliefs to searching psychological investigations. Kazan's yearning to direct plays that would "hit audiences in the belly"[31] in their assault upon comfortable assumptions about human values and behavior was carrying him further and further into the minds of his characters and the fund of personal experience that attracted him to them.

Kazan's next assignment, *A Streetcar Named Desire*, was to be a triumphant reckoning with this movement toward psychological complexity. In his article calling for a new drama, Kazan had cited Tennessee Williams's *The Glass Menagerie* as a recent example of what he meant.[32] Yet, impressed as he was by this delicate tragedy, Kazan was not the natural match for Williams that this commendation suggested. Two years after *The Glass Menagerie*, Williams finished a more violent play depicting the nervous visit of a faded southern belle to the cramped apartment of her married sister. Hoping to find refuge from her humiliations, defeats, and distress, Blanche DuBois winds up insulting and offending her lower-class brother-in-law Stanley, who retaliates by raping her and completing her slide into madness. Convinced of his drama's power, annoyed by Eddie Dowling's handling of *The Glass Menagerie*, and impressed by *All My Sons*, Williams pushed his agent Audrey Wood to get Kazan to direct *Streetcar*. But, after reading Williams's creation, Kazan was reluctant to accept this assignment. Recognizing the drama's originality and emotional intensity, he uneasily sensed himself to be in alien territory. *Streetcar* departed sharply from the tightly knit plotlines and well-focused social commentary of *Deep Are the Roots* and *All My Sons*. The play's bruising struggles were caused by primal sexual urges suffused with madness and rage. As filtered through the characters' peculiar psyches, these desires eluded understanding, at times even subverting it. They were simultaneously confusing and convincing. Thus grounded in the murky depths of the subconscious, they did not adhere to the assumptions of Kazan's previous work. The drama of social criticism on which he had cut his teeth and to which he had recently returned was an ideal vehicle for his skill in making its message emanate from the characters' actions and speeches; each aspect of a production could be studied and shaped for the point it was supposed to communicate. Williams's actions, on the other hand, defied such neat definitions. As Kazan himself once explained: "the playwright I found myself furthest away from in material and closest to personally and I can't tell you why except that I admired him so much, was Tennessee Williams. I felt very close to him. I thought he had genius. With Miller I could always see where he had derived his materials. Although I could see the excellence of what he did, I was never surprised. But with Williams there was always something that would startle me, there was always a new brilliant illumination. I was overwhelmed by Williams."[33]

This remarkable collaboration, which began with *A Streetcar Named Desire* and continued through *Camino Real, Cat on a Hot Tin Roof, Baby Doll,* and *Sweet Bird of Youth,* was made possible by a shared wish to move beyond the limitations of their theatrical proclivities. In his playwriting, Williams was forever translating the turbulent currents of his psyche into colorful characters and charged conflicts. His multiple revisions expressed a compelling personal need to define his intuitive sense of their drives. When questioned about his source of inspiration on the eve of *Streetcar*'s opening, Williams replied, "Perhaps my unconscious could tell, I can't. . . . My chief aim in playwriting is the creation of a character. I have always had a deep feeling for the mystery in life, and essentially my plays have been an effort to explore the beauty and meaning in the confusion of living."[34] In relying so heavily upon intuition and impulse, Williams worried that he might lose his audience and, in Kazan, he was seeking a skillful mediator. Up to this point, Kazan had assiduously cultivated this role. Shrewdly he would evaluate the tenor of the times and assess the prospective audience appeal of the profferred assignment. Once he agreed, he would carefully work out what the play was saying. In his notebook he defined the play's theme and the important attributes of each character. Then he arranged and shaped each aspect of the production so that these points were communicated. On the other hand, Kazan had always believed that a character had to be more than a placard to produce moving drama. After all, the foundation of his Group training and experience had been a cultivated appreciation for the root motivation within each character. Moreover, he had recently come to believe that the mystery, eccentricity, and twistedness in Williams's characters was as important as the orderly lines of development he customarily mapped out. Kazan's skill in evoking a vivid sense of realism, of believable characters with commonly understood goals who behaved in a manner audiences readily accepted, had always accomodated warped motives and bizarre, frightening compulsions just beneath the surface of life. Moreover, in his own psychiatric sessions, Kazan was discovering these same knots and tangles in himself. Thus in their exposure to the different cast of the other's sensibility, Kazan and Williams discovered a basis for fruitful collaboration. Still, given Kazan's initial reservation, he and Williams first had to forge a reconciliation of their differences.

After reading *Streecar*, Kazan informed Williams of his high regard for his work, but, after hard deliberations, had decided against directing it. Williams refused to give up on Kazan. As he had explained to Wood at the outset of the production planning, "We . . . are going to hold out for exactly the right people."[35] Consequently, Williams responded to Kazan's decision with a long letter explaining the intent of his play in a manner designed to overcome the director's reservations.

I am sure that you must have had reservations about the script. I will try to clarify my intentions in this play. I think its best quality is its *authenticity or its fidelity to life*. There are no "good" or "bad" people. Some are a little better or a little worse but all are activated more by *misunderstanding* than malice, a *blindness* to what is going on in each other's hearts. . . . *Nobody sees anybody truly, but all through the flairs of their own ego*—that is the way we all see each other in life. . . .

Naturally a play of this kind does not exactly present a theme or score a point, unless it be the point or theme of *human misunderstanding*. When you begin to arrange the action of a play to score a certain point the fidelity to life may suffer. I don't say it always does. Things may be selected to score a point clearly without any contrivance toward that end, but I am afraid it happens rarely.

Finding a director aside from yourself who can bring this play to life exactly as if it were happening in life is going to be a

79

problem. But that is the kind of direction it has to have (I don't necessarily mean "realism": sometimes a living quality is caught better by expressionism than what is supposed to be realistic treatment). I remember you asked me what should an audience feel for Blanche. *Certainly pity.* It is a tragedy with the classic aim of producing a catharsis of pity and terror, and in order to do that Blanche must finally have the understanding and compassion of the audience. *This without* creating a black-dyed villain in Stanley. It is a thing (misunderstanding) not a person (Stanley) that destroys her in the end. In the end you should feel—"If only they all had *known* about each other!"—But there was always the paper lantern or the naked bulb! (Incidentally, at the close of the play, I think Stanley should remove the paper lantern from the bulb—after Blanche is carried out and as he goes to resume the game.)

I have written all this out in case you were primarily troubled over my intentions in the play. Please don't regard this as 'pressure.' A wire from Mrs. Selznick and a letter from Audrey Wood indicates that both feel you have definitely withdrawn yourself from association with us and we must find someone else. I don't want to accept this necessity without exploring the nature and degree of the differences between us.[36]

Williams tried to change Kazan's mind by arguing that the strength of *Streetcar* resided in "its authenticity or its fidelity to life." This, he realized, was Kazan's forte, the quality which distinguished his best work. Yet his ensuing discussion reveals that he was not thinking of realism in the formal conventional sense. His play was "real" or "authentic" in that it was not divisible into good or bad people. Moreover, though it appealed to a common or shared understanding of life, its purpose resisted reduction to a thematic statement. No one character or set of characters was responsible for what happens to the others. Both the drama and the action of the play came from the complex motivation informing the characters' interaction. The realism here departed from the commonplace settings and familiar behavior in Kazan's preceding assignments. This was psychological realism whose truth lay in its convincing depiction of a disintegrating mind and the distressing reactions of those who contribute to its collapse.

Whether or not Kazan was persuaded by the terms in which Williams couched his appeal, he reversed his decision. Appropriately, his preparations then dwelled upon many of the same points. The main challenge, as he was to define it in his notebook, lay in "turning Psychology into Behavior." This was "a poetic tragedy" necessitating "a stylized production" because the "subjective factor—Blanche's memories, inner life emotions are a real factor." As he went on to explain to himself, "stylized acting and direction is to realistic acting and direction as poetry is to prose. The acting must be styled, not in the obvious sense. (Say nothing about it to the producer and actors.) But you will fail unless you find this kind of poetic realization for the behavior of these people."

For Kazan, as for Williams, *Streetcar* was a play about Blanche. His initial notes urge "Try to keep each scene in terms of Blanche." There follows a breakdown of the play's plot into eleven points which all stress what happens to Blanche. She is the character he first analyzes. Beneath a headline assertion that "Blanche is Desperate," Kazan decides that the spine of her character is to "find Protection: the tradition of the old South says that it must be through another person."[37] She constitutes the assumed basis for his ensuing definition of Stella, Mitch, and Stanley. The differences in these characters measure the failure of her efforts and its consequences.

In his conception of *Streetcar* as a dramatized dissection of a single personality, Kazan persisted in seeing the play as a commentary upon social conditions, but one which came from *within* the character rather than from the situation. For him, the play's theme was "a message from the dark interior." For all her peculiarities and eccentricities, Blanche was "a social type, an emblem of a dying civilization, making its last curlicued and romantic exit. All her behavior patterns are those of the dying civilization she represents. In other words her behavior is *social*."[38] Blanche embodies a romantic attitude, associated with an outworn past, that is oddly out of step with the modern world. Her quest for an accommodating refuge is futile, and because she senses this, an incipient madness informs all her actions. Her manner is flighty, affected and hyperbolic. She alone speaks in a syrupy southern accent. Her clothes are rich with folds and airy in texture. She is linked with the mottled lighting effects created by her Chinese shade. Melodrama envelopes her.

As her nemesis, Stanley reflects the "basic animal cynicism of today." At the core of his being, Kazan concluded, "he's deeply dissatisfied, deeply hopeless, deeply cynical." He considers no one but himself. His thoughts rivet singularly upon his needs and wants. "The immediate pleasures," Kazan decided, "if they come in a steady enough stream quiet this [inner discontent] *as long as no one gets more.*" When this happens, "then his bitterness comes forth and he tears down the pretender."[39] He is earth to Blanche's fire, physical drive to her flights of imagination, selfish determination to her helpless dependency upon others. His manner is brash, surly, and insensitive. Marlon Brando, whom Kazan selected to play Stanley and who went from an unknown to a star in this part, spoke in a flat drawl devoid of any regional association, though emphatically lower class. He wore jeans and a T-shirt, which insisted upon his physicality. He was associated with the harsh light of naked bulbs. He embodied the realism that threatened Blanche. In effect, theirs was a battle of styles.

But Kazan thoroughly agreed with Williams's assertion in his letter that Stanley "was not a black-dyed villain." Kazan believed that the audience should respond favorably to Stanley's initial aversion to Blanche. She provokes his hostility. In her own tragic way, she even invites it. His response comprehends a legitimate claim to the privacy of his own home and to whatever he and his wife enjoy doing. His behavior is such that it, too, comments upon existing social conditions without being reducible to a simple statement. Not until rehearsals did Kazan grasp the full ramifications of his preliminary analysis: Stanley is fundamentally as neurotic as Blanche. In countering her behavior with one that is radically different yet no less strange, he rivals her demands for the audience's attention. Brando's acting possessed a power and eccentricity that caused Stanley to appear both malevolent and maligned. When Kazan characterized Stanley as a "hoodlum aristocrat"[40] in his notebook he probably made no connection between Stanley and the gangster roles he had played ten years earlier, but unwittingly he touched upon a quality that was to emerge from his direc-

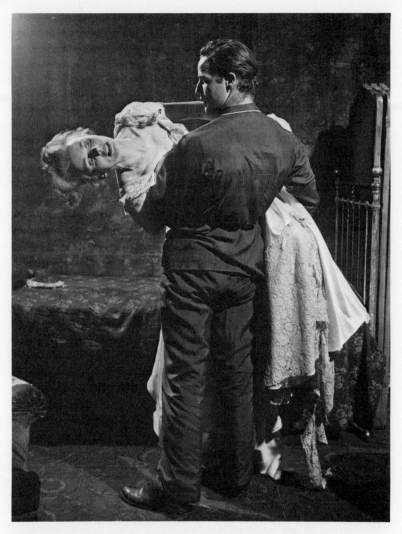

Stanley (Marlon Brando) and Blanche (Jessica Tandy) in *A Streetcar Named Desire*: A fateful antagonism grounded in mutual vulnerability and lack of self-understanding. (Photo by Eileen Darby; reproduced by permission.)

tion. Like Eddie Fuseli, Stanley was a man of powerful feelings made to appear insensitive by the conditioning of his lower-class background. His visceral antagonism toward everything for which Blanche stands is understandable and in many respects justifiable. His contemptuous wit, willful aggressiveness, and manifest insensitivity smack of a defensive insecurity. For this reason, his anguished cry for Stella expresses a need larger than mere sexual desire. That is to say, he has been warped as much by his background as Blanche has been by hers. Brando was so convincing in this respect that he was able to stick a cigarette up his nose during one of Blanche's speeches without ever being out of character. This gesture was perfectly consistent with the way he drank beer, played cards, and ate his food.

In no way did Brando's unanticipated command of the audience's attention upstage Blanche or detract from her plight. On the contrary, it made their struggle more balanced (or unbalanced) and enriched the drama. John Garfield turned down the role of Stanley because he felt Blanche dominated the play. With Brando playing him, Stanley was not simply illuminating Blanche's needs. Their relationship expanded into a fateful antagonism grounded in vulnerability and lack of self-understanding. During rehearsals, Kazan spurred Brando to develop the possibilities he opened and shaped the play's design to accomodate them.[41] Stanley's opening response to Blanche was made to appear a therapeutic corrective to her excesses. His candor cut through her affectations and enabled *him* to command the audience's sympathy. As the ensuing developments reveal the desperation of Blanche's plight and the malice in Stanley's response, the flow of sympathy was completely reversed, thereby deepening Blanche's tragedy.*

In his original review, which despite its implied fault finding, was at once a perceptive evaluation of Kazan's interpretation of Williams's play, and an anticipation of the very different one he was to communicate with his handling of the road show starring Uta Hagen and Anthony Quinn, Harold Clurman was to write:

*In making the movie version of *Streetcar*, Kazan got into a heated dispute with Vivien Leigh over how Blanche should appear in the opening scenes. Leigh felt the character should be sympathetic throughout as she had played the part in London under the direction of her husband, Laurence Olivier.

There are elements in the production—chiefly in the acting—that make for a certain ambiguity and confusion. This is not to say that the acting and production are poor. On the contrary, they are both distinctly superior. The director, Elia Kazan, is a man of high theatrical intelligence, a craftsman of genuine sensibility. . . . But there is a lack of balance and perspective in the production of *A Streetcar Named Desire* due to the fact that the acting of the parts is of unequal force, quality and stress. . . .

Marlon Brando, who plays Stanley Kowalski (Blanche's brother-in-law), is an actor of genuine power. He has what someone once called "high visibility" on the stage. His silences, even more than his speech, are completely arresting. Through his own intense concentration on what he is thinking or doing at each moment he is on the stage all our attention focuses on him. Brando's quality is one of acute sensibility. None of the brutishness of his part is native to him: it is a characteristic he has to "invent." The combination of an intense, introspective, and almost lyric personality under the mask of a bully endows the character with something almost touchingly painful. Because the elements of characterization are put on a face to which they are not altogether becoming, a certain crudeness mars our impression, while something in the nature of the actor's very considerable talent makes us wonder whether he is not actually suffering deeply in a way that relates him to what is represented by Blanche rather than to what his own character represents in the play. When he beats his wife or throws the radio out the window, there is, aside from the ugliness of these acts, an element of agony that falsifies their color in relation to their meaning in the play: they take on an almost Dostoevskian aspect.[42]

Instead of a one-sided contest in which a beleaguered survivor of the past is brutalized by a calloused representative of the present, Kazan crafted a battle with twisted psychological overtones in which Blanche bore greater responsibility for what happened to her and Stanley's strength was shot through with weakness.

To communicate these nuances, Kazan had to modify his accustomed style of realism. Blanche's whole behavior expressed a desperate flight from it. For all his insistent exemplification of it, Stanley was anything but familiar or commonplace. Not only were these characters sharply at odds with one another, but the constant mental pressure of their relationship lent a measure of exaggeration or aberration to every action. Blanche's influence was such that life ceased to be routine or normal; everyone including Mitch and Stella evidenced strain and neurosis. Like her Chinese shade, Blanche colored the atmosphere so that it seemed eerie and surreal. Kazan realized that these conditions called for exaggerated acting, extreme lighting effects, and a complex sound track. Plausability and unity demanded theatrical flair in the handling of every aspect of the production. The set was practically a statement about the imaginative synthesis that was demanded. It was at once a believable low-life scene and an environment of deterioration, a slice of life and a mental condition. By presenting the audience with a simultaneous view of the building's exterior and interior, the Kowalski flat communicated the psychoanalytic nature of the drama taking place there. As its designer, Jo Mielziner, was to observe, "Throughout the play, the brooding atmosphere is like an impressionistic x-ray. We are always conscious of this house of terror."[43]

A Streetcar Named Desire was a thoroughgoing psychological drama. In a reflection upon the uniqueness he sensed in *Streetcar*, Brooks Atkinson was to raise a point that would be widely discussed following *Death of a Salesman*—"ordinary people can suffer as terribly as men of distinction."[44] He was, of course, referring to Blanche, but it was this same quality of suffering that made Stanley such a formidable opponent and frightening architect of her downfall. Williams created the characters and Kazan brought them to life. Their success helped revive a jeopardized theatrical heritage. The theatre of social consciousness the Group had formerly fought to bring to Broadway had been practically eliminated by the war effort. When the war's end created "new audiences" looking for serious fare, they came looking for dramas that reflected the changes the veterans perceived. Their interests were different from those that marked the depression years and so was their outlook. Kazan sensed that their mood disposed them toward a more introspective drama and he found himself having to make crucial adjustments to capture it. Blanche DuBois was an electrifying embodiment of the neurosis that had suddenly erupted, though the troubled defensiveness of his Joe Keller and Stanley Kowalski were more revealing of the direction in which Kazan was moving.

For Kazan, *All My Sons* and *A Streetcar Named Desire* were to be important steps toward the attainment of more satisfying, more self-fulfilling professional identity. By once more eliciting sympathy for victims of social injustice, these dramas reasserted the injured sense of alienation Kazan had been harboring for years, and, in their innovative concentration upon the disturbed psychology of this condition, they reflected Kazan's movement into psychoanalysis. These were dramas in which the director's introspection was playing a strong supporting role.

FOUR

The Fox Way

On September 13, 1944, Kazan signed a contract with Twentieth Century–Fox to direct a film a year for the next five years. This agreement left him free to handle whatever Broadway assignments he wanted and even to work for another studio if he had the time and inclination. Drawn as he was to this contract's lucrative salary and multi-year guarantee, he was also fulfilling the longstanding wish to direct films that he had expressed on his application to the Yale Drama School. If his Group perspective had caused Hollywood to appear a temptation to high salaries and inferior artistry, this estimate, like that of his fellow members who defected—Clifford Odets, Franchot Tone, John Garfield, and Kazan's classmate, Alan Baxter—was attended by a contravening belief that his talents could elevate the quality of what was being offered. Thus when Kazan signed, he did so both to gain financial security *and* to make his presence felt.

If the fat paychecks of Hollywood's employees testified to the fruits to be gained from the vast audiences movies attracted, they were an equally telling index to their constraints. The complicated equipment and the large number of people involved in making and circulating a single product made all filmmaking an expensive, industrial process. This high cost of production was, in fact, responsible for Kazan's lack of filmmaking experience. His eager participation in the Theatre of Action's film program had been confined to three very modest ventures in large measure because the organization lacked funds to do more. On the other hand, given the studios' sophisticated systemization of the filmmaking process, Kazan's employers were not bothered by his inexperience. Within Fox's carefully structured network of delegated responsibilities, Kazan would not be expected to do more than instruct his performers on how they should move and behave—essentially what he had already been doing for some time. One of reasons Kazan turned his back on Hollywood back in 1937 was his realization that, as a virtual unknown, he would find it difficult to penetrate this system. Although Kazan's contract now accorded him first-class status, these conditions still circumscribed his sphere of influence. Consequently, the films Kazan was to direct in fulfillment of his initial Fox contact were, for the most part, important lessons in the studio process. Kazan associated himself as much as possible with films whose commentary upon social injustice complemented his stage work, and through them he became one of Fox's premier directors. However, his efforts cannot be understood apart from this studio process and Darryl Zanuck's efforts to make Fox a prosperous, premiere studio.

At the time he signed with Fox, Kazan was offered a similar contract by Warner Brothers, which had an equally strong commitment to the kind of film toward which he gravitated. Both studios, Kazan realized, had reputations for doing "contemporary, down-to-earth subjects."[1] During the Depression years, Warners specialized in fast-moving, low-budget features focusing upon pressing issues of the day in such films as *Little Caesar, I Am a Fugitive from the Chain Gang, G-Men, Black Fury, They Won't Forget,* and *Angels with Dirty Faces.* By 1944, however, its best work had been done, though this was by no means clear at that moment. Fox, on the other hand, was a relatively new operation. Darryl Zanuck, who had been one of the moving forces behind Warners' venture into more timely, controversial material, became production head when the Fox chain merged with Twentieth Century Productions in 1935. Under his leadership, Fox grew adept at turning out sequels and remakes. His choice of subject matter was distinctly chauvinistic. "The characteristic Zanuck picture of that period," Mel Gussow has observed, "was a romanticized look at American history: the building of a city, the founding of a religion, the finding of a musical sound, the making of a president, the invention of the telephone. As Zanuck saw America's past, it was the same movie over and over again, one huge, brawling, sprawling

Quint-and-Flaggian epic, where in the end, usually with the help of motherly love, all conflicts were resolved."[2] But Zanuck was too ambitious, too enterprising, too flamboyant to confine himself to the tried and true. By the late thirties, in a manner reminiscent of his earlier undertakings at Warners, he made a bold move into the area of serious social drama in a determined effort to bolster his studio's prestige. Out of this came *The Grapes of Wrath* and *How Green Was My Valley*. Though both these films were to reflect strongly Zanuck's influence and familiar Fox biases, John Ford was to garner much of the credit for their achievement. And rightly so. Within the constraints of the studio process, Zanuck allowed Ford an exceptional measure of authority and recognized its effect upon the results. Because of this success, Zanuck started according the director an importance and responsibility which was to gain Fox a reputation for being the "directors' studio."

When the increased movie attendance generated by the war brought it a landslide of profits, Fox invested heavily in a collection of directors whose work was to make Fox the most innovative studio during the decade following the war's end. Joseph Mankiewicz, who was lured to Fox from MGM during the war, would win back-to-back academy awards for both directing and scriptwriting in 1949 and 1950 for *Letter to Three Wives* and *All about Eve*. Otto Preminger was recruited from Broadway in 1943 and a year later handed Fox one of its biggest successes, *Laura*. During this same period Louis de Rochemont, the moving force behind *The March of Time*, was signed as was the director Henry Hathaway. Their collaboration on the *House on 92nd Street* (1945) and *13 Rue Madeleine* (1946) demonstrated the fruits to be gained from applying the documentary technique of photojournalism to Hollywood production. Of these men, none was to do more to enhance Fox's reputation than Kazan.

At that time—coming from Broadway as he did—Kazan was more inclined to notice the lack of respect a film director received. (In dwelling so much upon his numerous fights for concessions, Kazan has never noticed how exceptional Fox was in listening to and granting his demands.) What was important to him about Fox was Zanuck's resolute commitment to social drama. While serving in the armed forces in 1943, Zanuck published an article in *Saturday Review* in which he posed the question, "Is it possible to make pictures which have purpose and significance and yet show a proper return at the box-office?" His answer that entertainment could be a "device to make the serious, worthwhile pictures palatable to mass movie audiences"[3] was not the hollow declaration it had been for so many filmmakers. On the contrary, he had written his article to justify the three million dollars he was about to sink into his ill-fated production of *Wilson*.

Zanuck was no crusader. He had spent too many years in the entertainment business to place social relevance above public appeal. His primary concern was for films that would attract paying customers. If properly handled, he believed, these two objectives were complementary rather than opposed. *The Grapes of Wrath* and *How Green Was My Valley*, which Zanuck proudly cited as support for his argument, exemplify his approach to this tricky marriage. Their critical view of unhealthy social conditions affirmed ingrained beliefs. As proclaimed departures from Fox's more conventional fare, both were basically sentimental testimonies to the importance of family solidarity. Their attacks upon an unjust economic system were cleverly mixed with Fox's usual celebration of individual determination and fortitude. In short, the social criticism of *The Grapes of Wrath* and *How Green Was My Valley* was daring in a way that attracted audiences.

Both also derived from books which topped the bestseller list the year they were released. Throughout the war and the ensuing years of readjustment, Fox was consistently to outbid rival studios in purchasing rights to best sellers. Fox moved to snap up these novels in the belief that they showed what audiences preferred. They were proven properties and good indices to current interests. By late 1946, *Variety* would identify Fox as having "the heftiest shelf of best-selling novels any studio has stacked away."[4] While Fox was wooing Kazan, it was busily negotiating for rights to *A Bell for Adano* and *The Razor's Edge*, number five and nine on the bestseller list for 1944. Both were among Fox's most successful productions of the next two years. Yet its prize became Kazan's first assignment. *A Tree Grows in Brooklyn* was the fourth most popular novel of 1943, and after moving up to number three in 1944, it was second only to *The Robe* in wartime sales.

With her turn-of-the-century setting, Betty Smith fashioned a sentimental tale around an obsession of the war years—the problem of keeping the family together. Smith's Katie and Johnny Nolan are parents whose differences are as insurmountable as their situation. Manifestly unable to provide for his family's financial needs, Johnny is a singing waiter who works too little and drinks too much. Though he is well liked for his expansive warmth of spirit, he is mired in his childish imaginings of a better world. Katie, in contrast, is enterprising and determined. She strives to compensate for her husband's failings and provide the ballast necessary to keep the family going. Katie denies Johnny's enthusiasm for Saturdays with an insistence upon workday responsibilities.

The Nolan's cramped tenement is a harsh world of poverty, small pleasure, and enforced compromises. Each saving, like each expenditure, carries a measure of loss and leaves the family painfully divided over its priorities. The one bond remaining from Katie's and Johnny's youthful love is their dedication to the welfare of their children, but this has evolved into a battle of influences that further strains their marriage. Yet these conflicts and deprivations are muted with a sentimentality that causes them to bring compensatory joys and opportunities. For all their frustration and antagonism, the different outlooks of Johnny and Katie endow their children with a balance they each lack and thereby assure them of a brighter future.

"I read *A Tree*," Kazan has commented, "and saw in it material I knew something about, the streets of New York and the lives of the working class."[5] Still, in turning this poignant novel into an equally touching film, Kazan came to look upon himself as no more than a cog in an assembly line. That is to say, *A Tree Grows in Brooklyn* was very much a Fox production. Although Kazan's role was confined to getting effective performances from the actors that were photographed and assembled by someone else, he still did an impressive job. His work was crucial to the academy award James Dunn won for best supporting actor and the special Oscar awarded to Peggy Ann Garner. The fragile image of innocent delight and adult concern that Kazan got Garner to project as the daughter is unforgettable. Much of the film's impact hinges upon the effectiveness with which this image is conveyed. Conventional pictures of the era tended to show children

A Tree Grows in Brooklyn: With its evocation of sympathy for the contrasting situations of the wage earner and the homemaker, it surpassed other lachrymose movies of the war years in communicating the emotional cost of conquering adversities. *Left to right:* Francie (Peggy Ann Garner), Johnny (James Dunn), Neeley (Ted Donaldson), Katie (Dorothy McGuire). (The Museum of Modern Art/Film Stills Archive, New York.)

as adults like to think of them: happy, optimistic, talented. But *Tree* presented an adult world seen through the eyes of a child. Francie's view was naïve, tinged with affection, yet pained by a dawning realization of her parents' shortcomings. Kazan understood that the child she was playing demanded a radical departure from the roles Shirley Temple had played for Fox, so he downplayed "performance" and concentrated on "look." Much of his effort went into "get(ting) the light in that little girl's eyes, the expression of her face, the feeling in her soul."[6]

The effectiveness of Dunn's performance, its power and credibility, demanded Francie's perspective. Johnny's actions are consistently coupled with cuts to Francie's face or else framed so that the

94

audience sees Francie watching him, as in the scene of his singing "Annie Laurie." The trust she accords him, which combines skepticism with loving devotion, convinces the audience that he is essentially the person he repeatedly fails at trying to be. Dunn, according to Kazan, was very "uncertain" and "so dependent on me."[7] His career had slipped into decline and the animated characters he had once played were no longer coming his way. While he jumped at the opportunity to play Johnny Nolan, he was uncomfortably aware that the melancholy of the character ranged beyond his acting experience. This problem Kazan deftly turned into a source of strength. Dunn's very uneasiness made his performance arresting. Johnny, Francie, and the audience intensely long to believe his unconvincing view of life. Full of wistful optimism and a fanciful imagination like so many of Kazan's future father figures, his manner is nonetheless forced and exaggerated, so that only a child could believe his stories. At the same time he is betrayed by fears and doubts no child could miss. Johnny does not appear in many scenes, but they are so well set up that they are invariably the most memorable. The uplifting cheer of Johnny's first appearance, which partakes of the vitality of the streets, makes Francie happy, but her hesitation, her instinctive skepticism, erodes his conviction and produces his dark, unfinished observation "Oh, this could be a fine world, if . . ." The even better scene of his return from a wedding follows the same pattern, Johnny's exaggerated swing from joy to despair, from clown-like animation to flat, soft-spoken frankness is moving because the audience is so aware of its impact upon Francie.

A Tree Grows in Brooklyn was melodrama of a very high order. In the sympathy it evoked for the contrasting situations of the husband and the wife, the family head and the homekeeper, it surpassed the more conventional lachrymose movies of the war years in communicating the cost of the effort to make things better. Equally deft was its balance of brooding preoccupation with death and poignant straining for joy. When Francie said, in the film's last scene, "I feel like I'm saying goodbye to something," she could almost have been speaking for the audience she was addressing. Once the war was over, the divided family took on a different meaning and movies like A Tree Grows in Brooklyn lost a significant measure of their appeal. For

Kazan, who was anticipating this shift even while he worked on this film, this would be a similar farewell. Never again would he associate himself with an environment of impoverishment and misery in which merry music echoed from the streets and people smiled behind their tears. Already he sensed that to hold audiences in the future, the divided family would have to be presented more in the spirit of *Deep Are the Roots* and *All My Sons*.

Kazan's next film, *Sea of Grass* (1946) which he did as an assignment for MGM, was a disaster and a harsh reminder that the transition from stage directing to film would not be altogether smooth. The result is so lifeless it is hard to believe Kazan directed it. The pacing is slow and ponderous. There are no "scenes"; the dramatic action builds to no peak and leads nowhere. Kazan's complaint about MGM's penchant for overdressing everything, the background film forced upon him, and the recalcitrance of its stars (Spencer Tracy and Katherine Hepburn) inadequately account for the botched results. Because *Sea of Grass* is more a domestic melodrama than a Western, which would have been well afield of Kazan's expertise, one cannot help wondering why it is so devoid of intensity. Was this not a classic case of misunderstanding? "And I truly hoped that my following film, *Sea of Grass*," Kazan has observed, "would allow me to do something in accord with my own background."[8] This curious comment most probably refers to the drama's background conflict between the cattlemen and the farmers over how the land was to be used. The fight between the wealthy cattleman with his huge land holdings and the host of poor disenfranchised squatters who are further hurt by a devastating drought was a holdover from the depression years that would have naturally appealed to Kazan. But such themes found little accommodation at MGM. To the extent that Kazan gravitated in this direction he strayed from the epic romance MGM was geared for producing. It was this mismatch of sensibilities that doomed the foundering marriage on which the film focused.

The studio environment in which Kazan had worked on *Tree* and *Sea of Grass* had left him with the familiar feeling of being the outsider. Each element of the filmmaking process, he had to learn, was clearly defined and rigidly controlled. He never saw the writers. The script was to be shot as they had written it.[9] In-house experts were inclined to tell a newcomer the way things should be done rather than consider the alternatives he might suggest. But by 1947 Hollywood's confidence and convictions were being badly shaken. Movie attendance was dropping and costs were rising. Audience tastes were no longer predictable. Management was exercising tighter control over budgets and searching for alternatives to expensive backlot productions. In short, the assumptions that for so long had been the foundation of the studio system were starting to crumble.

Kazan's next film was an outgrowth of these changes. *Boomerang* (1947) won no awards, created no critical stir, turned only a small profit, yet this low budget, on-location creation was to bring Kazan enormous personal satisfaction. Willingly he accepted the headaches of curious crowds and difficult scene arrangements[10] in return for increased control over the finished product. Freed from the defined responsibilities of backlot production, he selected the camera setups and the scenic layouts. This film's use of actual settings and real townspeople rather than pasteboard props and made-up professionals accorded with Kazan's belief that drama should impress audiences with its likeness to life outside the theatre, not its differences. For the first time he participated in casting decisions and was so pleased with the results that he retained Arthur Kennedy, Ed Begley, and Dudley Sadler for the ensuing production of *All My Sons*. Most of all, *Boomerang* realigned Kazan with the style of documentary realism toward which he naturally gravitated.

If *Boomerang* was a product of Kazan's peacetime push to get back to social problem drama and an important precursor of his future work, it also illustrated the compromise and modifications which necessarily resulted from the studio process. Despite Kazan's influence, *Boomerang* carries the unmistakable imprint of its producer, Louis de Rochemont.

DeRochemont's first film, *House on 92nd Street* (1945), gave an impressive demonstration of how feature presentations might be enriched by the slick techniques he had developed for his famed *March of Time* series. Through a skilled use of narrative overlay, location photography, and flashy montages of informational footage, the actual was dramatized, and de Rochemont came up with a flattering portrait of the F.B.I.'s scientific resources and bureaucratic know-how. Bene-

Boomerang: Using his former Group colleagues Cobb, Malden, and Kennedy, Kazan modified de Rochemont's usual glorification of governmental agencies into an indictment of civic disregard for truth and justice. (The Museum of Modern Art/Film Stills Archive, New York.)

fitting from the fact that his film's depiction of a Nazi attempt to steal a formula for a top-secret mega-explosive had the uncanny good fortune to appear within weeks of the dropping of the A-bomb, *The House on 92nd Street* produced impressive returns on its modest investment. The followup *13 Rue Madeleine* did almost as well with its use of the same techniques to dramatize a discovery by U.S. Intelligence of a Nazi attempt to infiltrate one of its secret operations.[11]

Boomerang was planned as one more variation. Again the presentation sought to personalize and celebrate the operation of an important branch of the government. This was to do for the American judicial system what the previous films had done for the F.B.I. and Army Intelligence. This was another factual account intended to be as current as the news and immediately relevant for the audience. In order to prevent this formula from appearing overworked, wartime maneuverings between foreign espionage agents and governmental sleuths were dropped and the plot dealt with a prosecutor's efforts to prevent a discharged serviceman from being convicted of a murder he didn't commit. In this case, civic demands that the killer of a popular local priest be brought to justice lead to the hasty arrest of a serviceman passing through town in search of work. On the basis of circumstantial evidence, he is brought to trial. The local attorney appointed to prosecute the case is assured of professional advancement if he secures a speedy conviction. However, he concludes the veteran is innocent, and, in a dramatic (but implausible) display of professional responsibility, proceeds to disprove the very evidence from which he should be building his case.

Boomerang was to bring together opponents of ten years earlier and thus to be a telling measure of interim changes. As a former director for Frontier Films, Kazan was joining with the founder of *March of Time*, whose innovative use of documentary techniques Frontier had set out to rival. In effect, de Rochemont's customary defense of established institutions was being teamed with Kazan's drive toward exposing social injustice. Significantly, it was *Boomerang's* shading of de Rochemont's position toward Kazan's that was to distinguish it from the two de Rochemont productions that immediately preceded it. *Boomerang* was another artfully contrived true story, but its drama questioned the values *House on 92nd Street* and *13 Rue*

Madeleine had upheld. Under Kazan's direction, *Boomerang*'s intended glorification of the American judicial process became an effective indictment of the populace's inveterate disregard for honesty, truth, and justice. The montage that de Rochemont had used so effectively to show the complex but synchronized workings of federal bureaucracies here reveals how a "typical" American town operates. Every concern is quickly transformed into a political issue. All the community's moral energy is dissipated by hesitation, confusion, and self-serving power struggles. By the time a suspect is found, the demand for conviction has preempted all concern for justice.

Such is the gap the district attorney Henry Harvey (Dana Andrews) rises to fill. Initially he appears to be no better than anyone else; he too bows to the mounting pressure for action. Only when everyone is confident the killer has been caught, the upheaval is about to settle, and Harvey is on the brink of professional advancement does he consider that there might be more to the case than he had thought. Although Harvey's sudden skepticism at the mountain of incriminating evidence is most improbable, it allowed Kazan to dramatize how Harvey's commitment to justice alienated him, by turn, from the town, his party, the police chief he respects, and even his wife. Each scene intensifies the painful loneliness demanded by his stand. In this way the plight of the innocent serviceman develops into a struggle of righteous conscience against a mean, prejudicial, small-town mentality. The account of the case (identified in the opening credits as the film's source) concluded that "it is just as important for a State's Attorney to use the great powers of his office to protect the innocent as it is to convict the guilty."[12] But the thrust of Kazan's handling differed. At the film's climactic turning point, Harvey asserts, "One man's life is worth more than the community" and explains that this realization necessitates his fighting the whole town. Consequently, the final courtroom scene turns the serviceman's trial into an indictment of the local citizenry. They are the ones found guilty.

With its concentration upon a returning veteran as victim of a false accusation, *Boomerang* departed from the wartime premise of *House on 92nd Street* and *13 Rue Madeleine*. The spirit of searching critical appraisal Kazan communicated did even more to relate it to the circumstances of postwar readjustment. However much Kazan's use of

100

de Rochemont's documentary techniques seemed a revival of the styling he cultivated in the *People of the Cumberland,* his grafting of them to a drama of developing doubt and alienation caused the result to resemble the darkening introspection of his stagework more than that film's militant confidence in civic cooperation.

Nine months after the courtroom scene for *Boomerang* was filmed there, Stamford, Connecticut became the site of a second trial at which 250 of the local residents were found guilty of another injustice. Although Kazan did not participate in this affair, it would indirectly link *Boomerang* to his next film. This time the Stamford trial was a civic pageant showing the townspeoples' discovery of their unrealized anti-Semitism. The immediate inspiration for this mass testimony came from Laura Hobson's *Gentleman's Agreement,* which had topped the bestseller list through the spring of 1947.[13] Starting from a situation in which Phil Green is assigned to write a series on anti-Semitism, Hobson has her character decide that the only way in which he can get the truth is to lead everyone to believe he is Jewish and to make his account a record of their reactions. The result is a series of rejections that are surprising, depressing, and finally infuriating. His child is abused and his mother is denied badly needed medical care. Even his fiancée turns against him. Although the book contained no trial scenes and none of its action was set in Stamford, its sharp attack upon the discreet anti-Semitism of nearby Darien struck the citizens of Stamford as applying to them as well. Their courtroom drama was a publicity stunt acknowledging their shared sense of guilt and their determination to rectify this injustice. The residents of Stamford were showing what they had learned from Kazan a few months earlier about making a trial a vehicle for this point.

The popularity of Hobson's novel indicated a growing public willingness to examine festering social problems that would have been unthinkable only a few years before. Zanuck saw that this willingness was not confined to the publishing world and Broadway. The resurgent social consciousness that made *The Best Years of Our Lives* a box-office and critical triumph created a strong market for films such as *The Lost Weekend, Mildred Pierce, Smash-Up,* and *Till the End of Time.* With an emphasis on the corrosive effect of time's passage seldom found in the prewar fights against more concrete, personalized evils, all had drawn well. Fox's own *The Razor's Edge, Kiss of Death*, and *Nightmare Alley* had been tailored to capitalize on this use of social problems as vehicles for dramatizations of distress. In view of this trend it was almost inevitable that anti-Semitism should be seized upon as the basis for such a film. Still Zanuck was not especially concerned that his film adaptation of Hobson's novel be a profitable venture. *Gentleman's Agreement* was supposed to prove that, despite the failure of *Wilson*, Zanuck surpassed his peers in his willingness to take on controversial material.*

The spirit in which Zanuck approached this project is evidenced by a scene not in Hobson's novel. At a luncheon gathering of the staff of *Smith's Weekly* magazine early in the film, a faceless executive voices his belief that the proposed series on anti-Semitism is unwise: "The less talk about it the better," he advises. Minify, the editor, sharply responds, "Pretend it doesn't exist and add to the conspiracy of silence? I should say not." *Gentleman's Agreement* was a top flight production conceived to speak out on a matter of current concern, and in doing so, to demonstrate just how outspoken the producer behind it was.

The result was a slick Hollywood package presenting a conventional production in bold wrapping. Zanuck recruited Moss Hart to prepare the script, accorded the production a first-class budget, and assembled a cast of star performers and technicians. Thus Kazan found himself in much the same position as he was in with *A Tree Grows in Brooklyn*—that of another cog in the Fox assembly line. Hobson's book was first serialized in *Cosmopolitan* magazine, and in recent interviews, Kazan has latched onto this origin to characterize the work: "*Gentleman's Agreement* was like an illustration for *Cosmopolitan* magazine. Everyone was prettified. It was a series of clichés."[14] *Gentleman's Agreement* starts as though it is to be an extension of *Boomerang*'s documentary styling. The opening shots of Phil Green (Gregory

*The typical Hollywood response to this issue just a year earlier is reflected in the change of the veteran's name in *Boomerang* from Harold Israel to John Waldron. For the film version of the Broadway play *Home of the Brave*, the traumatized veteran was changed from a Jew to a black. Nonetheless Zanuck was to be upstaged by RKO's *Crossfire*, which dealt with anti-Semitism and opened several months before *Gentleman's Agreement*.

Peck) show him before the Plaza Hotel, at Rockefeller Center, and in Saks Fifth Avenue. He is in New York and not on a set. However, the very choices suggest a Hollywood point of view. The lush greenery outside the magazine's offices, the palatial grandeur of the editor's home, the imposing view from the apartment of Phil's girlfriend and the glut of furniture in her country house pander to the viewer's eye. In effect, they promote the pretentious sophistication and respectability the movie was supposed to be attacking.

However different the film's visual texture may have been from that of *Boomerang*, Kazan crafted a rather similar drama of conviction being undermined and giving way to soul-searching reevaluation. When Laura Hobson first sat down to write her novel, she undoubtedly found herself in the same quandary as her protagonist when he receives his assignment. How can anti-Semitism be presented so that a large percentage of the general public would pay attention? Her solution was to have a typical white middle-class citizen adopt the identity of a Jew. When people discover that Phil is a Jew, the comfortable, accommodating world around him suddenly turns frightening and infuriating. This certainly was the effect Kazan strove for in his direction. Scene after scene starts out with commonplace occurrences—a chance meeting with the apartment manager, a conference with a doctor, an idle conversation with a secretary, an exchange with a desk clerk— that lead to shocking transformations when Phil is discovered to be Jewish. People cease talking and acting in their normal manner. Acceptance and trust dissolves and Phil becomes an object of suspicion. Within seconds he moves from being an accepted, respected member of society to a rejected ousider.

Fox certainly did all it could to bring out the *Cosmopolitan* in *Gentleman's Agreement* by joining its controversial subject matter to a romance involving the triumph of love over adversity. Behind the upright but unsure journalist stands the woman who is supposed to give valuable support and reassurance. Yet this romance was to be unique in its inversion of this convention and its aggravation of Phil's growing alienation. Wrongly perceiving inconsistency in Kathy's behavior, Phil judges her to be as hypocritical as everyone else and rejects her. As Kazan had Gregory Peck and Dorothy McGuire play the exchanges between Phil and Kathy, their words fail to express their emotional

Gentleman's Agreement: As a premiere Fox production dealing with anti-Semitism, it boldly proclaimed Darryl Zanuck's determination to handle controversial social issues. *Left to right:* Minify (Albert Dekker) and Phil Greene (Gregory Peck). (The Museum of Modern Art/Film Stills Archive, New York.)

Pinky: Although designed to expose white middle-class audiences to the effects of racial prejudice as *Gentleman's Agreement* had done, it presented a very different atmosphere. *Left to right:* Pinky (Jeanne Crain) and Aunt Dicey (Ethel Waters). (The Museum of Modern Art/Film Stills Archive, New York.)

confusion and communication breaks down. The total silence of Phil's walk through Kathy's private retreat eloquently states the end to their affair. Kazan's skillful orchestration of these effects is particularly evident in the liveliness he gets from the the subordinate characters played by Celeste Holm and John Garfield to counterbalance Peck's brooding and suppressed outrage.

Gentleman's Agreement was roundly acclaimed a fine motion picture. The film's caution and qualification, so apparent to the modern viewer, went virtually unnoticed in 1947 amidst the widespread surprise that Hollywood would dare to treat such a sensitive issue. The talent recruited for the undertaking made the result seem compelling, and it demanded recognition. At the annual balloting of the Motion Picture Academy, *Gentleman's Agreement* was voted the year's outstanding picture, and Kazan was awarded the Oscar for direction. The New York Film Critics' Circle, which cultivated the practice of disagreeing with the Academy's selections, reaffirmed these two awards. In a feature-length article for the leading Jewish intellectual journal *Commentary*, Elliot Cohen went so far as to declare: "It is a pleasure to report that for once in a lifetime, Mr. Zanuck is even better than his billing. The plain fact is that *Gentleman's Agreement* is a moving, thought-provoking film, which dramatically brings home the question of anti-Semitism to precisely those people whose insight is most needed—decent average Americans."[15]

One of the few with second thoughts about the film was Zanuck himself. Under a headline proclaiming "Drop Message Pix," which appeared just after *Gentleman's Agreement* went into general release, *Variety* reported, "Highly publicized production of 'message' pictures has been virtually abandoned with no attendant fanfare. Twentieth–Fox's 'Quality' planned as a follow up to *Gentleman's Agreement* has been placed on the shelf."[16] *Quality* was a novel, developed by Cid Ricketts Sumner from a story she had published in *Ladies' Home Journal*, about the struggle of a mulatto nurse to overcome the racial prejudice she encounters on a return to her native South. Because she appears white, has been North and therefore acts white, "Pinky" is initially taken to be white. But as the truth comes out, she is rebuffed, derided, and attacked as a black—often as one who does not understand her "place." Fox had purchased this property just following its acquisition of *Gentleman's Agreement*. The later decision to stay this follow-up did not represent a loss of confidence so much as a fear that Fox might be overextending itself. The impending appearance of a host of social commentaries prompted Zanuck to wonder if the market for this type of film would dry up. Was not the appeal of these movies a momentary fancy that would soon pass? To his surprise, Zanuck discovered that *Gentleman's Agreement* had not only far exceeded its expected box-office returns, but also, in the South, was running up the second largest gross receipts in the company's history. Meanwhile, *The Snake Pit* appeared and drew much better than anyone expected. Immediately Zanuck reversed his estimate and decided to invest as heavily on "Quality," now entitled *Pinky*, as he had on *Gentleman's Agreement*. Philip Dunne, one of the studio's top writers, was assigned to the project. John Ford was persuaded to serve as director. After lengthy discussion, it was decided that the white Jeanne Crain would play the lead role of Pinky. She would be buttressed by the impressive talents of Ethel Waters and Ethel Barrymore in the two major supporting roles.

Pinky represented a rather obvious attempt to do for blacks what *Gentleman's Agreement* had done for the Jews. The calculated sensationalism of Pinky's encounters with Mrs. Wooley, the matriarch who condescends to her, the midnight revelers who try to rape her, the local storekeeper who refuses to wait on her, the police who do not protect her, and finally the assembled townspeople who support the trial disputing her inheritance, follow the pattern of Phil Green's experience. *Pinky* further resembles *Gentleman's Agreement* in that the protagonist's progression from confidence to uncertainty changes her essential character. Everyone presses Pinky to come to a better understanding of herself. The human injustice and degradation she patiently suffers justify her concluding decision to fight back. Given this similarity to *Gentleman's Agreement*, Kazan would have been a more logical choice for director than Ford, but Zanuck was intentionally avoiding everyone involved in the earlier film. He didn't want this follow-up to appear a remake. *Pinky* was to have a distinctive styling of its own. Unfortunately, even before the first week of shooting had been completed, disagreement broke out between Ford and Ethel Waters over how the role of Pinky's grandmother should be played. Abruptly Ford departed and Kazan was pressed into replacing him.

Arriving on such short notice, Kazan concentrated his efforts upon making Pinky's humiliations as upsetting as possible and realizing Zanuck's wish for a unique film. Although *Pinky* and *Gentleman's Agreement* were both shot on the same lot at Fox, they look as different as night and day. The world of *Gentleman's Agreement* is neatly arranged and sharply defined; the overall effect is one of clarity, order, and precision. The dark, heavily shadowed shot of Peck brooding in his bed before Garfield and Holm burst in on him is a sharp break in styling used to stress an exceptionally bleak moment. *Pinky*, on the other hand, appears congested and ominous. The psychological anxiety, so central to the drama of *Gentleman's Agreement*, is developed more in the atmosphere and styling of *Pinky*. Characteristics of *film noir* are strongly felt. Working closely with his new cameraman, Joe MacDonald, who would remain with him for *Panic in the Streets* and *Viva Zapata!*, Kazan dwelled on the fecundity and poverty of the southern setting. Some of the most dramatic scenes occur when the foliage and undergrowth press between the camera and its object. What seems to be a regional difference is essentially a matter of aesthetics. Except for Miss Em's house, the interiors are portrayed as messy gatherings of people and objects. Everywhere Pinky turns she finds herself confined and overwhelmed. Most disturbing of all is the darkness constantly threatening to engulf her. The high contrast lighting that makes the darkened surroundings menacing also makes her bright image seem overexposed.

The uneasy mood of *Pinky* was familiar enough to filmgoers of the forties. The opening shot of an arriving train, followed by one of an anxious girl walking with her suitcase, let viewers know that this would be another upsetting journey down memory lane. The source of Pinky's uneasiness is certainly revealed with startling effect when Ethel Waters looks up wonderingly from her wash and hears Jeanne Crain reply, "Yes, granny, it's me." How, the viewer immediately asks, can this black woman be related to this lily-white visitor? If *Pinky* dispenses with the conventional dissolve into the past that typically followed such dramatic, question-raising openings, its kinship to the flashback film is fully apparent in the psychological cast of the scenes that follow. Pinky's restless dreams, the telegram she considers sending, and the disturbing echo of the train whistle communicate all the anxiety attendant upon her return home. Her waking moments are filled with painful reminders of what it means to be a southern black and how different her situation is from that of the white she was taken to be up North. The iron fence surrounding Miss Em's property, anticipatory of the one Kazan would employ in *On the Waterfront*, makes Pinky uncomfortably aware of the sharp division between black and white in this locale, while the groping uncertainty of her approach captures the spirit of her response. Pinky does not possess Phil Green's strength of will. Her development is fueled by fear and confusion rather than smouldering anger. She is torn apart by the discontinuity of her various identities—downtrodden black, devoted lover, and skilled professional. The radically different reactions caused by the type of person she is taken to be (black or white, poor or well-to-do), set off against her democratic assumption that people should be treated with equal respect, leave her feeling hurt and helpless. Pinky's journey to resolution stresses an introspection and insecurity that was not a part of Phil Green's. Like *Gentleman's Agreement, Pinky* was a vehicle for exposing white audiences to a prejudice they were more accustomed to practice than to feel. But *Pinky* was an educational experience offered in a very different spirit.

Kazan's sensitivity to these qualities led to a frustration with the casting of Jeanne Crain to play Pinky. "She was cast already," he has said, "and I had to take it or leave it. And not only was she white in her face but also white in her heart. She was the blandest person I ever worked with. She had no rebellion in her whatever. She is not a bad person, a sweet girl in fact, but she has no inner conflict that I have seen."[17] When Kazan agreed to take over for Ford and realized Crain's lack of acting ability, he immediately began searching for ways to get around it. Cagily he devised distant shots, shadows, and context to transmit the effects he wanted. Crain was reduced to a fixture the camera made meaningful. Close-ups were reserved for moments of troubled introspection that Kazan communicated by having Crain look worried and shift her eyes from the camera.

The result was a surprising success. Few critics found fault with

Crain's performance. One critic even found Crain "deeply stirring,"[18] while another went so far as to declare that "Pinky captures the largest share of the audience and the honors" and praised Crain's impressive breakaway from her roles of the past five years "in which she had come to typify the pretty, vivacious co-ed of American University life."[19] Crain wound up receiving an Academy award nomination for best actress, and the film itself went on to reap the year's second largest gross returns.

The problems Kazan overcame with *Pinky* suggest the achievement of his early years at Fox. Crain's limitations were the result of an industry that placed too high a premium upon a particular appearance and paid too little attention to the thought and feeling the character might convey. When Kazan was working on *A Tree Grows in Brooklyn,* Zanuck had complained in a memo: "In his [Kazan's] searching for illusive moods and inner emotional motivations there is the danger that we may talk ourselves into a perfectly psychological story that is emotionally magnificent but lacking the true elements of entertainment that will appeal to the masses."[20] Yet Kazan believed such "embellishments" were crucial to his characters and engaging for audiences. And they were not the only ingredient lacking in Hollywood's bland fare. Pressed as he was to conform to preordained expectations, Kazan could see how Fox's smooth, well-established, well-integrated, well-controlled method contravened the distress in which this material was grounded. He knew the phony set fashioned for *Pinky* bore little resemblance to actual Southern poverty. A real shanty town would have been more convincing—and more dramatic. People who came from this environment did not look like Jeanne Crain and they did not act like her. The pressures on their lives, as Kazan well knew, marked their faces and twisted their souls. Their behavior was surprising and disturbing, not reserved, well-mannered, and formulaic. Reality and psychology went together. A skilled fusion of the two actually stood to enrich the entertainment for which Zanuck was calling.

To be given an opportunity to show what he might do, Kazan first had to be able to relate to the studio mentality. He had to win Fox's respect and understand its thinking. Each of the four major productions on which he worked at Fox had exceeded its commercial projections. None had been a disappointment. These successes, combined with the favor he won as Ford's replacement, earned Kazan the right to more concessions. He was eager to have more say in his assignments and the casting. He wanted power to get script modifications and to explore the possibility of outside script preparation. From his experience on Broadway, he could envision benefits to be derived from outsiders whose talents were not so well honed to industry expectations. At the same time, Kazan himself had benefitted from his apprenticeship. Thrust as he had been into the complex process of filmmaking, he had been saved from clumsy errors of inexperience and had profited enormously from the skilled technicians assigned to assist him. He had received valuable education in the filmmaking process and proven that he had much to offer.

In 1947, Kazan told Murray Schumach, "I want to make folk movies, not folksy movies. Odets discovered the Bronx; but no one had discovered America."[21] In looking to the future, Kazan was inclined to reference his past; what he hoped to accomplish was envisioned as a departure from Odets and his view of drama as it was shaped by his Depression experiences. Amidst Hollywood's sudden willingness to examine defects within the American scene, Kazan could sense opportunities nonexistent only a few years earlier. Fox was growing more and more receptive to his crusading fervor and emotional dramatizations. *Gentleman's Agreement* and *Pinky*, which followed on the heels of Kazan's remark to Schumach, were to be "folk movies" in their calculated effort to generate broad-based interest in a problem faced by minorities, but as such, they were still a dubious fulfillment of Kazan's projections. However much they affirmed Kazan's impressive skills, their use of WASP protagonists and backlot artifice bespoke the costly compromise in Kazan's efforts to accommodate his theatrical heritage to the studio environment. Nonetheless, Kazan was making his presence felt. One of the best measures of the uniqueness of *Gentleman's Agreement* and *Pinky* is their departure from the "folk movie" that made Frank Capra so successful a decade earlier.

During the 1930s, Capra had fashioned rousing social fables from the conventions of screwball comedy. Angered by sophisticated urban skepticism of democratic principles and essential human needs, the Capra hero was transformed from a bumbler into a resolute fighter who eventually converts an uncertain public to his cause. By the for-

111

ties, however, Capra's films assumed a darker cast, dwelling less on the hero's antics and more on his agonies. As the behavior of his characters grew strained and the frenzy of their desperation snuffed out the comic spirit, Capra lost control of his material and his audience. Kazan's films reformulated Capra's premise and brought it into accord with the very different spirit of the times.

The conditions of postwar readjustment were such that films dwelling on discontent and injustice suddenly enjoyed renewed popularity. The widespread problem of the unappreciated, displaced serviceman, which had immediate appeal, predisposed audiences toward the plight of abused, misunderstood minorities. Now rejected by the decent citizens the Capra film once assumed, the hero of Kazan's films broods over both his alienation and the flawed character of the society rejecting him. He turns inward and the social battle becomes psychological. The strong-willed, compassionate elders who counsel these restless seekers are foils who make audiences more aware of their troubled gropings. At the same time, their confidence comes across as forced, almost nostalgic, not just because the times were less confident of solutions but also because the problems had become more complex. The crusaders of these films notably fail to win the final communal approval so characteristic of the Capra film and the agit prop drama on which Kazan cut his teeth because theirs is a very different premise: the problem they confront is so inherent to the existing social structure that their efforts to remedy it isolate them and turn them into loathsome pariahs. The frustration of their hopes is an essential part of their characterizations. Yet as key examples of this shift, *Gentleman's Agreement* and *Pinky* never quite realized their potential. Neither contained enough complexity of situation or characterization. To accomplish this, Kazan was to learn, demanded a different type of scriptwriting and acting. It necessitated an appreciation for inescapable pressure and consequent desperation. It demanded a fuller understanding of how the drive of the thirties for social solidarity had been eroded by a new sense of hopelessness and alienation.

FIVE

Taking Charge

The success of *All My Sons, A Streetcar Named Desire, Gentleman's Agreement,* and *Pinky,* made Kazan a leading director on Broadway and in Hollywood. His skill was above question. Still, he chafed under the constraints of the production process. His sphere of influence was too limited. He wanted more control and more responsibility—more power. In many respects, this enterprising ambition was its own worst enemy. Quite simply, Kazan was too busy to shoulder more responsibilities. For the past five years, he had been leading a frenetic double life rushing back and forth between Hollywood and Broadway. His work schedule had been straining the outer limits of his time and energy. Repeatedly he had found himself having to pass up an attractive project or to race into production. His characteristic preference for the latter course necessarily restricted the amount of effort he had to invest. He had only three weeks between finishing *Boomerang* and rehearsals of *All My Sons.* Less than six weeks separated completion of *Gentleman's Agreement* and *A Streetcar Named Desire.* He came to *Pinky* after filming had actually begun. To do more Kazan would have to do less. He would have to handle fewer productions and invest more effort in the preparation of the ones he did.

Although he was still inclined to capitalize on opportunity as it presented itself, Kazan's ambitions were shifting. Shrewdly he had assessed the commercial prospects of each project. Ambitiously, even ruthlessly, he had pursued those with strong promise. His recent list of credits showed his maneuvering to get his name associated with premiere productions. The risks he took with *All My Sons, A Streetcar*

Named Desire, and *Boomerang* were neatly coupled with his participation in the heavily promoted *A Tree Grows in Brooklyn, Gentleman's Agreement*, and *Pinky*. Kazan had been fortunate that the climate of postwar readjustment had favored his return to dramas exploring current social problems. While these undertakings had enabled him to say something important and to earn a professional identity in which he could take pride, they communicated more an orientation and disposition than a strong conviction or deep feeling. Kazan's short-lived acting career had already demonstrated that his best work sprang from material eliciting a strong personal involvement. His drive for recognition was such that he was at his best trying to express important components of his own personality. Attracting audiences to conditions of alienation seemed to alleviate a compelling personal need while his sensitivity to the attendant stresses carried him ever further into the psychology of motivation. That is to say, the dramatic center of most of his plays and films was continually verging upon his own psychoanalysis. What Kazan now needed was a vehicle which would extend this overlap and inspire him with the sense of purpose as Group Theatre and his left-wing activities once did.

Death of a Salesman, Panic in the Streets, and the film version of *A Streetcar Named Desire*, were to be major steps in this direction. In *Death of a Salesman*, Kazan had material with strong reminders of his family background. An even more important factor in this landmark undertaking was the challenge the play posed in communicating the complex nature of Willy Loman's psychological breakdown. This presentation compelled Kazan to fashion behavior that in itself communicated the social conditioning that determined it. Willy was a victim of a defective society—not so much in his particular circumstances as in his ingrained ways of thinking. The key to staging Miller's play properly lay in dramatizing his cast of mind and its consequences. *Panic in the Streets*, on the other hand, was a vivid depiction of the conditions and atmosphere capable of producing distress of this sort. Though nowhere near the achievement of *Death of a Salesman*, it helped Kazan to envision the powerful results to be gained by fusing these two dramas so that complex motivation verging upon breakdown could be dramatically amplified, more than explained, by a sensitive depiction of its context. Conceiving his film version of

114

Streetcar to be such a union, Kazan discovered the stage version to be ill-served by this approach and decided upon a closer adherence to the play as originally written. Still the challenge of this adaptation and the experience of his battles to come up with an acceptable script were valuable preparation for future pushes toward this objective.

Despite Kazan's balance of plays and films since the war's end, it was inevitable that one of these represent a stronger commitment. Up to 1948, it still was the theatre. "Kazan complains," ran a 1947 profile, "that Hollywood movie making is too much of a community affair. Only in the theatre does he feel completely free, and so he returns to it constantly."[1] For this reason, the assumption of additional responsibilities naturally inclined him in this direction. In part, this was a matter of expedience. Kazan did not want to spend any more time in Hollywood than he absolutely had to. New York was his home and he did not care for the West Coast. Also the theatre was his heritage. Despite the formidable economic obstacles against repertory theatre, he explored the possibility of reviving the Group. Rather than give up when the project proved unworkable, he began speculating on a viable alternative.

Out of these efforts came the Actors Studio, which he founded in 1947 and fought to keep alive over the next two years. Kazan and his fellow organizers, Cheryl Crawford and Bob Lewis, averted the snag that had sundered previous efforts by avoiding the question of whether Actors Studio could or should be a production company. Helping actors to develop their skills and versatility was to be the main objective. Consequently the Studio was to concentrate upon its acting classes. Kazan agreed to assist Lewis with these responsibilities as he could. They devoted the first year principally to selecting members, setting up a site, and planning classes. These activities were accompanied by a production of Chekhov's *The Sea Gull*, but this was played for a small invited audience and intended to be no more than a test case for the Studio's training techniques.

The bulk of Kazan's time was invested in continuing discussions on the school's scope. Should the Studio confine itself to workshop exercises? Was the estimate of the membership an adequate gauge of the results? Was not something essential being lost in not exposing the students' work to the judgment of audiences who were the ultimate

115

source of their livelihood? Did such in-house activity increase the students' prospects for employment and theatrical success? The answers were not easy. Again and again the theatrical considerations were at odds with the practical and realistic.

During the second year, Kazan decided to mount a Broadway production of *Sundown Beach,* by Bessie Breuer. This was not to compete with regular commercial offerings. Whether or not it made money, it was decided, was unimportant.[2] The production was aimed at exposing Broadway audiences to the higher level of skill and innovation for which the Studio was striving.

Kazan was attracted to *Sundown Beach* because he wanted to use a large number of students, and it was almost a gallery of cameo roles. Its theme was a familiar Kazan obsession: a collection of individuals wishing greater interaction and exchange, yet faced with adverse conditions. The setting of the play is a café frequented by injured air force veterans undergoing rehabilitation at a nearby hospital. Here they initiate contact with civilian life and meet women who hold out the prospect of help. Unfortunately the potential is seldom realized. Since the women all have strong needs of their own, the problem of understanding is unusually acute. Characteristically, the pairings are made with a good deal of awkwardness and turn out poorly. Besides offering a convenient vehicle for showing the intrusion of confused emotions upon behavior, which would become a trademark of Studio training, this play was an obvious extension of Kazan's preoccupation with the agonies of postwar adjustment. Several reviewers even noted the play's resemblance to *Truckline Café*, and, like that fiasco, *Sundown Beach* was a washout, closing after only eight performances.

From this debacle, the Studio learned nothing it had not already suspected. The public confirmed that it wanted assured excitement and had little interest in experimental departures. Debate over the Studio's purpose came to an end: there would be no more commercial productions. In the future it would concentrate its energies upon training promising talent. Scenes and improvisations would be its staple. With this decision that the Studio would be a school and not a production company, Lewis resigned. Though Cheryl Crawford remained willing to lend her administrative support, the future of the Studio's operation again fell to Kazan. Sanford Meisner and Daniel Mann were recruited as a stopgap measure. They oversaw the Studio's operation until Lee Strasberg was finally persuaded to become its permanent head, thus freeing Kazan of a responsibility he never intended to assume. In the future he would be a patron, rather than a director or instructor. Because Kazan would long remain a loyal Studio supporter, connections between his work and the Studio have been greatly overblown. In the future Kazan would utilize the Studio as a resource for acting talent and a testing ground for dramatic material and styling, but always quite sparingly. Although Kazan taught classes during the Studio's first year of existence and would do so later from time to time, he involved himself very little in the training of actors. Most of the unknowns Kazan cast in major roles—Marlon Brando, James Dean, Lee Remick, Warren Beatty—were not Studio products. Moreover, the performances he got from them were almost entirely the product of an astute judgment of talent and a resourceful skill for evoking the effects he wanted. That is to say, the Studio is more important for what it reflects about Kazan's objectives—especially his quest for acting skill and versatility in the projection of psychological effects—than for its influence upon his work.

By the time *Sundown Beach* closed, Kazan was already off to New Haven for rehearsals of a musical entitled *Love Life*, which brought together a wealth of talent. Alan Jay Lerner had written the story and lyrics. Kurt Weill had composed the score. Michael Kidd was handling the choreography. The male lead, Ray Middletown, was just coming off an impressive performance in *Annie Get Your Gun*, while Nanette Fabray was highly respected for her work in *Bloomer Girl* and *High Button Shoes*. Unfortunately, these ingredients never blended. The freewheeling vignettes, ranging from spirited comedy to poignant introspection, presented strong possibilities and pronounced dangers, and Kazan was not up to the challenge. Whether he was too hurried, too constrained, or just not interested, he failed to synthesize this material. Just as everyone acknowledged that the show had impressive moments, they all agreed that the second act was flat and the result uneven.

What Kazan lost with his brief return to musical comedy, he soon regained with his stunning follow-up, *Death of a Salesman*. For this play, Arthur Miller fashioned a family situation strongly rem-

117

iniscent of the Kellers in *All My Sons* but without any of the earlier work's wartime associations. As a simple salesman who has never achieved the wealth and distinction he desired, Willy Loman is a far cry from Joe Keller the corporate head. But, like Joe, Willie is the father of two sons who, having long been cornerstones of his strength, end up driving him to suicide. Again the sons are mere agents, the true cause being a disparity between the actuality of the father's situation and his long-held dreams. Willy believes that a friendly, confident manner is the key to success. Rather than confront how these dreams and beliefs have contributed to his own lackluster career, he optimistically endows his sons with them in blind trust that their achievements will compensate. When pressed to confront the failure of his sons, especially Biff, who has been the most promising, and the loss of his job, Willy becomes deranged. In a final desperate effort to uphold the validity of his dreams and vanquish the doubts weighing down upon him, Willy kills himself so that his family might receive his life insurance benefits.

Kazan once observed that his best films "spoke of this country, of the life of this country and of nothing else." "That they described it or criticized it," he continued, was "in the spirit in which one can criticize one's father, or one's mother, or one's children. They are people whom, first one loves or admires. Then one can say to them, yes, you are admirable, but you do bad things. . . . With that ambivalence between attack and love."[3] This spirit is clearly evident in Arthur Miller's *Death of a Salesman* and in directing this masterpiece, Kazan had an ideal vehicle for his obsession with America and his complementary preoccupation with family relationships. For him, the two were interconnected, at once admirable and deficient. Kazan's early films frequently contained an impassioned encomium of the American way of life being held up to critical examination, and almost invariably its defender was an older relative or close friend of the central character. Grandmother Nolan, Mrs. Green, Miss Em and Aunt Dicey all declare an unwavering trust in America's unique opportunities and potential for constructive change. By presenting these stereotypes as overzealous or somewhat senile, Kazan qualified the reliability of their pronouncements. Impressive as their strong convictions are, they always come across as questionable assertions of belief, unsure ramparts against threatening adversities.

Willy Loman shares these figures' resolute belief in America, the value of hard work and the importance of being well-liked. Moreover, Willy possesses the same human qualities that compel the audience's regard. He is passionately devoted to the welfare and well-being of his offspring and to a world in which man can command respect and be master of his destiny. In him, the most distinctive characteristics of these parental figures are concentrated, showing *not* the redemption of these beliefs but rather their devastating betrayal. His manifest failure, his helpless slide toward madness, and the *cul de sac* of his unacknowledged lies expose painfully the folly of Willy's optimism. Willy is a patriarch who wishes to pass on the fruits of his experience, but he has nothing to give. Age has endowed him with no legacy. He is merely old. Hoping to achieve prosperity and personal satisfaction from his efforts, he has lost both his job and his family. Evolving conditions have bewildered him and, by the opening of the play, he no longer understands even himself. Like Blanche Dubois, he is a past with no future. In him the postwar sense of displacement and reevaluation has become a fully realized psychological condition.

Kazan felt that *Death of a Salesman*, more than any other directing assignment up to this point, related to his personal background. Noting that Arthur Miller's "father was a salesman like mine," Kazan told Michel Ciment that *Death of a Salesman* "is a play that dealt with experiences I knew well in my own life."[4] Kazan's recollections of his father invariably dwell upon his demoralization over the financial reversals he incurred during the Depression or his badgering of Kazan to work for financial success. Given the hostility that infuses these comments, it was inevitable that Kazan would sense keenly Willy's failings and his deleterious influence upon his sons. Having himself been the wayward son who felt compelled to reject his own father in order to make his way, Kazan naturally understood the older son's hostility toward Willy. He therefore presented Biff (played by Arthur Kennedy) with the same exceptional sympathy as his Stanley. He also capitalized on Biff's opposition to Willy to achieve a result like that of Stanley's hostility to Blanche: in getting the audience to understand Willy's deficiencies much as Stanley exposes Blanche's, Biff is guilty likewise of a harshness that finally provokes audience compassion for his adversary. Nonetheless, Kazan realized that the power of Miller's play lay in what is finally a tragic view of Willy's plight and the terrible confusion that overwhelms him. Thus, as director, Kazan strove to convey the kind of understanding for Willy that Biff bitterly refuses.

"This play has to be directed with COMPASSION," Kazan scrawled in his notebook.[5] Earlier, in his list of "basic" points, he observed, "This is a story of love—the end of a tragic love—between Willy and his son Biff. What the audience should feel at the end of this performance is only one thing: Pity, Compassion and Terror for Willy. Every dramatic value should serve this end. This Willy is a fine, tender, capable, potentially useful human. He is just socially mistaught." Characteristically Kazan conceived of this personal drama in terms of its relevance to the contemporary social climate. He added, "Society, our present society, is the 'heavy'—its current philosophy."[6] The society being indicted in this play is not one comprised of the bigoted, narrow-minded, lawless individuals who peopled so many of Kazan's previous works. Rather, it is the society of *prevailing attitudes* that Willy tragically relied upon to give his life direction. "This play is a dramatization of the process in the mind of Willy," Kazan wrote. "The play dwells within the interior process. All its values and meanings are Willy's."[7] Then repeatedly he reminded himself of this throughout his notes. "The play describes the *Process*—dramatizes the Process in Willy's mind."[8] Willy was the sum of his thoughts. All his actions—past and present—were to be viewed in terms of what they said about the cast of his mind.

In *All My Sons,* Kazan had pushed Miller to revise the third act so that Joe Keller would be driven to suicide by his corrosive guilt rather than by a devastating exposure. *Death of a Salesman*, by way of extension, was a thoroughgoing psychological study. What distinguishes *Death of a Salesman* from *All My Sons*, despite its similar presentation of a patriotic, well-intentioned father, a devoted wife striving to allay her husband's fears, and two sons who remind him of betrayal and wrong-doing, is its concentration upon the effect the unfolding action has upon Willy's mind—his determined disregard of

Death of a Salesman: In Willy Loman (Lee J. Cobb), the postwar sense of displacement and searching re-evaluation became a fully realized psychological condition. (Photo by Fred Fehl; reproduced by permission of Hoblitzelle Theatre Arts Library, Humanities Research Center, The University of Texas at Austin.)

what he does not want to admit colliding with the inescapable crush of its disastrous consequences. According to Kazan's approach, every aspect of the production had to be honed so that not only was Willy a constantly felt presence but his suppressed, misdirected, and misunderstood feelings were the *measure* of all that happened.

Death of a Salesman was a full fruition of the type of drama toward which Kazan had been gravitating since the war's end. With it, he had a play grounded in the tenets of social realism, inherited from Odets and the Group Theater, that at the same time concentrated upon the twisted inner workings of the mind in a way that moved toward expressionism. It presented a pitched battle between reality and fantasy that almost defied the director to come up with a controlling style. In this respect, *Death of a Salesman* compounded the problem of *Streetcar*. Kazan immediately recognized that the crucial decision lay in the presentation of Willy's daydreams. He decided that Willy "has imaginary conversations with other people, because of some compulsive reason. Usually to defend himself, re-enact some scene to prove himself, to *attack* someone that he failed to defend himself against properly in the real world." The distortion in Willy's actions and their motivations are the natural, albeit extreme, extension of a prevalent disposition. Willy, Kazan concluded, "built his life and his *sense of worth* on something completely false; the Opinion of Others. This is the error of our whole society. We build our sense of worth not within ourselves but thru our besting others and at the same time having their constant perfect approval."[9] In this respect, Willy's daydreams constitute a desperate straining to revive and relive his past. The credibility and poignancy of this behavior hinges upon Willy's refusal to accept change. Within a section entitled "Characters in the Past," Kazan wrote with special emphasis, *"None of these dream figures are actually in the past!"*[10] Again later, he reiterated in his first note under "Style": "There are no flashbacks!"[11] He saw these sequences to be the keys to Willy's thought process. As he went on to explain, "The only laws of these scenes are the laws of Willy's own mind. And all the figures in Willy's mind are distorted by Willy's *hopes, wishes, desires*."[12] Thus all actions associated with the past are to be understood as thoughts running through Willy's mind at different times following his weary return at the play's outset. Being still vividly alive to Willy, this past remains colored by all his original expectations and delusions.

In order to communicate these difficult effects, Kazan had Jo Mielziner design his famous set so that the Loman home was reduced to an elemental structure stripped of its rear covering. The audience's penetrating view of the goings-on in the various rooms had the effect of exposing the inner lives of the inhabitants. It was a specific, commonplace dwelling with familiar drab furnishings, and a fluid locus for the drama, an actual house that could be freely disregarded but never forgotten when Willy's mind came into play. As a variation upon Mielziner's set for *Streetcar*, it was an even more vivid illustration of a realistic setting doubling as a psychological condition. Kazan then carefully planned the action and pacing so that this atmosphere would not be oppressive. His notes on the acting show that he took great pains to insure that the displays of vigor which held the audience's attention be solidly grounded in a psychologically sound behavioral pattern. "In this play," he wrote, "all movement must come from *Character* impulse. No crosses, etc., with *Energy Substituted for Emotion*. General energy instead of particular emotion. This play has a line which is all down the inside of Willy's spine."[13] Everyone, especially Willy, was *not* to brood over his problems. Ostentatiously they were to display strength, conviction, and vitality. Willy's instinctive preference for activity over thought, which embues the whole family's outlook, establishes him as being typically American while calling attention to the underlying cause of his failure. Willy's refusal to question the premises behind his efforts or to admit defeat, in spite of his nagging uneasiness, doubt, and disillusionment, deepens the poignancy of his plight. His tragedy lies in *never* realizing where his life went wrong. This demanded an exceptional actor, who had the formidable task of showing the audience what Willy failed to see. Though Fredric March was first offered the role and later played in the film version, Lee J. Cobb achieved such a full realization of these effects that his performance was to be definitive. "Lee Cobb," Kazan would observe in commending his portrayal, "was the deepest of the Willys."[14]

Death of a Salesman was a gargantuan success, rivaling that of *A Streetcar Named Desire*. The play ran 742 performances (vs. *Street-*

car's 855) and produced a similar avalanche of profits. It won all the major awards including the Pulitzer Prize. The genius of the playwright had been matched with the imaginative skill of Kazan's direction. Playgoers now had reason to believe that the plight of the common man might be presented so as to rival classical tragedy. In his creation of a style that verged upon expressionism, never before had Kazan journeyed quite so far into the terrain of the mind. Describing how Kazan's handling of "areas for acting imaginatively rather than literally" complemented the play's attempt "to break the conventional mold of realism," John Gassner judged the play "a consummation of virtually everything attempted by that part of the theatre which has specialized in awareness and criticism of social realities . . . a culmination of all efforts since the 1930s to observe the American scene and trace, as well as evaluate, its effect on character and personal life."[15] *Death of a Salesman* had its roots in the tradition of social drama, but it attained something new. Here was a fully developed character whose troubled mind and compulsive behavior reflected the defects of his society. Flushed with success and eager to collaborate on more projects, neither Miller nor Kazan suspected that the past might return to haunt them just as it did Willy.

Between *Love Life* and *Death of a Salesman*, around the spring of 1948, Kazan started to branch out and take a more active role in the planning and preparation of his filmscripts. From his work both on studio sets and on location, he could see that the environments in which people actually lived—the rooms, buildings, and streets—were potentially more convincing and more atmospheric than anything that could be achieved with a contrived look alike. The courtroom in which he shot the final scenes of *Boomerang* had a believability and authority notably lacking in the apartment and country home sets especially built for *Gentleman's Agreement*. By the same token, his use of the downtown section of White Plains enriched his presentation of the priest's murder, while opening shots of Gregory Peck in front of New York's tourist attractions contributed nothing to *Gentleman's Agreement*. What was important was that the setting enrich the flavor of the scene— that they complement one another so that the dramatic effect was enhanced.

From his experience, Kazan could see how the standard compartmentalization of director and scriptwriter frustrated this possibility. Working with a finished script, the director had to close his eye to whatever possibilities he might see in either the location he was using or in the exchange between the characters. Having emerged at the forefront of what was happening on Broadway, Kazan also believed that he was in a unique position to adapt his discoveries to the film-making process. Moreover, he realized that he might never get a chance to work with the kinds of drama and settings which interested him most if he settled for the scripts being offered. In short, to get more of his ideas and his experience into films, Kazan concluded that a close interaction with scriptwriters was imperative.

One of Kazan's first moves in this direction was a project for which he recruited Richard Murphy. Murphy had been scriptwriter for *Boomerang* and, during the shooting, he had been both willing and helpful in modifying the script to take advantage of certain effects Kazan wanted. During the spring of 1948, after the film's completion, Kazan became interested in a story about a colony of Greek sponge fishermen whose livelihood was threatened by an approaching red tide and contacted Murphy on the possibility of developing it into a film-script. Conceiving this to be another location film concentrating upon an ethnic enclave close to his own heritage, Kazan proposed that they go on a research outing together and decide how their material could be most fruitfully rendered. Together they set out for Tarpon Springs, Florida, which contained an enclave of immigrant Greek fishermen.[16]

While Murphy was preparing this script, Kazan struck up a friendship with John Steinbeck, who was currently living nearby in the Upper East Side of New York. Many of Steinbeck's well-known novels had been made into films, and some of them—most notably *Grapes of Wrath*—with impressive results. Though Steinbeck had studiously avoided having anything to do with these adaptations, he was clearly a skilled dramatist. One of the reasons his books lent themselves so readily to the screen was that they contained such vividly imagined scenes. His own stage versions of *Of Mice and Men* and *The Moon is Down* had been Broadway hits. In 1941 he prepared the script for a documentary film about a small Mexican mountain town entitled *The Forgotten Village*. As Kazan and Steinbeck talked, they discovered a common interest in Emiliano Zapata. In their speculations on the po-

Panic in the Streets: A photojournalistic dramatization of a lonely individual battling a suspicious community reluctant to support his efforts to save it. The film inspired Kazan to do an even better one about the waterfront. (The Museum of Modern Art/Film Stills Archive, New York.)

tential of this material, Kazan persuaded the novelist to draft a script, assuring him that he could convince Zanuck to come up with the necessary backing. At the time, Steinbeck was going through a costly divorce and could use the money such a venture would generate. Given Steinbeck's proven talent with scripts and Kazan's with cinematic rendering, both were excited about the prospects and convinced that their reputations would be well served by this collaboration.[17] Late in the summer of 1948, Steinbeck made a quick fact-finding trip to Mexico so that his script would allow Kazan to document the village life of Mexican peasants in the same fashion he was proposing to do with the Greek fishermen of Tarpon Springs.

About the time Steinbeck took up his pen, Darryl Zanuck killed the great fisherman script and put Murphy to work on a story about a manhunt for a killer infected with a plague virus that could produce an epidemic. The script had already been through multiple drafts. Kazan was presented Murphy's results along with the sweetener that he be free to handle "Outbreak," as it was then called, in the same fashion he had *Boomerang*. Anxious as Kazan was to work more upon the documentary effect of *Boomerang*, the drama struck him as lacking relevance for either himself or the prospective movie-goer. In the process of reconsidering the script, Murphy thought of shifting the locale from the cool, windy climate of San Francisco to the steamy, semi-tropical climate of New Orleans in order to make both the killer's environs more squalid and the threatened epidemic a more believable concern. Kazan was enthusiastic about this idea. Since he was then formulating plans for a film version of *Streetcar,* this would be a splendid opportunity to experiment upon locations that could be used in this followup. Now favorably disposed to the project, he and Murphy sped off to New Orleans to search for setups and to tailor their script to them.[18]

Given this collaboration between Kazan and Murphy, it is hardly surprising that *Panic in the Streets* should contain notable resemblances to *Boomerang*. Again the drama dwells upon an agent of the government (here the public health service) who gets embroiled in a lonely battle to save the community from a dangerous threat to its well-being. Again his dedication to the responsibilities of his position causes him to become a pariah. Once more the police hesitate to give him support. Captain Warren, like Chief Robinson, is a tough cop with a pessimistic view of human nature, a man of experience skeptical about the course the hero is pursuing yet capable of respecting him for it. In the background there is the same reporter clamoring after a story and making the protagonist's task more difficult. His outspoken concern for the public interest is a transparent cover for a vanity and ambition that sharply contrasts with his counterpart's humble dedication. He spurs the town fathers to impede the doctor's actions. Meanwhile the enormous physical and emotional strains upon the public servant once again fray his relationship with his devoted wife.

Even though Kazan concentrated upon fleshing out this drama with the same on-location styling, *Panic* is no mere remake of *Boomerang*. Its documentary styling—which now derived more from the

influential, much celebrated *The Naked City*, than from de Rochemont's techniques—was combined with the atmospheric effects of
popular *film noir* crime thrillers like *Double Indemnity*, *The Killers*,
Out of the Past, *Cry of the City*, and *Kiss of Death*. Scenes accentuating stark realism were coupled with ones charged and obscured by
high-contrast lighting. Conditions of order and calm gave way to
squalid, claustrophobic ones recorded with nervous camera work.

Kazan once observed that the plague "was a device, a way of
getting into the various sides of the society and the city."[19] That is to
say, the dramatic issues allowed Kazan enormous latitude in his choice
of setups. He could select sites for their dramatic potential and then
modify a given scene to exploit it. As in so much of his work, and
in even the wording of the remark itself, Kazan's aesthetic was determined by a sociological interpretation of his material. Kazan's association of the disease with a ghetto-like environment links its threat to
conventional middle-class fears. Certainly this is the logic of his
studied contrast between the familiar, accommodating world of Dr.
Reed (Richard Widmark) and the menacing conditions into which this
case carries him. The film opens with an ill immigrant (Kazan made
him an Armenian) being stalked by a group of low-life hoods who
want to prevent him from escaping with the money he has won in a
poker game. This chase amidst rundown warehouses in the enveloping
darkness of night (its menace further accentuated by abrupt cross
cutting), is followed by an autopsy conducted in a bright clinic, with
routine casualness. The camera moves little while the examiner chats
with his friend. Gradually an edge comes into his tone, his concentration shifts, and abruptly he orders his associate out of the room.
Quickly the camera cuts to another "everyday" scene between Dr. Reed
and his son that is interrupted by the examiner's phone call. The tension then climaxes when Dr. Reed confirms the sample to be "pure
culture."

These contrasting scenes set up the ensuing pursuit, which carries
the viewer on a journey through the bowels of the city. With a carefully regulated pacing of the unfolding events, Kazan builds to the
breathless desperation of a magnificently choreographed warehouse
chase that culminates with a final shot of the killer (Jack Palance)
hanging from a ship mooring like a doomed rat. However, the social

128

implications of the chase go beyond locating and eliminating a threat from within the lower class. Dr. Reed's quest is complicated by people's reluctance to help. His scramble through the city—from city hall to skid row taverns—becomes an unnerving lesson in the public's opposition to what it does not want to hear and its ingrained suspicion of governmental agents. He must battle widespread rejection in order to save the populace.

Naturally, Kazan is at his best in his depictions of people balking at Reed's appeals for help. And this happens many times. In a scene anticipating *On the Waterfront*, Reed goes to a crowded seamen's hall and offers fifty dollars to anyone who will give him information about the victim. Movement ceases and he is met with the same suspicious antagonistic stares directed against the victims of prejudice in Kazan's films. "Fellows around here are not liable to talk," he is told. When he finally penetrates this barrier of suspicion and locates the ship from which the victim came, he runs up against the same silent hostility of the seamen's hall. Only luck prevents this from being another dead end. "Widmark is at his best," one reviewer observed, "in the frustrating scenes in a seamen's hiring hall and later aboard the ship which smuggled the plague carrier into the country."[20] Richard Widmark's effectiveness derives largely from the circumstances of these scenes and their vivid illustration of a lonely individual battling an immovable community that refuses to act on its own behalf.

As he observed the troubling drift of international developments and sensed the nation growing increasingly nervous over how it might be affected by them (the "red tide" of the aborted Greek script being only a slightly more obvious metaphor than *Panic*'s plague in this respect), Kazan was left with a lingering impression that Reed's lonely battle comprehended material from which another even better movie might be made. Perhaps a more violent, more emotionally complex struggle could be created from conditions on the waterfront, the brutality of its way of life, the fearful, suspicious reserve of its residents. Shortly after he finished *Panic in the Streets*, over the winter of 1949–50, he proposed that Arthur Miller prepare a filmscript dealing with the current labor struggles at the New York docks, hoping that Miller might be able to give him a character possessing some of Willy Loman's psychological depth to project against such a backdrop.

At this point, Kazan was moving toward a union of the psychological bent in his stagework with the increased sensitivity to setting in his film work. While oppression and deprivation were commonly understood to engender defensiveness, Kazan realized that an outstanding dramatization of this process demanded a special combination of drama and context. With the unique conditions of the waterfront and writing skill of Miller, he believed he might be able to unify the somewhat different emphasis of his stage work and his filmmaking.

Meanwhile, thinking along similar lines, he immersed himself in preparations for filming *A Streetcar Named Desire*. As already noted, Kazan was attracted to *Panic in the Streets* because the switch of its setting from San Francisco to New Orleans enabled him to scout locations for *Streetcar*. At this point, Kazan was planning major modifications in Williams's drama so that the film version would be more cinematic. As part of his intent to "open up" the script, Kazan conceived his film as starting with a view of Blanche's life in Laurel, which is only referred to in the actual play. By using location setups, as he had in *Boomerang* and was then preparing to do in *Panic in the Streets*, he hoped to show the background that turned Blanche into the flighty, neurotic woman who arrives at the Kowalski flat. Yet after exploring the kinds of scenes this would involve and how this approach would change both the characterizations of Blanche and the effect of the drama, Kazan decided the film should instead adhere to the play's original design. He came to realize that the heart of Williams's drama lay in starting with a vivid impression of this curious woman and then, with bits of information introduced at key moments, illuminating her cloudy past so as to alter the flow of audience sympathy—away from her in the early stages and towards her later on. Still, as a woman who persistently avoids any glaring light that might expose her, Blanche had to remain veiled in mystery. Any documentary rendering of her story would harm it. Whatever the viewer saw of Blanche's life in Laurel would not only diminish the dramatic impact of the subsequent revelations but it would also detract from the defensiveness coloring Blanche's admissions and the hostility influencing Stanley's findings.

Nonetheless, when Kazan decided that his film should be as true to the original as possible, his problems were far from over. Even more threatening to *Streetcar* than a documentary probing of its mystery was the censor. Since *Streetcar* dealt with so many sexual taboos—joyous lovemaking, nymphomania, homosexuality, and rape—Williams's play needed a knowledgable, strong-willed defender to prevent the Breen office from emasculating it. If Kazan had to abandon the innovative film he envisioned, the achievement of the finished product came from shrewd, determined negotiations with the censors and a sensitive but cautious exercise of his filmmaking skills.

First came the script. Because Williams himself wanted no part of the adaptation, Oscar Saul was recruited to prepare the filmscript with Kazan closely overseeing the results. In the sixty-eight major and minor changes from the Broadway version,[21] the dominant concern was to satisfy the demands of the Breen Office. During the initial flurry of interest in *Streetcar*, Paramount had sounded out Joseph Breen on what sort of changes would be required in order to get the seal of approval that most exhibitors would demand before they would show the film. Breen responded that the homosexuality and rape would both have to be eliminated.[22] In other words, the film would have to do without the cornerstones to Blanche's behavior. It is no wonder that studios were reluctant to bid for the film rights. When Saul and Kazan sat down to hammer out some form of a compromise, they faced additional demands that Blanche's background of sexual activity be laundered and that there be no vulgar or profane language. Of these, the last point was easiest to dispatch. Saul and Kazan debated each point and where changes were deemed imperative, they strove to preserve the concreteness and ribaldry of Williams's language. Where the actual meaning was at issue, they fought to preserve as much as possible, often resulting in an explicit point being reduced to an inference. For example, Blanche's "many intimacies" with strangers became "many meetings."

As a result, especially sexual points were shaded into emotional ones. This shift is most evident in the handling of the homosexuality, which Kazan persuaded Williams to accept. In the film version, Blanche explains that her young husband was driven to commit suicide, because his exceptional sensitivity rendered him weak and unable to cope with life's normal demands. Regarding this modification Kazan wrote to Breen: "I wouldn't put the homosexuality back in the picture if

131

the code had been revised last night and it was now permissible. I don't want it. I prefer debility and weakness over any kind of suggestion of perversion."[23] Kazan did not want the boy's vulnerability to have a specific source. This vague, generalized disposition reduced the possibility of an adverse audience reaction without invalidating Blanche's sense of failure. If Allen Grey's deviance still retained homosexual connotations, Kazan preferred that it be presented to the audience as a meritorious sensitivity that his immediate, narrow-minded society would not tolerate rather than as a specifically sexual impulse, especially one that was generally disapproved of. Already Kazan was gravitating toward an issue that would assume the character of an obsession several years later with *Tea and Sympathy, On the Waterfront,* and *East of Eden.*

This capitulation to Breen's demand was also a calculated ploy. By acceding to this demand, Kazan hoped to gain bargaining leverage against a requested change that would undermine the play's meaning. Kazan and Williams were adamant that the rape be retained. In an impassioned defense of this aspect of his drama, Williams wrote:

"Streetcar" is an extremely and peculiarly moral play, in the deepest and truest sense of the term. . . . The rape of Blanche by Stanley is a pivotal, integral truth in the play, without which the play loses its meaning, which is the ravishment of the tender, the sensitive, the delicate, by the savage and brutal forces of modern society. It is a poetic plea for comprehension . . . we are fighting for what we think is the heart of the play, and when we have our backs against the wall—if we are forced into that position—none of us is going to throw in the towel! We will use every legitimate means that any of us at his or her disposal to protect the things in this film which we think cannot be sacrificed, since we feel that it contains some very important truths about the world we live in.[24]

Breen responded with a willingness to allow the rape to be retained if it could be presented so that there was no question of Stanley's villainy. He objected to the stage version in which Brando spoke the line, "We've had this date with each other from the beginning" as he

A Streetcar Named Desire: Kazan battled the censor in defense of Williams's creation and his direction. (The Museum of Modern Art/Film Stills Archive, New York.)

lifted the limp Tandy and carried her off stage, leaving the impression that, despite her traumatization, she was yielding to her assailant.[25] As an alternative, Kazan had the scene end with an abrupt cut away from the advancing Stanley to a shot of a beer bottle smashing a mirror. The act is now totally implied, though its violent, illusion-shattering effect upon Blanche is only suggested.

Finally, in line with the Breen policy that all wrongdoing be finally punished, Kazan was told that "Stella should not return to Stanley and supposedly live happily ever after."[26] Kazan proposed that Stella end the film saying, "We're not going back in there. Not this time. We're never going back. Never, never back, never back again."[27] When this was approved, Kazan then created a context that qualified the literal meaning of these words. Stella addresses these remarks not to Stanley, but to her baby, and then leaves for Eunice's. The audience cannot view this repeat of her response to the first poker party without suspecting that it will lead to another passionate reunion. Her condemnation appeased the censors without totally forsaking the play's insistence of her dependency upon Stanley.

There were, of course, other matters which had to be decided upon every bit as carefully. When Kazan initially accepted this assignment, he did so with the intention of "opening" the play up. The more he reviewed his original conception, the more he realized that Williams's drama would be ill-served by an insistent realism, even if it were a modified version such as that of *Panic in the Streets*. Williams had originally envisioned his play as taking place in a bizarre environment of decadence, raffish charm, and plainness. Because the strength of the play lay in its claustrophobic press toward confrontation, Kazan decided that the film should insist upon the dilapidated, crowded quarters of the Kowalski flat. Thus everything except the initial footage of the arriving train was shot on the Warner lot, with three quarters of the action occurring on a set only slightly larger than that of the original stage production. Kazan relied on set-ups rather than locations to keep the presentation lively, but the camera was not to call attention to itself. It was to be an intent observer, not a participant. When appropriate, as with the fight that erupts during the first poker game, Kazan would display a flurry of camera movement and cutting. The more characteristic pattern of establishing a scene with a long or middle shot and then following with a probing series of close-ups created an effect of narrowing encroachment and looming confrontation.

The film's opening, the one major addition to the play, followed along these very lines. In order to define Blanche as the central character and utilize some of the freedom that film offered, Kazan started the film with a series of telescoping cuts charting Blanche's arrival. Despite its obvious resemblance to the opening of *Pinky*, this was carefully planned to call attention to key elements of the ensuing drama. The train bringing Blanche prefigures the unnerving effect of Stanley's raw power in the same way the sounds of passing trains did in the play. The burst of steam from which she first appears anticipates the film's stifling atmosphere of hot baths, boiling kettles, and recurrent images of people sweating. The sailor who proposes to help Blanche is an initial example of the strangers she futilely turns to for support in the course of her descent into madness.

In similar fashion, Kazan's shift of the later second act conversation between Blanche and Mitch to the dockside dance pavilion was no mere change of scene. This open-air setting, so different from the cramped quarters of the Kowalski apartment, was specifically intended to communicate the sense of relief and hope Blanche derives from this exchange. The background music echoes the delicate melodies, notably the Varsouviana, into which she retreats to ease her troubled thoughts. The search lights in the background are blurred by the camera's focus and made romantic in the same way Blanche's lantern softened the glare of the naked bulb. With night favoring both her and her illusions, she has momentarily escaped the hard reality associated with Stanley. Being the site of a dance, not unlike the one at which Grey committed suicide, it is an appropriate site for Blanche's recollection of the event, especially since the love she elicits from Mitch with the revelation of her husband's suicide eventually brings her an equal measure of trauma.

To make his film of *Streetcar* duplicate the effect of the stage version, given all the constraints under which Kazan was laboring, demanded enormous patience, understanding, and skill. Understandably he was outraged when he discovered just prior to its release that changes had been made without his being consulted. After screening

135

the finished product, the Catholic Legion of Decency advised Warners that the film would probably receive its Condemned rating. Immediately Warners initiated an indirect series of negotiations to circumvent this possibility. The terms of the agreement demanded additional cutting. Once Kazan determined how this exchange had been conducted and what had been eliminated he wrote an article of outrage for the *New York Times*. He maintained that the sound track had been damaged by cutting the words "on the mouth" from Blanche's statement of her intent to kiss the newsboy. He explained that the elimination of Stanley's last line to Stella in the rape scene, "You know you might not be bad to interfere with," struck the implication that only here, for the first time, does Stanley have any idea of harming the girl. He was angry that Stanley's famous stairway reunion with Stella had been recut, a scene crucial to his sympathetic view of Stanley and to the revised ending. After the months ironing out these issues with the Breen Office, he felt that such calloused disregard amounted to outright betrayal:

> I could not help wondering where this process left the moral responsibility of the makers of the picture, including the author and myself, or how the end result differed from direct censorship by the Legion. . . . Warners just wanted a seal. They didn't give a damn about the beauty or artistic value of the picture. To them it was just a piece of entertainment. It was a business, not art. They wanted to get the entire family to see the picture. They didn't want anything in the picture that might keep *anyone* away. At the same time they wanted it to be dirty enough to pull people in. The whole business was rather an outrage.[28]

Despite the setback, Kazan won the war. The public flocked to see his film and it was roundly proclaimed a masterful adaptation of Williams's play. *Streetcar* was to be the first and last time that Kazan was to film one of his Broadway efforts. Even before he agreed to handle *Streetcar*, he could see the trap in this practice. The film would inevitably reflect carry-over from the staging and he would be branded a limited director trading on his theatre reputation. Out of

136

respect for *Streetcar*'s special artistry, Kazan had decided to jettison his preliminary plans for "opening up" the play and instead to preserve as much of Williams's meaning as possible. Thereafter, however, he would take on only original screenplays. With confidence and ambition, he would participate in their preparation so that the results would profit from his filmmaking skills—and attest to them. He was determined to make better movies.

"Most important of all movies," Murray Schumach observed in his history of Hollywood censorship, "in forcing censors to broaden their interpretation of the code and to consider the realities of American behavior was *A Streetcar Named Desire*. This film was truly a Hollywood milestone."[29] However, in his conclusion that "the way was now open for men of courage, taste, and artistry to make films that would elevate a business commodity to art,"[30] Schumach goes too far. By 1952 Breen's office and the Catholic Legion of Decency were increasingly thrust into the position of fighting a rear guard action. But the thorny problem of censorship was not limited to sex. By the end of 1950, when Kazan finished filming *A Streetcar Named Desire*, politics and economics were equally touchy issues, and the Breen office was but one of many Kazan headaches. If *A Streetcar Named Desire* exposed Kazan to the time-consuming demands and frustrations attendant upon his deepening commitment to filmmaking, critical and popular acclaim still made the effort worthwhile. Over the years that followed, when the evolution of his career was to embroil Kazan in more controversies, he would continue to be an equally fierce defender and promoter of the dramas in which he believed.

SIX

"Man of Individual Conscience"

Kazan was in trouble and too preoccupied to heed the dangers rising up around him. Throughout the 1940s, through the war years and their wrenching aftermath, he had perceptively read the shifts in the cultural climate and come up with dramas cued to them. But his remarkable success had significantly altered his outlook. He had become a visionary eager to make his presence felt and his voice heard. Having spearheaded innovative breakthroughs on Broadway, Kazan had come to believe that he might creatively refashion what he had learned and accomplish a similar revolution in filmmaking. He now saw directing films as presenting him a greater challenge and opportunity. His impressive film adaptation of *A Streetcar Named Desire* was at once an initial expression of this belief and a precursor of original efforts to follow. In thus growing more confident of his power and committing more of his energy to working with scriptwriters and producers, Kazan lost touch with his audience and America. First he failed to notice and then he badly misread the menacing turns in the commercial and political conditions over the next two years. And he paid dearly.

By 1950, Americans had gotten over the trauma of return to civilian life and altered domestic conditions, but regained security and prosperity eroded movie attendance and the appeal of social problem films. A key factor in this deterioration was the demand for television sets. Between 1948 and 1950 television purchases had quadrupled and everyone believed that future increases would be even greater. Disturbing as this situation was for moviemakers, it was symptomatic of even more worrisome developments. Coupled with sharp increases in

139

marriages, births, and house purchases as well, the television figures suggested that America was becoming a nation of families whose interests were concentrated within the home. The sharp drop in movie attendance from eighty-six million a week in 1946 to sixty million in 1950 (fifty-one million by 1952) confirmed that the habitual moviegoer was a disappearing species.[1]

Hollywood's mounting concern for these developments was aggravated by a series of jolting blows to the industry itself. First, the postwar years produced a sharp escalation in production costs. Meanwhile, in an effort to protect their shaky currencies, foreign countries enacted legislation to prevent American companies from removing the profits their movies were running up. Then in 1948, after a time consuming ten-year appeal, the Supreme Court upheld the earlier court decision that studios would have to give up their theatre chains and block-booking practices.

All this upheaval plunged studio executives into tense reappraisals of their strategies and methods for coping with these adversities. As always, the crucial issue was profits. Initially studios decided that all production costs should be pruned to minimum, with no project being allowed to exceed a two million dollar limit. Here the reasoning was clear: smaller investments reduced prospective losses. This decision favored Kazan, with his preference for low-budget, on-location assignments.

However, there were some notable dissenters to this approach. One prominent exception was Cecil B. DeMille, who was currently laying plans for a lavish portrayal of Samson's fatal attraction to Delilah. To many within the industry, this return to Biblical epics, which DeMille had made back in the 1920s and 1930s, smacked of a disastrous self-indulgence. Yet DeMille's decision was premised upon a very different interpretation of recent developments, one which, if correct, gravely threatened the kind of film with which Kazan had become identified. The recent change in audience habits from regular moviegoing to weekend outings clearly increased the attraction of a big draw feature. With their opulent, panoramic displays of clothes and crowds, pageant and action, Biblical epics presented an ideal vehicle for capitalizing on the Technicolor that moviemakers were realizing to be a necessary defense against television. According to

140

this argument, low-budget, black-and-white realism was such a natural route for the emerging television industry to follow that movies, which demanded paid admission, would have to offer alternative, more lavish fare to remain competitive. Finally, the then impending Supreme Court decision on the case demanding that the studios divest themselves of their theatres, if upheld, would give exhibitors greater choice in their offerings. The theatre owners would certainly be eager to pay more for the right to exhibit films that could lure the prosperous middle class away from its television sets and through their turnstiles. Certainly the eleven million dollars *Samson and Delilah* returned in 1950 on the three million dollar investment provided persuasive support for this logic. These receipts were two and a half times those of its closest competitor that year; measured against all Hollywood films, only *Gone with the Wind* had harvested more dollars. On the heels of *Samson and Delilah*'s release, Twentieth Century-Fox rushed into production with *David and Bathsheba* which then proved to be the top grossing film for 1951. MGM fielded *Quo Vadis* the following year and turned the second largest box-office profit for 1952. Thus DeMille's portrayal of Samson's dazzling triumph over his humiliating debasement showed his fellow filmmakers how to overcome the hobbling setbacks their once mighty industry had sustained.[2]

At the time Kazan could not be bothered by all this worry and debate; his record of success was too strong. His major undertakings of the past three years had all yielded handsome returns and even the modest *Boomerang* and *Panic in the Streets* had been profitable. However, these threatening signs of change ranged well beyond industrial economics and patterns of movie attendance. The political climate had turned equally dark and stormy and Kazan was uneasy over the growing public suspicion of any social criticism directed at the country itself. Able to defend his work's economic viability, he faced having to justify its political intent.

For some time now Hollywood had been suspected of engaging in subversion with its films. As far back as 1938, Martin Dies had chaired a House Committee on Un-American Activities to investigate the extent of Communist influence within the movie industry, but little had come of it. With America's eyes focused on the restless armies of Nazi Germany and its unpredictable leader, the danger of Communism spawned by the earlier Depression years seemed a diminishing threat. Then, even before the war ended, John Rankin sounded the opening shot of a new campaign by calling Hollywood "the greatest hotbed of subversive activities in America" and charged it with devising "one of the most dangerous plots ever instigated for the overthrow of the American government."[3] Again these remarks fell on deaf ears, but over the next two years as Russia's menacing expansion caused this former ally to seem a reincarnation of the enemies just defeated, Rankin's fellow Republicans began to see how these cries of Communist subversion could be converted into tactical strategies for defeating New Deal liberals left over from the War.

In 1947, S. Parnell Thomas, a dedicated anti–New Dealer who had participated in the original 1938 HUAC hearings, sought to capitalize on these developments by launching a new investigation of Hollywood. Although the outspoken Rankin was missing from his committee, which included a young California Congressman named Richard M. Nixon, his flair for hyperbole set the tone for the hearings that opened in October. The Congressional inquisitors were ostentatious in their display of gravity and presumed authority. The twenty-four "friendly" witnesses included enough renown to more than compensate for their lack of solid evidence; with all the resultant publicity they lent credibility and notoriety to the Committee's cause. The "unfriendlies" who followed, especially the first two, John Howard Lawson and Albert Maltz, were defensive and unruly. Having already announced their opposition, the "Hollywood Ten," as they would come to be known, attacked the Committee's violation of their Constitutional rights and refused to answer questions about their Communist affiliations. The fight was on. Supporters of the Committee branded the conduct of the Ten an outrageous attempt to hide information that corroborated the Committee's allegations, while its attackers charged that the Committee was putting citizens on trial without respect for their guaranteed rights. Suddenly the hearings were cut short. No reasons were given and no conclusions were drawn. The public was left with theatrical flourishes and few facts and called upon to judge for itself. The Committee rested its case on the citation for contempt of Congress it filed against the Ten.

The only undisputed loser was Hollywood. The film community

was irremediably split and on the defensive. The question of Communist entrenchment grew more insistent, and, as they had done in the past, the studios moved quickly with a show of self-regulation to defuse criticism and prevent further government intervention. On November 27, 1947, less than a month after the hearings closed and on the same day that the House of Representatives voted to find the Ten in contempt, fifty executives representing the major studios gathered in New York and drafted the famous Waldorf accord stating that they would not employ a known Communist. Thus the curtain went up on the era of blacklisting. All of the Ten were put out of their jobs. How many others were to find themselves in the same situation? Was this accord quickly applied "make up" aimed at creating a favorable appearance and leaving the situation unchanged? Or was this the first cut of major surgery? Would producers take no further action against current employees, as Dore Schary originally assured representatives of the Directors' and Screen Writers' Guild? Or was Schary's speech just another part of the publicity campaign the industry was launching to improve its image? Had the Waldorf declaration been a deal that would put an end to further Congressional investigation? Only time would tell.

Over the next two and a half years an uneasy lull hung over Hollywood. There were no more investigations and few lost their jobs. Then in June of 1950, the situation took a sharp turn for the worse. Within days of the outbreak of the Korean War, the lower court conviction of the Ten, which had worked its way to the Supreme Court, was upheld. The Ten would have to go to prison. With the spectre of Communism looming ever larger, the message was unmistakable: henceforth anyone working in Hollywood had better be prepared to account for his political activities or face the likelihood of unemployment. From now on all script proposals would be closely scrutinized for any possible Communist influences. In this charged atmosphere of mounting concern, any film that drew attention to deficiences in American society or government immediately became suspect of being subversive. When these charges were raised against *All My Sons* back in 1947, they created enough stir to force cancellation of its presentation at military bases abroad but had little impact upon the domestic road shows. Hollywood was more vulnerable than Broadway to the shifting political climate. Between 1947 and 1950 the percentage of social problem and psychological films being made dropped from 28 percent of the total to 11.7 percent.[4]

One particularly revealing example of this worsening state of affairs was another move made by Cecil B. DeMille, this time in August, 1950, as part of a determined effort to get the Screen Directors' Guild to make a loyalty oath requisite for membership. He had recently founded his DeMille Foundation for Political Freedom in order to alert his fellow Americans to the threat of Communism and now he wanted his fellow filmmakers to start cleaning their own house. DeMille felt confident that the current president, Joseph Mankiewicz, would try to thwart his intentions. Through friends on the board, he spearheaded a drive to unseat Mankiewicz while he was out of the country on vacation. But when Mankiewicz subsequently learned of the rigged vote DeMille had engineered, he returned, challenged its legality, and steered the matter to an open vote. Mankiewicz outmaneuvered DeMille and, in a tense confrontation involving Hollywood's most prominent directors, affirmed his position.[5]

In this drama Kazan was to play a small, but telling role. He, of course, knew Mankiewicz well. Both were Fox directors who had recently won Oscars for their work. Because of Kazan's prominence, Mankiewicz was most anxious to enlist his support. Kazan even rode in the same car that carried Mankiewicz to the recall vote. When Mankiewicz asked Kazan to accompany him into the meeting, Kazan declined, explaining that his presence could only damage Mankiewicz's case.[6] Kazan had a valid point. Mankiewicz finally defeated DeMille because he insisted that his retaliation was prompted by DeMille's violation of procedures and was not to be construed as a reflection of his views on Communism. For him to enter this critical showdown in the company of a person well-known for his radical, left-wing background would be to blur this distinction, creating the unwanted impression that the upcoming vote was a choice between purging suspected Communists and abetting them.

Kazan's response also implied, of course, that he simply did not want to get involved. Since Jack Warner had fingered Kazan as "one of the mob" in his 1947 HUAC testimony, he knew he was a marked man.[7] He realized that he might one day be subpoenaed and asked to account for his Communist involvements. He did not want to be linked with political actions that could be held against him. Though he signed petitions of support and contributed to defense drives for the Hollywood Ten in 1947, he ceased to allow his name to be used to promote left-wing causes shortly thereafter.[8] Sometime following the opening of *All My Sons,* Bertolt Brecht, who was to be grouped with the Hollywood Ten at the 1947 HUAC hearings though he left the country before the hearings opened, expressed a willingness to have Kazan direct his *Galileo,* but Kazan refused, according to Harold Clurman, because he was already worried about Brecht's reputation as a Communist.[9] Though Kazan attended the Chasen's dinner that produced the petition forcing the Mankiewicz recall to an open vote, his name was notably absent from that document. With more battles over Communism looming on the horizon, the man who once played Agate was disassociating himself from his past, and the voice that had once called stridently for reform was suddenly silent.

Kazan's next film, *Viva Zapata!,* was to be strongly influenced by these developments. Against this backdrop of deepening concern over the spread of Communism and the subversive influences emanating from Hollywood, *Viva Zapata!* dared to present a sympathetic depiction of a leader of a peasant rebellion. Moreover, in spite of concerted efforts to convert this drawback into a source of strength, the film was a resounding commercial failure.

Significantly the origins of *Viva Zapata!* stretched back to the Depression years and the commercial success of *Viva Villa!* (1934), which confirmed that moviegoers could be attracted to the fight of oppressed citizens against their tyrannical rulers. In 1938, Thomas Pinchon, the author of the book on which *Viva Villa* was based, approached MGM to purchase the film rights to a projected book on Emiliano Zapata and "Mexico's long years of struggle for a democratic government." They agreed and Pynchon finished "Zapata the Unconquerable" in 1940. At this point, the property was shelved where it remained until after the war when Jack Cummings revived the subject. By 1948, his production plans had progressed to the point where he had eighty pages of script, with Robert Taylor cast to play Zapata.

Then suddenly the project was scrapped, probably because mounting concern over the fallout from the 1947 HUAC investigations had made MGM executives fearful of the project's "Communist" overtones.[10]

What frightened the studio appealed to Kazan. He and John Steinbeck were drawn to Zapata like moths to a flame; they convinced Fox to secure rights to this controversial property from MGM. It was not Zapata the revolutionary who appealed to Steinbeck and Kazan. They were interested in his final rejection of a cause that could easily be paralleled with Communism. "What fascinated us about Zapata," Kazan was to write in a letter to the *Saturday Review* following the film's premiere, "was one nakedly dramatic act. In the moment of victory, he turned his back on power."[11] That is to say, they saw Zapata as a revolutionary who rejected revolution. Kazan and Steinbeck, of course, had both won fame during the 1930s with material calling for social reform. In their abiding commitment to very much the same kind of material following the war, both had begun to delve into its personal significance to them and to downplay its political ramifications. Both were successful leftwingers who had severed ties with the political positions with which they were originally identified. With Zapata, they had an actual historical personage with whom they could explore how success and experience altered an initial revolutionary fervor. They also had a figure whose original impulsive adoption of radical extremes was checked by a conservative orthodoxy.

As a film about an armed overthrow of an existing government, *Viva Zapata!* was to be about the cost of revolutionary commitment and ultimate betrayal. To be the leader of a peasant insurrection, Zapata finds he must deny the side of himself that respects authority and yearns for refinement. Not a revolutionary by nature or inclination, he cannot abide the social injustice which engulfs him. In the opening scene, he arrives with a group of peasants obsequiously requesting that the president restore their lands, which have recently been appropriated. When the president treats them like children and presents to them unworkable solutions, Zapata stands alone as his fellow peasants go to leave and humbly exposes how they are being put off. On the heels of this reluctant move toward defiance, he impulsively destroys a machine gun trained upon helpless villagers, then jeopardizes his position to defend a starving boy who is being beaten, and finally assaults soldiers to free a badly abused peasant prisoner. Carried by these actions into command of a peasant uprising, Zapata finds himself in the uncomfortable position of attacking a social system he basically reveres, a man of action unsure of his course, a leader uneasy with the power thrust upon him, a revolutionary social reformer devoid of political ideology or aspirations. Futilely he pleads, "I don't want to be the conscience of the world."

To his dismay, Zapata discovers that social improvement demands more than good intentions and new government. Zapata's fight yields only painful alienation from all those closest to him. His trust in Madero, the idealistic leader who gives Zapata his word and his watch, almost carries him into the trap of giving up his guns. His fervent, devoted peasant friend Pablo is revealed to have leaked information that has cost lives, thereby compelling Zapata to shoot him. His passionate, beloved brother Eufemio turns into a derelict who abuses his own people and dies a dishonorable death. Overwhelmed by this tangled web of treachery, Zapata finds that he has even betrayed himself as he angrily circles the name of a defiant peasant just as the president had circled his own name at the outset of the film. At this point, with the same impulsiveness that he once attacked injustice, Zapata rejects the presidency and returns to his native Morelos.

Zapata's decision to turn his back on the peasant cause precipitates a fatal break between him and Fernando. Throughout the film Fernando (Joe Wiseman) has been the cold, tight-lipped revolutionary, immune to pleasure and totally dedicated to the massive killing he considers inevitable and imperative. The tacit symbiosis that develops between him and Zapata recalls the relationships between the lawmen and the protagonists in *Boomerang* and *Panic in the Streets*—basically opposed outlooks forced into collaboration in order to deal with the problem at hand—but these two men turn out to have nothing in common. Zapata's renunciation of power, which Kazan called "the high point of our story" and "the key to Zapata," is dramatized as a flat disavowal of Fernando and his arguments.[12] Fernando then defects to the enemy and sets up a fatal meeting at which Zapata is shot to ribbons by a hidden army of federales. Although primarily concerned with the character and motivations of Zapata, Kazan retained a strong interest in the dramatic potential of the Mexican revolution and the possibility of crafting a film of excitement and movement.[13] In this he succeeded brilliantly. Except for *Streetcar, Viva Zapata!* turned out to be Kazan's finest film to date, and one of its greatest strengths was its accomplished cinematography. The exchange and understanding that grew up between Kazan and Joe MacDonald since their first collaboration on *Pinky* had greatly facilitated Kazan's attainment of a more sophisticated cinematic style. With *Zapata*, for the first time, Kazan finally allowed his camera to break free from the constraints of his theatrical orientation and to play a lead role. In many ways, *Viva Zapata!* was a Western. The fighting and brutal violence played out before an expansive arid landscape and small agrarian villages, movement and action rather than dialog, was quite different from Kazan's usual concentration upon the claustrophobic pressures of urban life.

"Man of individual conscience" torn to pieces at the end of *Viva Zapata!*: Heroism, vanity, or political naïveté? (The Museum of Modern Art/Film Stills Archive, New York.)

Never before, as he commented during the filming, had he "operated on such a broad geographical scale outdoors," and in none of his films to date was his camera work so impressive.[14]

Nowhere is Kazan's cinematic flair more apparent than in the film's action sequences. In the early scene in which the federales sweep down on the trespassing peasants, there is a confident sense of pace and purpose in the rapid intermingling of long shot with close-up. The scene of Fernando's arrival, his echoing call to Zapata as the camera looks down on the tiny figure swallowed up by the vast, rugged landscape, sets up an interplay of sound and image that is distinctive and impressive. The harsh angle of the up-down shots of Fernando's approach, the disconnected dialogue of the ensuing discussion, accompanied by shots of waving scrub bushes and the sound of whistling wind, create an ominous tension in this first meeting between Zapata and the Judas who later betrays him.

Kazan staged the action with equal impressiveness. His handling of the scene in which Zapata is rescued and made the peasants' leader is executed with bravura flourish. Zapata's escort, with the rope stretching from his neck to the soldiers on their horses, recalls his attempted rescue of a fellow peasant in a similar situation. The stones the villagers click build an electric atmosphere of tension and danger. The ensuing montage creates a powerful double image of peasants joining together and looming confrontation. Shots of individuals give way to ones of bands rising from fields and spilling down the mountainside. When this vast gathering finally fills the road and forces the soldiers to a standstill, the audience expects the killing to begin. But, quietly, Zapata is released. Kazan stresses the peasants' inherent pacifism by having it thwart the developed expectations for an eruption of violence. Only after Zapata is released, without bloodshed, does he dramatically raise his machete, cut telephone wires, and signal the start of this preferably non-violent revolution.

Zapata's final massacre is another masterful orchestration of shifts from calm to violence. The risks involved in Zapata's visit to the garrison are first discussed in hushed tones, which his wife shatters with her hysterical outbursts at Zapata's decision to go. The ominous still of his arrival at the courtyard is intensified by Zapata's disregard for the telltale signs of danger the camera systematically records—the fateful looking peasants and stealthy movements of the sinister Guajardo. The sudden eruption of Zapata's annihilation from this calm is devastating.

Despite the accomplishment of its cinematography, its dramatic effects, and its carefully contrived look of authenticity, *Viva Zapata!* was to be a critical and commercial failure. One of its main faults, according to many reviewers, was its historical inaccuracies. Zapata's brother, Eufemio, for example, was not the libertine hedonist Anthony Quinn plays. While there was a person named Pablo whom Zapata sent to Madero, he had no resemblance to the noble peasant of the film. Anything but a man of principle and sincerity, Madero actually connived to defeat Zapata and sent Huerta to capture him. Zapata never had any dealings with either a character like Fernando or the sort of ideology he intrudes. And with numerous illegitimate children to his credit, Zapata was not particularly enamoured of his well-to-do wife.

Perhaps the biggest distortion, and the one to generate the most heated debate, was the film's characterization of Zapata as an impulsive, reluctant revolutionary, wracked with doubt over the road he was travelling. Kazan never took criticism lightly, but the charges of historical falsification deeply offended him for they cast grave doubts about his lifelong commitment to social realism. He wrote angrily to the *Saturday Review*, insisting upon the care and research that went into the script, explaining how he and Steinbeck had to focus on certain aspects of Zapata's character to give direction to their efforts. Curiously, instead of disproving any of the charges brought against the film, Kazan dwelled upon the pressures that influenced the project's development. "Your readers may be interested to hear how the political tensions of the present bore down upon us—John Steinbeck and Darryl Zanuck and me—as we thought about and shaped a historical picture," he stated in the opening paragraph. "These pressures, though nerve-wracking, forced us to clear our own perspectives and in this sense were useful. They also brought to me a realization of the relationship between abstract politics and personal character which I had not formulated before." Then Kazan took great pains to point out that the film, far from appealing to Communists, would offend them, especially the climactic "act of renunciation" in which Zapata rejects both

150

Fernando and his advice. "By showing that Zapata did this," Kazan explained, "we spoiled a poster figure that the Communists have been at some pains to create. . . . The man who refused power was not only no Communist, he was that opposite phenomenon: a man of individual conscience."[15]

The political implications that so obsessed Kazan and were so distasteful to his "man of individual conscience" were not an after-the-fact interpretation of the film. They were, in fact, central to the characterization of Zapata and key factors in the script's evolution through some six preliminary drafts stretching over a period of more than two years. Steinbeck started by writing a bulky four hundred-page manuscript about Zapata, which he then concentrated into a "first draft continuity," bearing the date November 26, 1949. This contains a number of scenes that would survive to the shooting scripts. It, in conjunction with the long narrative account, shows that Steinbeck originally planned the film to be a sweeping epic with panoramic scenes of festive celebration and fighting that would rely heavily on the camera's ability to record action. The characters are only roughed out and there is no ending. This was followed by a manuscript screenplay and two revised versions, which were the result of various conferences between Kazan and Steinbeck and between them and Darryl Zanuck. From these emerged a "final screenplay," dated February 6, 1951, though an outside screenwriter was called in for yet another round of revisions.[16]

Amidst the countless changes of these drafts one concern emerged paramount: to contrast Zapata with a character of identifiable Communist traits. This goal involved the character of Fernando, named Pablo when he first appears and Bicho in a subsequent revision. Of this character, Kazan was to write in his letter of defense:

there is such a thing as a Communist mentality. We created a figure of this complexion in Fernando, whom the audience identify as "the man with the typewriter." He typifies the men who use the just grievances of the people for their own ends, who shift and twist their course, betray any friend or principle or promise to get power and keep it.[17]

151

Early in the development of *Viva Zapata!* this revolutionary figure was not a stereotypical party hack but a man of some sensitivity and insight. The Pablo of an early undated typescript is the man with the typewriter but also a courageous comrade concerned with Zapata's well-being. He remains sober while Eufemio gets drunk and urges Zapata to become leader of the revolution. Amidst the celebration of Diaz's defeat, he reminds the weary Zapata "these few days may destroy everything you've done in your life." He prevents Zapata from following Villa into retirement. But, rather than the good-hearted, peasant Pablo of the finished film who questions the meaning of the revolution, this early Pablo represents an educated understanding of the frustrating complexities of a revolution. He is a sympathetically portrayed man in the middle, who calls attention to deficiences of both the rulers *and* the oppressed. His prodding of Zapata to become leader of the revolution comes with insistence that Zapata's fight extend beyond immediate battles. But Zapata lacks the dedication, sensitivity, and understanding. When Zapata rejects the presidency and returns to Morelos, the original Pablo makes a final impassioned plea:

PABLO: You're throwing the whole thing away . . . You want to go home. When these people need you most you run away. Let me tell you that even before you have left your enemies are on the move. They're in the field and in the palace. . . . And they won't stay in the palace. They'll start after you . . . they won't let you rest . . . you don't trust anything except your own horse and your countryside . . . and you don't trust learning . . . you don't trust yourselves. (now hysterical) I think you're traitors . . . I think you'll be killed and I'm not sure you shouldn't be. (frantically) Do you trust anyone . . . name anyone!! Let him be leader . . . do you trust anyone?

EMILIANO: (looks at the crowd) Them? . . . what can they do without a leader? Look at them. . . .[18]

In this speech, which was later deleted, Pablo articulates an irony central to the characterization of Zapata: in turning his back on his

152

supporters, on Fernando, and on the presidency, he is also betraying himself.

Kazan and Steinbeck introduced the character of Pablo to personalize the issues and to define the nature of revolutionary fighting. But the character, while providing clarity, was fraught with difficulty. Here was a man of wisdom and vision who could command the audience's respect even when advocating that the people rise up to overthrow the established government. His insight into leaders' vulnerability to corruption could affirm, rather than qualify, the need for revolution. A Pablo of such sensitive revolutionary character would jeopardize the entire film by providing support for HUAC's contention that Hollywood films were promoting the cause of Communism. Kazan found himself confronting the same problem he had run into with *A Streetcar Named Desire*: either remove the objectionable elements or have the project scrubbed. In an effort to protect their invested effort, he and Steinbeck decided to split Pablo into two characters. The Pablo pushing for insurrection became Bicho, then Fernando, whose desire for power is a transparent mask for his selfish, ignoble motives. His duplicitous conniving for his own advancement was turned into a blatant symbol of Communism as incipient totalitarianism. The compassionate dedication of the original Pablo was channeled in a new Pablo who was now a peasant.

Such revisions enabled Kazan and Steinbeck to get their script back on Fox's production schedule. Their distortion of Mexican history grew more obvious—and much less dangerous. Yet there were dramatic reasons for altering Pablo's characterization that were as important as the political ones. By the time the original Pablo broke with Zapata he had almost supplanted Zapata as the script's central character. The Zapata of the second draft was essentially a noble but simple-minded peasant. Pablo, on the other hand, clearly saw the formidable obstacles to reform and suffered a growing disillusionment. He interpreted the drama. His constant fretting over the implication of what was happening made him, in effect, Zapata's conscience. For Zapata to become a complex "man of individual conscience" Pablo's moral sensibility had to be transferred to Zapata and internalized.

By splitting Pablo into two opposed characters, Kazan and Steinbeck began their effort to convert Zapata from inarticulate giant to an

153

emotionally beleaguered Gulliver brought down by relative Lilliputians. The two more conventional, less complex characters into which Pablo was divided no longer rivaled Zapata but merely added to the chorus of conflicting voices that would eventually push the hero to a breaking point. Zapata now shouldered the emotional burdens, weighed the cost of commitment, became the man of individual conscience. Thus Zapata's hesitant espousal of social reform winds up alienating him from *everyone* closest to him not just Fernando; the climactic sense of annihilation being somewhat of a commentary upon Zapata's emotional condition by this point.

The result presented Marlon Brando, Kazan's obvious choice for the part of Zapata, with a much more demanding role to play. This Zapata challenged his exceptional ability in projecting restless, ineffable emotions, his skill in portraying characters whose lack of educated understanding seems to intensify their responsiveness. This role marked an important step for him from the brutish Stanley Kowalski, a man whose elemental feelings strained for an inevitable release, to a truly admirable figure who found himself increasingly hemmed in by the consequences of his instinctive behavior. This modified Zapata embodied the ambivalence Kazan strove for in his best work. However, the product was to remain more important for what it represented than what it achieved. Most reviewers were to trace the movie's problems to Zapata. For some the fault was Brando's makeup, which seemed to immobilize his face in trying to get him to look like a Mexican. To others, Brando's performance seemed eccentric; his posturing, his mumbling, his paradoxical concentration of passivity and intensity were unbelievable. However, these were essentially symptoms of a much deeper problem—Kazan's belief that Mexican culture could be equated with his own ethnic heritage. It seemed to present an opportunity to portray alien values and conduct that had special meaning for him. Nowhere were the liabilities of Kazan's cross-cultural transpositions more apparent than in the painful scenes of Zapata's courtship of Josepha and his request to marry her. Most viewers find these scenes especially awkward and tedious. Kazan's later dramatization of Stavros's relationship with Thomna in his very personal *America America* were to contain many of the same elements.

Fumbling though these scenes are, they illuminate the motivation responsible for the film's weakness and its objectionable politics. Kazan's interest was intensely personal and had very little to do with Mexican culture or politics. The central act of renunciation that attracted Kazan and Steinbeck to Zapata was basically a springboard to issues of particular moment to them. All the political ramifications of this act that figured so prominently into their original conception and exercised such a profound influence on the script's evolution were peculiarly American. *Viva Zapata!* was a timely movie set in the wrong place at the wrong time. Kazan's *Zapata* was a brooding embodiment of American social tensions, and its characters were an extension of a type of behavior by which Kazan had been successfully dramatizing those tensions. In the blend of stoicism and passion conventionally associated with Mexican culture, Kazan felt he had the makings for another tense battle between a conditioned behavioral mask and repressed emotion. Yet his growing tendency to translate sociological problems into psychological effects resulted in a view of Mexican culture that was not convincing. Most of the charges of *Zapata*'s distortion of Mexican history were reducible to the simple fact that audiences did not believe Brando's portrayal of Zapata. As a reflection of Kazan's efforts to capitalize on developing interests and to extend his filmmaking skills, he needed material much different from *Viva Zapata!* to forge the kind of drama for which he was aiming.

One telling measure of Kazan's and Steinbeck's failure to come to terms with the mixed feelings being channeled into this project was the movie's ending. When he wrote his original first draft continuity, Steinbeck considered Zapata's death sufficiently incidental to his abdication that he did not write an ending, but the conclusion wound up posing serious problems before the film's completion. In the different possibilities they considered, Steinbeck and Kazan agreed that Zapata's death should be a vindication of his controversial act of renunciation.[19] In the final version, when Zapata's bullet-ridden body is dumped in the town center, the people persist in believing Zapata too wise and too strong to have been slain. Their reactions, coupled with Zapata's earlier speech proclaiming "There's no leader but yourselves," leave a final implication that Zapata's conscientious defiance is more important than anything he alone has done or might do. The final shot

155

of Zapata's white horse looking down from a distant mountain top was inserted to suggest that his *spirit* could not be killed. However, Kazan's dramatic staging of Zapata's death, set against the background of previous actions, notably his rejection of the presidency, intruded a very different possibility: that Zapata died for his failure to comprehend the dangers threatening him. Zapata's blindness to the trap Fernando set is almost impossible to believe. Why is he so oblivious to all those tell-tale signs that bring the audience to the edge of its seats? That Zapata could have been betrayed not for his refusal to become a crafty politician, but for his impractical idealism, his wish to be "a man of individual conscience," his political naïveté would have violated the respect that Kazan and Steinbeck wanted his rejection of the presidency to command. *Viva Zapata!*'s failure to resolve the unrealized. implications of its reevaluation of Communism not only marred its characterization of Zapata but also bristled with ironies that were to return to haunt Kazan during the turbulent months following its release.

Shortly after the filming of *Viva Zapata!* was completed, Kazan found himself in the position he had long feared. He was subpoenaed to testify before HUAC in a *closed* hearing set for January 19, 1952. A year earlier HUAC had resumed its investigation of Hollywood with a solid confidence that if the witness summoned could not clear himself of the charge raised, the nervous industry would move to block him from employment. Kazan's job was on the line. In his testimony, Kazan strove to appear cooperative. He openly admitted that he had once been a Communist and carefully explained how he had dropped his membership well before the Second World War. He stressed how his current opposition to Communism originated years earlier. Striving to give as little information as possible, he resisted naming Communists he had formerly known though he apparently mentioned one or two. The result pleased no one.

With a terse explanation to the press that "in the past weeks intolerable rumors about my political position have been circulating in New York and Hollywood," Kazan made a *voluntary* reappearance before HUAC three months later on April 10, 1952.[20] For this he prepared a public statement regarding his association with Communism and its relation to his professional undertakings. In it, he acknowledged his membership in the Communist Party from the summer of 1934 to the late winter or early spring of 1936 and identified various Communists he had known, including his previous Group associates J. Edward Bromberg, Morris Carnovsky, Phoebe Brand, Clifford Odets, and Pamela Miller, who was Lee Strasberg's wife at the time. Kazan also offered a thumbnail description of his plays and films stressing again and again their expression of a basic democratic spirit. For example, *Viva Zapata!*, which was currently showing throughout the country, Kazan identified as "an anti-Communist picture" and cited his article in *Saturday Review* for a fuller explanation.[21]

The most important feature of this testimony was the spirit in which it was presented. As the accomplished director of dramas insisting upon the exposure of painful, unacknowledged truths, Kazan took the position that his recent thoughts about Communism had had the same effect upon him. He had come to believe that all the secrecy surrounding Communists and their activities should be revealed. Having been forced to this hard realization by current events, he felt obligated to be outspoken about what he had learned. Two days following his testimony and one day after the public release of his remarks, Kazan paid for a large ad in the *New York Times* that elaborated upon this point.

I believe that Communist activities confront the people of this country with an unprecedented and exceptionally tough problem. That is, how to protect ourselves from a dangerous and alien conspiracy and still keep the free, open, healthy way of life that gives us self-respect. . . . Secrecy serves the Communists. At the other pole, it serves those who are interested in silencing liberal voices. The employment of a lot of good liberals is threatened because they have allowed themselves to become associated with or silenced by the Communists.[22]

A month later, he gave a major address at Harvard describing the catastrophic effects Communism was having on the motion picture industry and why he had decided to act as he did.[23] These remarks he then reworked into a forty-page discussion he tried unsuccessfully to get Viking to publish.[24] Though this project was eventually dropped,

Reader's Digest was persuaded to reprint the text of his *New York Times* ad under the title of "Where I Stand."[25]

Right or wrong, Kazan certainly approached this disavowal of his political past much differently from the other "friendlies," including his fellow Group associates John Garfield, Clifford Odets, and Lee J. Cobb, who used the same argument. Unlike them, he zealously proclaimed his new found beliefs. To the extent that these activities constituted a performance, they partook of his directorial styling. "My wife used to say that when I felt uncertain about a scene," Kazan once observed, "I would make it more forceful. That's been true. I'm uncertain, therefore, you *must* believe this."[26] Rather than groveling as his left-wing critics charged, he insistently promoted his decision as the difficult, but compelling act of "a man of individual conscience." Correspondingly, he pictured Communism as consisting of the very same duplicity, malevolence, and quest for power he had concentrated into his characterization of the fictitious Fernando. Proclaiming to his audience at Harvard that cooperation with HUAC was necessary to dispel the prevailing climate of secrecy, fear, and repression that was enabling Communism to spread, Kazan anticipated a crucial plot line in his later triumph, *On the Waterfront*. As he had done in his testimony, Kazan reiterated the democratic principles he had made the premise of his stand with a concluding assertion, "I realized that it won't be the Committee which will settle the issue of Communism and Civil Rights, it will be the people, and I was happier."[27] Like the ending of *Viva Zapata!*, he stoutly maintained that the ordinary citizens, rather than he or the Committee, would determine the final outcome of the ongoing turmoil.

The months following demonstrated that Kazan had badly miscalculated the impact of his bold assertions. He received little support. In their aversion to his decision, Kazan's professional colleagues began to desert him, and he them. This rejection was compounded by Kazan's own defensiveness. Kazan even avoided his mentor and longstanding friend Harold Clurman, who held that Kazan had the right to do what he believed.[28] His close relationship with Arthur Miller dissolved and the playwright began searching for a new director for the play on which he was working. His detractors were legion. "Without doubt," one historian of the HUAC investigation has commented,

158

"Kazan's performance . . . aroused a greater hostility, a more biting contempt, than that of any other Hollywood informer."[29] Even major periodicals took notice. Conservative *Time* gave an account of his testimony and openly posed the question, "Why did he wait till now to tell his story?"[30] In its account of Kazan's testimony, the *Nation* seized upon his ad in the *Times* and observed that it "must have put him considerably out of pocket if not out of conscience."[31] Meanwhile, the public remained on the sidelines and watched the controversy rage.

The personal impact of Kazan's decision—his aggressive statement of his position giving way to a pained sense of rejection—was perhaps best revealed in a casual remark Steinbeck sent to his agent two months following the testimony: "You know of course," he wrote just after seeing Kazan, "this Congress thing tore him to pieces."[32] Having made a very bold move that gained little support, Kazan suffered an emotional annihilation not unlike that which befell his idealistic Zapata. As with Zapata, Kazan's sense of himself as a man of principle and conviction had blinded him to the possible outcome of his actions.* His wife Molly ventured a similar interpretation of her husband's testimony in her play *The Egg Head* (1957) in which a college professor's bold proclamation of his beliefs regarding a suspected Communist is exposed as strong-willed naïveté.

While Kazan could accept that his testimony might have been naïve, he was deeply hurt by charges that it had been totally self-serving, a product of fear and ambition. "A man must want to make pictures very badly to be willing so to degrade himself in public," the *Nation* proclaimed and then hastened to add, "After all, 'The Informer' has already been filmed; even the redoubtable Mr. Kazan could hardly improve upon it."[33] Tony Kraber made the same point during his HUAC appearance when he responded to Kazan's identification of him as a Communist with the question: "Is this the Kazan that signed the contract for $500,000 the day after he gave names to this Committee? Would you sell your brothers for $500,000?"[34]

There can be little doubt that Kazan was anxious to avoid black-

---

*Significantly Kazan's more recent comments on *Viva Zapata!* (Michel Ciment, *Kazan on Kazan* [New York: Viking Press, 1974], p. 89) have downplayed his original interpretation of this film as a tract on Communism in favor of it as an illustration of his unrealized confusion at the time.

listing and preserve his filmmaking career to which he had grown increasingly committed. He even admitted as much when he explained to the students at Harvard how he had had two contracts cancelled when he refused to give names in his first appearance before HUAC.[35] Yet his second testimony was not the action of one driven by motives that were purely selfish or monetary, but rather that of a man who, after intense soul-searching, came to believe that a decisive stand was necessary and that reluctance to speak out on Communism increased its current threat. Also, Kazan did not sign any contract as Kraber charged. In fact, within the next year, the one he currently held with Fox was to be thrown into limbo. This was but one of a series of crushing setbacks Kazan was to have between January, 1952, and May, 1953. Rather than protecting or advancing his career, Kazan's testimony led to continued reversals in the tides of fortune that formerly favored him. On the brink of gaining the authority for which he had been pushing, he found everything going haywire. Molly Kazan once observed that her husband's confrontation with HUAC destroyed the image of the "fair-haired boy" he enjoyed up to that point,[36] but this setback would have been much less disturbing had it not been followed by the resounding commercial failure of his next three directorial assignments.

Just after the completion of *Viva Zapata!*, Kazan told an interviewer, "You've got to risk your life every six months if you want to keep living."[37] This was the spirit in which Kazan had approached his two HUAC appearances and the results had been devastating. From now on risk was unavoidable. By putting him on trial for expressing social criticism, HUAC backed Kazan into a corner. After building his career around dramatizations of what was wrong with America, Kazan found himself having to shy away from such material. The outspoken social commentary that sparked Kazan's creativity could no longer be applied to America without discrediting his testimony and raising more questions about his true allegiances. For the past six years he had consciously been honing his skills to the special demands of this kind of drama. Moreover he had grown increasingly dependent upon it to communicate important feelings and to alleviate his need for personal expression. In short, Kazan had salvaged his career and, in doing so, had cut himself off from its life blood.

Ironically, Kazan wound up doing what many who were black-listed did—going abroad, not so much literally (Kazan would shoot his next film in Germany) as in the foreign setting of his next assignments. Kazan was out of his element and his persistent efforts to think of this material as commenting upon American obsessions and deficiencies added to its confusion. Audiences failed to understand or appreciate what goings-on in Egypt, Czechoslovakia, and Mexico said about conditions in the United States. Still, the hard fact was that all three were failures, leaving behind a pronounced impression that audiences had lost interest in Kazan's dramas and that he was perhaps finished.

Rather than brood over the consequences of his first HUAC appearance, Kazan chose, in characteristic fashion, to take up a heavy workload. First, just prior to his first voluntary HUAC appearance he and Williams discussed the possibilities of mounting a production of *Ten Blocks on the Camino Real*. While they were deciding instead that Williams should expand this one-act play into a full-length offering, Irene Selznick presented Kazan with a handsome contract to prepare *Flight into Egypt* for a March 1952 opening. This depiction of an Austrian family's efforts to escape their adversities in Cairo and to relocate to the United States was conceived by its unknown Hungarian author, George Tabori, as a commentary upon the pressures of American life. Discussing how his reaction to the United States came to inform a play so little concerned with America itself, he explained in an article for the *Herald Tribune*, "I found that my experience was not particularly special or exotic. Displacement was not necessarily geographical—the refugee seemed to have invaded the drug store and the country club."[38] What he meant by this equation was clarified in an interview for the *New York Times* in which he characterized the average American as "a refugee, fleeing from his real problems and his own reality, marching desperately for all the certitudes—economics, political, sexual security."[39]

Tabori's hopes that American theatregoers would identify with the Engel family and their frustrations were sadly misplaced. *Flight into Egypt* proved a crushing blow for everyone involved. The pre-production planning had been buoyed by an optimistic belief the play would rival *Death of a Salesman*, but the out-of-town run soon ex-

Man on a Tightrope: Another refusal to yield to Communist demands. (The Museum of Modern Art/Film Stills, Archive, New York.)

posed its defects. Kazan's efforts to gloss these over with displays of intensity only compounded the play's problems. Reviews of the Broadway opening showed unusual agreement that the drama was an unrelieved catalog of misery that numbed, rather than moved, the audience. Kazan's direction was faulted for sensationalizing the family's suffering. Repeatedly, reviewers attacked the sadistic excesses of Lutik's futile struggle to walk and his upping his radio's volume to drown out his cries of pain. It was almost as though Kazan was using the play as an opportunity to parade all the anguish he himself was suffering. *Flight into Egypt* closed after forty-six performances and lost $90,000 of its original $100,000 investment.[40]

Brooks Atkinson was one of several critics who noted how the Engels' belief in America as an ideal and Tabori's intended criticism of its way of life hamstrung the play. Citing the scene in which a fellow Austrian urges Lutik to return to his homeland to face up to the problems he is vainly trying to flee, Atkinson observed that such an act would have compelled Tabori to deal with the Iron Curtain and given "real integrity" to his play.[41] Whatever Kazan thought of this reaction, the film he undertook just following *Flight into Egypt* represented a much more obvious attempt to disassociate himself from his previous dramas criticizing America and to express the aversion to Communism his testimony had proclaimed.

Man on a Tightrope depicted the escape of a Czechoslovakian circus from behind the Iron Curtain. Fox intended this project to show the grim conditions of life under Communism—the tyrannical oppression, the constant surveillance, the poverty, the threats, the fears, the unrelieved wretchedness. The circus was judged an unusually good vehicle for communicating these effects by allowing the filmmaker to dwell upon the anguished desperation behind the painted smiles and feigned merriment. Cernik, the circus owner, is under suspicion for not being loyal to the state. Most of his troubles are traceable to the fact that the state imposes such restrictions on where his circus can play and what kind of acts it can present that the whole operation is teetering on the verge of bankruptcy. This pressure has the effect of turning Cernik into the traitor he is wrongly suspected of being; he concludes that a final break for freedom is the troupe's only hope of survival.

If *Man on a Tightrope* was conceived as a vehicle for the documentary styling Kazan had been cultivating since *Boomerang*, this was not a film Kazan planned to make. Henry Hathaway and Anatole Litvak had figured prominently in the pre-production planning.[42] Kazan was not called in until May of 1952, just two months before filming began. Given the dramatized desperation of Cernik's circus, one almost suspects that, in the same twisted logic of *Flight into Egypt*, Kazan was hoping to comment upon how American governmental surveillance of the entertainment world was destroying it. But he advanced no such claim. In a contemporary article entitled "The Movie That Had to Be Made," Kazan attempted to explain the meaning he saw in *Man on a Tightrope*. He opens by noting how he "felt uneasy" when he agreed to direct this circus story and found that this uneasiness lingered until he was in Germany working on final preparations. There his first view of the barrier between East and West Germany gave him a sudden awareness of "what this border means." The plight of those behind the Iron Curtain remained remote until he learned of the political pressures being brought to bear upon his East German cameraman, who had a home and family on the other side. Kazan was moved by his refusal to be intimidated by his government's insistence that he "quit or else." "If you can put a date to such a thing," Kazan concludes, "that was the moment I understood and was committed to the picture I was making."[43] Kazan, of course, wrote the article in an effort to generate publicity for the film, but his argument sounded a familiar note. Here was another man who refused to submit to Communist demands. Kazan's account is an extension of the views he expressed in his public statement to HUAC and his *New York Times* ad. Was it really the East German cameraman who made him see the importance of showing the Cernik circus struggling to break free from Communist domination? Was this not already very much on his mind when he first agreed to direct this film just six weeks after his second voluntary appearance before HUAC? Whatever the case, the political implications that attracted Kazan to *Man on a Tightrope* did little to inspire his directing. As with *Flight into Egypt*, weariness and futility were the dominant mood and box-office returns were disastrous.

Meanwhile Tennessee Williams had nearly doubled the size of

Ten Blocks on the Camino Real, the ten blocks being developed into sixteen, and then halved these additions. These changes subsequently underwent extensive rewriting and polishing. The original one act play had been built around Kilroy, who opens the play by arriving at an unidentified, Mexican-like piazza after an arduous journey referred to as "one continued hell." He is an ex–Golden Gloves champion with a bad heart, fallen upon hard times. Despite his obvious resemblance to Stanley Kowalski, he is a force that is waning rather than waxing. He is the champ turned loser. With his mementos and mannerisms that bespeak a faded glory, he is the confused, displaced victim of an unbeatable conspiracy. Back in 1946 when he wrote the play, Williams originally conceived of Kilroy as an embodiment of the disappearing roughneck vitality associated with America and the battling dog face whose graffiti, "Kilroy was here," charted his march to victory.[44] He was yet another version of the returning veteran facing altered circumstances in which his fighting skills no longer brought distinction. In his expansion of *Ten Blocks* into a full length play, Williams sought to reduce Kilroy's centrality by enlarging the roles of the town's other residents. Kilroy became only one of many romantic wanderers, including Quixote, Byron, Casanova, and Marguerite Gautier, who have come to the end of the line. Williams, in effect, updated the play so that Kilroy's plight was a shared social condition. Kilroy and his fellow exiles were to be an extravagant collection of misfits with whom Williams strongly identified.

Through all his myriad revisions, Williams maintained an unwavering commitment to his original conception of the play as a lyric, surrealistic defiance of damnation rather than a pessimistic statement about its inescapability. In his public comments on this play, which were to betray a pronounced defensiveness, Williams stated that he had attempted to write a plea on behalf of his characters. "The theme," he told a reporter from *Saturday Review*, "is, I guess you could say, a prayer for the wild of heart kept in cages . . . a picture of the state of the romantic nonconformist in modern society. It stresses honor and man's own sense of inner dignity which the Bohemian must reachieve after each period of degradation he is bound to run into. The romantic should have the spirit of anarchy and not let the world drag him down to its level."[45] This was not just a disposition toward which he was very sympathetic, but, as he further explained to readers of the *New York Times*, the spirit in which the play was written: "To me the appeal of this work is its unusual degree of freedom. . . . My desire was to give these audiences my own sense of something wild and unrestricted that ran like water in the mountains, or clouds changing shape in a gale, or the continually dissolving and transforming images of a dream."[46]

This belief that directionless, impulsive yearnings might triumph over the entrenched forces of restraint, backed by his wish to allow his imagination to throw off the bonds of realism, enabled Williams to create a panoramic range of effects—memorable scenes and bold theatrical innovation—but Kazan worried that audiences would not understand the play. On November 17, 1952, after he had finished reading Williams's expansion of *Ten Blocks*, Kazan drafted a long letter to the playwright cautiously trying to communicate his reservations. In a manner characteristic of his thinking and one quite at odds with Williams's, Kazan wrote:

> This play is moving to me because it describes to me what is happening in the world of 1952 to the people I love most in the world. The author is saying a few thousand words in defense of a dying race call them what you will, romantics, eccentrics, rebels, Bohemians, freaks, harum-scarum, bob-tail. . . .
>
> Even the hitchhikers are disappearing off the roads. Kilroy is the last of the eternal wanderers, and you don't see his name around much anymore. The world is being divided between two horrible standards. There is the standard Western model: the business man. There is the standard Eastern model: Stalin and his copies.

As he read it, *Camino Real* was concerned with the same political issues as his three previous assignments, but Kazan felt uncomfortable because the play inadequately sustained this interpretation. And so he observed, "I say if the play *is* about these people let's speak out and say so clearly because they are being killed off and ironed out, they are being shamed and trained out and silenced and shoved off the edge of the world. Let's speak out for them so everyone will hear and

166

Camino Real: "This play is moving to me because it describes what is happening in the world of 1952 to the people I love most." Eli Wallach appears as Kilroy and Frank Silvera as Gutman. (Photo by Alfredo Valente; reproduced by permission of Mrs. Alfredo Valente and the Billy Rose Theatre Collection, The New York Public Library at Lincoln Center, Astor, Lennox and Tilden Foundations.)

understand." Several sentences later, he reiterated, "We can speak up. Let's! Clearly!" The martial law scene and the play's ending are then cited as examples of the play's failure to fit its different pieces together.[47]

Kazan was upset because Williams's revisions did not fulfill an "architect's blueprint" he saw in the original one-act version.[48] But he was also wary of offending Williams. After all the revisions and modifications Kazan had already requested, Williams had reason to feel that he was being imposed upon. A month later the project was again up in the air and Molly was forced to intervene as mediator. "I could

167

shut up for peace sake," she wrote. "But a misunderstanding is going to make us all trouble in the end, whatever happens with the play. . . . Never before with you and never with any writer have I seen so desperate and absolute an identification. It's dangerous. If you lose the sense that you are more *than* anything you write, you lose your power to SEE it and you lose the power to bring it to its own full realization."[49]

Her appeal restored harmony, but it remained for Kazan and Williams to work out a solution. Describing the understanding they finally hammered out, Williams wrote:

> Elia Kazan was attracted to this work mainly, I believe, for the same reason—its freedom and mobility of form. I know that we have kept saying the word "Flight" to each other as if the play were merely an abstraction of the impulse to fly, and most of the work out of town, his in staging, mine in cutting and revising, has been with this impulse in mind; the achievement of a continual flow.[50]

Kazan himself explained that he sought to convey the feeling of "Tennessee speaking personally and lyrically right to you."[51] To achieve this sense of flow, Kazan decided upon a grand production that utilized a huge cast, fancy costuming, and flamboyant staging. The playing area was extended into the audience, using the aisles for exits and entrances. Movements were choreographed and given orchestral accompaniment. This was a pageant, a masque as fabulous as its featured characters. This was a lavishly staged avant-garde drama in which the Bohemians of the play's down-and-out environment bedazzled the audience. Instead of trying to integrate *Camino*'s strange mixture of the familiar, the abstract, and the symbolic, Kazan created a spectacular jumbling of movement and stage mechanics, as did he earlier with *The Skin of Our Teeth*, in order to suggest man's refusal to be defeated by external dangers and unnerving fears. But, because Williams's play did not sustain such optimism, as Wilder's did, whatever may have been his intentions, this type of presentation seemed false and contrived, finally exposing the hopes of those trying to escape as desperate illusions. In pointed contrast to *A Streetcar Named Desire*, Kazan's search for sociological relevance never got together with Williams's lyric introspection. Though *Camino Real* had enough defenders to be controversial, most critics judged Williams's work to be self-indulgent and Kazan's theatrics to be inappropriate. *Camino Real* had to fight to stay on the stage for sixty performances. Its loss of $115,000 of their bankers' $140,000 investment[52] made it an even greater box office debacle than *Flight into Egypt*. Many years would pass before Williams or Kazan would again try to range so far from their home ground of social realism.

On March 13, 1953, the same night *Camino Real* opened, Cecil B. DeMille's *The Greatest Show on Earth* was presented the academy award for best picture of 1952. The coincidence of this simultaneous triumph and defeat became a suggestive commentary upon audience preference two months later when *Man on a Tightrope* proved to be a box-office disaster as well. Like *The Greatest Show on Earth, Man on a Tightrope* explored the frustration and antagonism of circus life outside the ring. The audience witnessed the same vanity of the star performer, the same pathos and patriotism of the clown, the same heroic struggle of the manager to hold the troupe together. Gloria Graham not only appeared in both films, she even played the same role of a tramp. Few, however, noted these resemblances. In stark contrast to Kazan's grim indictment of Communism, DeMille's technicolor spectacle was a paean to the American way of life—its might, its resiliency, its flair, its extravagance. It was a collection of stars that glittered and acts that dazzled. This was a circus with size, color, and diversity, one whose ability to pull itself together and surmount adversity was above question. Most of all, here was a film that grossed twelve million dollars in receipts, giving it the second largest gross receipt in Hollywood's history. This was broad-based entertainment for middle-class America.

The dismal number of customers for *Man on a Tightrope* lent convincing support for the growing belief that the market for this type of film may well have dried up. For more than a year, Spyros Skouras, the executive president of Twentieth Century-Fox, had been reflecting upon the spectacular boxoffice returns of *Samson and Delilah* and its imitators. He concluded that the character and expectations of the average filmgoer were quite different from what they had been only a few years before. This coupled with his mounting uneasiness over the sud-

169

den popularity of the new screen processes, "3-D," "Todd-A-O," and Cinerama, caused him to believe that the motion picture industry was on the brink of a revolution that might be as earthshaking as the advent of sound. Convinced that big screen and spectacles were a natural complement to one another, he envisioned a landslide return for a successful marriage. Thus he spent most of 1952 arranging for Fox to buy rights to *The Robe*, which Frank Ross had been trying unsuccessfully to peddle since the Second World War, when Lloyd Douglas's novel topped the bestseller list, and to acquire the CinemaScope process which Dr. Henri Chrétien originally invented back in 1925.

Long before *The Robe* started harvesting its thirty million dollars in receipts, Darryl Zanuck scrambled to adjust his production schedule to this decision. In a memo dated March 12, 1953, just as filming on *The Robe* was starting, Zanuck advised his writers of the profound effect Fox's commitment to CinemaScope was going to have. Exempting several films about to be produced, including "Waterfront," he explained that future production plans would concentrate on the kind of subject matter which best lent itself to this new medium. He went on to explain how he was conducting a reevaluation of all project commitments and carefully assessing their ability to take advantage of CinemaScope.[53]

Just two months later, on May 7, 1952, Zanuck wrote Philip Dunne a follow-up memo in which he speculated on how this commitment to CinemaScope related to noticeable shifts in audience tastes and necessitated a sharp departure from the type of film Fox turned out a few years before. With emphasis upon "today," he observed how audiences had a decided preference for adventure or escape and wanted to get away from the gloomy news of the moment. Citing his disappointment at the poor returns of *Viva Zapata!* and *Man on a Tightrope*, he worried that the "excellent picture" had lost appeal. He noted the fact that there was not a single message picture on the list of recent successes and questioned how films like *The Snake Pit, Pinky,* and *Gentleman's Agreement* would have fared in this market. As an executive keenly aware that his studio's future hinged upon its continuing ability to generate profits, he concluded that, like it or not, Fox must cue its efforts to these changes.[54]

Zanuck was convinced audiences were no longer interested in

170

the sort of film Kazan had been making. Having gone far out on a limb with his testimony and the kind of films he directed to demonstrate that he was a fervent anti-Communist, Kazan was judged guilty of a worse offense—not being able to make money. Thus, shortly after the disastrous release of *Man on a Tightrope,* Zanuck scrapped the "Waterfront" project he had exempted from his reevaluation of production plans just two months earlier. The director, who had provided Zanuck with many of the films in which he took greatest pride and who had not made a real money loser until his two recent releases, was put into a holding pattern. Although his contract called for three more films, there was such disagreement between Fox* and Kazan over what these might be that both consented to a temporary separation as the best solution. Kazan was not washed up and neither was his "Waterfront." Zanuck believed message pictures were dead. In its derision of his testimony, *Nation* had confidently asserted that even Kazan could not make a film which could improve on *The Informer.* Kazan would show them both to be wrong.

SEVEN

Comeback

Like a champion who had suffered a jolting defeat, Kazan faced a tough uphill fight to regain his former preeminence. Bitterly stung by the outcome of his HUAC testimony, he had thrown himself into a rapid succession of directing assignments. And all three had proven resounding failures, yielding poor returns on their substantial investments. Not since the early 1930s, when he was just starting in the theatre, had Kazan felt the world to be so much against him. Again he was the outsider. Among his friends and colleagues, he was a turncoat and pariah. Fox no longer wanted his services unless he embraced the religion of CinemaScope. On Broadway he could not afford another debacle.

In his next efforts, Kazan would have to take risks. HUAC's suspicion of social criticism and the public's attraction for colorful, widescreen pageants were driving social problem dramas from theatres as World War II had once done. Still, Kazan could not forsake his commitment to this kind of material. It was the foundation for his creativity; he had honed his theatrical skills on social realism. Moreover, he had grown increasingly dependent upon this approach for self-expression. HUAC had been a painful lesson in the dangers of direct address, and as such had aggravated the intense need for recognition, self-justification, and approval that had always lay at the heart of Kazan's plays and films. Trying though these adversities were, they were also a source of inspiration. As in the past, rejection, pain, confusion, and defensiveness had the effect of firing Kazan's determination and giving him purpose. Now in a manner more insistently per-

173

sonal than ever before, Kazan's problems were to be his salvation, spurring him to another revitalization of his styling.

Realizing the dangers he was facing, Kazan reverted to his customary approach: venturesomeness allied with caution and calculation. His next four productions, *Tea and Sympathy, On the Waterfront, East of Eden,* and *Cat on a Hot Tin Roof* were to be highly acclaimed commercial successes that reaffirmed his command of his material and his audiences. Together they heralded a triumphant return to America and to an examination of defects within her way of life. They would reappraise those American values and preoccupations that caused oppression, intolerance, and suspicion. Likewise, they would concentrate upon a figure who challenged these conditions. In this respect, these dramas were to draw upon the returning war veterans and victims of racial prejudice in Kazan's earlier work. Although these elements bespoke carry-over from the past, they were tailored to the cultural conditions that had sharply breeched his professional ambitions.

All four handled social problems most gingerly. Where the dramas suggested defects within the existing social system, they were either generalized to the point of vagueness, or else localized so as to imply a specific distortion rather a widespread state of affairs. Instead of spotlighting an injustice, defining its nature, and tracing its operation, as Kazan's earlier work did, these dramas tended to present a climate of oppression and then dwell on its impact upon the thought and behavior of the victim. Where politics were involved, most notably in *On the Waterfront,* special care was taken to skirt potentially dangerous matters. Not only was this muted, indirect social criticism, it was insistently constructive. Each work advanced a final solution that was well within the grasp of the individual, though it necessitated relying on someone else—both to open understanding and alleviate a yearning for social acceptance.

These dramas would depart from Kazan's previous undertakings most noticeably in their use of social injustice as a stimulus to a featured romance. All four were to focus on a young, deeply troubled male protagonist whose reluctant, misunderstood waywardness was linked to a developing love affair that opened up the possibility of relief from his alienation. Consequently, the plight of this young rebel was less a social problem than a debilitating sense of self, which a generous, understanding woman helped him to overcome. These strong-willed but compassionate heroines demonstrated a stability that sharply contrasted with the anxieties of their male counterparts; through their love, they were able to offer these troubled males the sort of salvation associated with political action back in the 1930s. With a frank sexuality that belied their manifest propriety and increased their allure, these heroines were as striking as the men they strove to help.

If the romance and sex of these works tended to replace complex social problems with simplistic solutions, they made these dramas compelling. Moreover, this shift in emphasis from social problems to intimate relationships was no mere pandering to popular taste. These were tense, introspective dramas, and, as in *Death of a Salesman,* the significance accorded the anguished mentality of the male protagonists was premised on the assumption that unhealthy social conditions produced unsound minds. That Kazan should have continued to gravitate toward emotional-psychological struggles was almost to be expected. What was different was the special terms of these struggles. Each would present a man of exceptional talent who is condemned for his departure from agreed-upon standards of conduct. Each would explore the wounded defensiveness that results. Since these men were situated in a society in which pressures for conformity were unusually great, their strange deportment was believable in a way Zapata's was not. Perhaps most distinctive of all, though, was the fact that all four labored under a crippling burden of guilt for "mistakes" to the extent of suggesting an obsession on the part of the director. Further, these "mistakes" were persistently shown as innocent, even commendable, actions wrongly condemned by a narrow-minded society. That is to say, these were portraits of rejection that deeply involved the director whose HUAC stand had met with such disfavor. As much as they testified to Kazan's uncanny ability to stay abreast of changing audience tastes, they evidence a strong personal identification with the problems of these well-intentioned, misunderstood young rebels.

Tea and Sympathy, the production Kazan handled first and one which came to exercise a profound influence upon the three which followed, was by an unknown playwright, Robert Anderson. His play had already been rejected by many producers because it dealt with homosexuality within the setting of a conservative New England men's prep school. Molly, who first read the play and pressed her husband to consider it, sensed what the recently published *Catcher in the Rye* would demonstrate—that the prep school was a persuasive embodiment of the oppressive demand for conformity responsible for the so-called "silent generation." Although the play would be long remembered for being one of the first to treat the subject of homosexuality, Kazan saw that this issue was important primarily for its shock value to get the play going. Like the plague in *Panic in the Streets,* it was a device. It allowed Anderson to dissect the conspiratorial social pressures that made a conventional prep school an indoctrination in a lock-step code of behavior.

Young Tom Lee is a victim of this process. All the representative components of the school—the random students, Lee's roommate, the housemaster Bill Reynolds, and even his father the faithful alumnus—believe him to be guilty of a crime he has not committed. The case against Lee consists of inferences and suspicions. Although he is seen bathing nude with a school instructor, the most damaging evidence against him are traits of his character that set him apart from the other students. He does not go in for athletics and is content to be the team manager. He enjoys singing and frankly prefers the company of the housemaster's wife, Laura. Homosexuality is merely a convenient label for his deviance from the tyrannical norm; it brands his "off-horse" behavior reprehensible and legitimizes everyone's rejection of him. Anderson's play unfolds in such a way that the audience sees the root cause of this tragic misunderstanding to be Lee's innocence, his sympathetic sensitivity and naïveté. He is a guiltless victim of unjust standards of right and wrong, acceptable and unacceptable.

Although Lee's problem is the featured issue, he is not the main character. He registers confusion, inadequacy, and shame, but does not possess the strength and understanding that would give him stature. Through her growing awareness of this injustice, Laura takes over center stage. Her growing compassion for Lee's worsening plight compels her to abandon her cultivated detachment. Laura's position as the housemaster's wife commits her to the school and necessitates that she remain aloof from the students. This male environment forces her to suppress her essential beauty, artistic talent, feeling, and sexuality, but, in spite of her adoption of frumpy clothing and mannered behavior, she cannot accord herself to the school's values. Lee reminds her of all that she has given up. Her growing concern for the merit in his presumed faults brings a discomforting awareness of the drawbacks to her life. His distress provokes hers. Lee's systematic rejection by those who might be expected to come to his defense—the housemaster, his roommate, and his father—makes any form of support increasingly dangerous and, for Laura, more imperative. To act on Lee's behalf is a proclamation of her own worth. Her offer of herself to Lee at the play's conclusion, which stunned audiences with its violation of conventional morality, won their approval because it was presented as a heroic act of generosity and a realization of her own identity.

Kazan's appreciation for the potential in this material came with a dawning realization that more needed to be done to fulfill it. Initially, Kazan was uncomfortable with Anderson's characterization of Mr. Lee, the boy's father, and Bill Reynolds, Laura's husband. Reminiscent of familiar stereotypes from the 1930s, they virtually demand rejection. After getting Anderson to endow both characters with a limited concern for others that made them more sympathetic while still provoking the audience's antagonism,[1] Kazan found that actresses were reluctant to play Laura because they felt she was not enough of a participant to be a lead role; she was a silent force moved to final action by what happens around her.[2] She needed to participate more in the unfolding drama. In their discussions over how best to correct this drawback, Kazan and Anderson discovered that she could be made a stronger presence by having her show more feeling to those around her, especially her husband. Their revised Laura wants to get Bill away to Canada, where she can reestablish contact with the lovable, sensitive man the school has hardened. With the dimestore ring added to her wardrobe, she displays her fondness for the man who gave it to her, thereby allowing Bill's embarrassment over it to be an indication that he is not as unfeeling as he appears. The audience not only glimpses the man who called out for her help and won her love, as she explains in a key speech added to the second act, but also comprehends her sense of loss over the way the conditions of the school have hardened him.

This Laura represents something. She is a woman with a believable, well-defined commitment. She understands the vulnerability masked by masculine shows of strength and conviction. She possesses the ability to put men in touch with their unacknowledged feelings and needs. Before her denunciation of the school's deficiencies, this Laura first demonstrates the warmth and compassion she has to contribute. When she offers herself to Lee, she is acting upon her final realization that "everyone is everyone's responsibility," which Kazan defined as the play's core.[3] Her sexuality is integral to her nobility. Laura's decision to walk out on her husband and to go to bed with Lee is a final indictment of an inhumane, hypocritical morality, and it *affirms,* rather than violates, her exemplification of the conventional female ideal.

To appreciate both the subtlety and importance of this effect one only has to consider Laura Reynolds's latent kinship to Blanche DuBois, which resulted from the changes Kazan worked out with Anderson. Laura, like Blanche, was previously married to a young man uncertain of his manhood. While Blanche's husband shot himself, Laura's first partner got killed "being conspicuously brave" in the war. Laura then married Bill and won his love by being so understanding and helpful with the "need" he revealed on their honeymoon. Her final decision to go to bed with Lee recalls Blanche's seduction of a student, which leads to her dismissal. Both are driven by the same basic longing to use their sexuality to help needy males—but with sharply different consequences. While Blanche is unbalanced and pathetic in the extreme—frequently described as a "nymphomaniac"— Laura's behavior is supposed to suggest admirable compassion and inviolable virtue. The concluding scene of *Tea and Sympathy*, memorably staged with few words, tentative gestures, and silent pauses, so unlike the stiffled hysteria of Blanche's departure, effectively summarized the differences between these two women and the two plays. In acclaiming its power, Eric Bentley would write: "One doesn't ask just how the heroine's motives are mixed—to what extent her favors are kindness, to what extent self-indulgence."[4] Laura's behavior evoked no suggestion of Blanche's confused motives and lack of self-understanding in large measure because the spirit of this presentation was so unlike Kazan's previous efforts. Kazan concentrated upon getting *Tea and Sympathy* to be "light [and] delicate."[5] The production became almost synonymous with these terms. "'Fastidiousness' is an odd word to apply to the direction of Mr. Kazan who is better known for the power of his impact on a play," one critic observed, while a handful of others talked of the "Kazan Touch."[6]

On the Waterfront, which Kazan started filming just following the September 1953 opening of *Tea and Sympathy*, traced Terry Malloy's difficult progression from a longshoreman favored by his boss Johnny Friendly to an ostracized informer who exposes the thoroughgoing corruption of his union. Despite the pronounced differences in its subject matter and styling, *On the Waterfront* was to resemble *Tea and Sympathy* in important ways, most notably in the tortured confusion of the male protagonist and the crucial help he receives from a compassionate, understanding woman. Terry Malloy's union demands even more conformity than Tom's prep school: a good longshoreman does his job—what his superior dictates—and keeps his mouth shut. Like Tom Lee, Terry possesses a wayward sensibility that is sufficiently at odds with prevailing expectations to pose a dangerous threat. Terry's misgivings about his union allegiance are aggravated by his attraction to Edie. Edie's distinctive blend of propriety, understated beauty, and lambent sexuality likens her to Laura; her self-revealing observation on how teachers might have had more success with Terry if they had used "a little more patience and kindness" extends Edie's kinship to Laura to her very words.

Edie's resemblance to Laura is most pronounced in her appreciation of those qualities that make Terry offensive and out-of-step to others, even though Terry himself is quite different from Tom. She patiently endures Terry's rudeness and ill-considered remarks, showing a trust that he is better than his manner and superior to his fellow longshoremen. Nevertheless, in his confused efforts to open up to Edie, he justifies himself with the selfish, twisted thinking typical of the other longshoremen until it threatens their relationship. To his insistence upon the importance of looking out for oneself, she asks the very question Kazan singled out as the core of *Tea and Sympathy*—"Isn't everybody a part of everyone else?" Out of this clash of philos-

179

Marlon Brando as Terry Malloy in *On the Waterfront*: A portrait of defensiveness. (The Museum of Modern Art/Film Stills Archive, New York.)

ophies comes Terry's cry for help, an anguished admission that his adopted attitude is no longer tenable and the first in a series of confessions that climax with his taking the witness stand.

Behind these similarities to *Tea and Sympathy* lies a calculated appeal for the audience's attention. Even before the corroboration of *Tea and Sympathy*'s strong box-office returns, Kazan realized that the terms of the exchange between Laura and Tom possessed rich, romantic potential. Moreover, his experience with Fox had convinced him that the love motif would have a crucial bearing upon any film's success or failure. In a reflection some twenty years after *On the Waterfront*'s completion, Kazan himself observed, "The love scenes are the best thing in the film."[7] Still, what makes the featured romance of *On the Waterfront* so compelling is not its implementation of an increasingly popular formula so much as the integration of this romance with its dramatization of social injustice.

On the Waterfront richly deserved the eight Oscars it won in 1954. It demonstrated that hard hitting social drama could draw large audiences. Opening while the New York Crime Commission was still holding hearings on waterfront corruption, *On the Waterfront* possessed a currency and timeliness that were uncanny in light of the four-year struggle behind its completion. None of Kazan's undertakings up to this point, not even *Camino Real*, had demanded such an enormous investment of time and energy. None had been the object of so much personal anxiety and determination. *On the Waterfront* owed its success to the collaboration of many talented individuals, but Kazan was the guiding influence. He shaped good ideas into stirring drama and shepherded the film through the overwhelming adversities not recorded by the camera.

On the Waterfront reached back to the strike plays Kazan tried to write when he first joined Group Theatre. It drew upon the roles that heralded his emergence as an actor—the nameless rebel in *Waiting for Lefty*, who exposes his own brother to be a pawn of the corrupt union leadership; Agate, who sounds the concluding call for the membership to strike for their rights; Eddie Fuseli, in *Golden Boy*, who presses Joe to give up his soul in return for material gains; and finally Joe Bonaparte, the tough boxer whose exceptional sensibilities are brutalized by his fight to get ahead. However, the evolution of Kazan's thinking since the 1930s led to a work that was as striking for its differences from these touchstones as for its resemblances. *On the Waterfront* depicts a psychological struggle reminiscent of *Death of a Salesman*, played out against vividly portrayed waterfront conditions, in which Kazan achieved the psychological complexity and contextual definition that he envisioned when he first persuaded Arthur Miller to do a screenplay about the waterfront. The social problem in this film forced the protagonist to face long-suppressed thoughts and feelings with the result that his battle was finally with himself. However much Kazan's decision to name names before HUAC influenced the film's attempt to make a hero out of an informer, his testimony gave him acute insight into the emotional distress that an informer might suffer. What makes Terry's journey to the witness stand so memorable is his acutely pained defensiveness.

This personal, psychological dimension, so critical to the success of *Waterfront*, was integrally connected to its realistic, contemporary American setting. Back in 1949, some four years before the filming of *On the Waterfront* finally got underway, Malcolm Johnson wrote a series of articles for the *New York Sun* on the operations of the International Longshoremen's Union which controlled the New York docks. His exposé of the leaders' ruthless exploitation of the membership won him a Pulitzer Prize. Amid the mounting demands for a governmental investigation sparked by Johnson's findings, Kazan persuaded Arthur Miller to develop a script from this material as a refreshing departure from the tight familial situations of his last two plays. In sporadic bursts of effort between February 1949 and the summer of 1950, he drafted a screenplay entitled "The Hook." Miller conceived this as being about "the generally insulted man" who acts "as though a hand had been laid upon him, marking him the rebel, pressing him toward a collision with everything that is established and accepted."[8] Miller's "rebel" faced the same lonely fight of the protagonists of *Boomerang* and *Panic in the Streets,* only instead of being a respected professional—a lawyer or doctor—he was a working man. He looked at the world from the bottom up. Because "The Hook" pitted an individual against an oppressive, dictatorial union leadership, it is hardly surprising that Miller's hero prefigures Terry Malloy of *On the Waterfront.* Marty is a typical longshoreman who identifies with his fellow workers while possessing all the earmarks of a leader. At work he is annoyed by the concessions of his union to the shippers, which endanger the membership. When a man is killed, Marty walks out and secures the cushy job of a bookie. This brings him wealth, but at the expense of his fellow workers. Despite his efforts to remain aloof and to keep his mouth shut, his conscience drives him to throw up his job and to challenge the union leadership. Risking the prospective loss of his job and perhaps even his life, he resolves, "I gonna be an example, so the men should know there's a guy around here he ain't ascared to open his mouth."[9] The result is a crushing defeat. Marty is banned from work on any waterfront and reduced to grinding poverty. Broken, but not beaten, he returns for one last confrontation, a lonely symbol of defiance. Again he loses, but the union leadership is discredited in the process. Thus Marty's succession of defeats ends in victory.

These parallels between "The Hook" and *On the Waterfront* are somewhat misleading. None of the scenes are structured the same way; the lines are entirely different. "The Hook" could have been made into an interesting, perhaps even stirring, movie, but it would not have been *On The Waterfront*. In the first place, "The Hook" smacked too strongly of the outworn strike dramas of the 1930s. Marty's polemical fervor makes him more a cause than a character. His strength lies in his assertion of belief, rather than any searching quest for an appropriate course of action. Marty's anxiety for his family is surprisingly flat in view of the intermingled affection, friction, and misunderstanding in Miller's portrayal of the Keller and Loman families. Miller's script is also flawed by notable implausibilities in Marty's challenge to the union leadership. In order to show the enormous cost of his righteousness, Miller first has Marty betrayed by his fellow workers and driven into extreme poverty. This Marty stoically endures until his situation becomes desperate, at which point he again attacks the corrupt union. Miller obviously wanted this decline to be a test of character, but it leaves Marty only conviction with which to fight his return match. There is no reason to believe that Marty's second challenge could have more impact on either the men or the union than his disastrous first go around did.

These drawbacks, however, had little bearing on the aborted proj-

ect. "The Hook" fell victim to the same pressures that weighed upon
Viva Zapata!—money and politics. On the cover of the unpublished
manuscript Miller has written: "Unproduced screenplay about Brooklyn Waterfront. Written about 1951. Columbia pictures had agreed to
produce it until—(during the Korean War) pressure was applied to
change the gangster labor leaders to Communists, thus Americanizing
the story. The social situations described later by Kefauver investigation of waterfront."[10] Kazan, on the other hand, has said:

> the script was completed, and we arranged the financing from
> Columbia Pictures. Then I got a phone call from Art saying that
> he had decided he didn't want to do it. I still don't know why
> he did that. Anyway he called it off, and I was annoyed with
> him, because I'd spent a lot of time on it. It was an extremely
> abrupt and embarrassing decision. . . . I think Art saw the Un-
> American Activities Committee coming and there was something
> that had suddenly developed in his personal life that made him
> not want to have that film done. . . . The Hook is a section
> of the waterfront, 'Red Hook,' it's called, but it's also the
> longshoremen's hook which you hold with the handle, like a
> communist sickle.[11]

Clearly, the termination of this project impinges upon an area of
considerable sensitivity obscured by both men's self-defensive distor-
tions. To make the union leadership Communists was a patent absurdity
no audience would accept. At the same time, Miller's script lends little
support to Kazan's Red Hook explanation; Marty repeatedly maintains
that his attack upon the union is an affirmation of democratic principles. Still there is enough overlap in these differing accounts to suggest that "The Hook" was victimized by the same spectre of Communism that haunted *Viva Zapata!* Here was another sympathetically
portrayed revolution against social corruption by a disgruntled "proletariat," and studio executives would have been understandably leery
of these implications. Presumably, Kazan was ready to help Miller
forge, a compromise solution as he had with *Streetcar* and *Viva Zapata!*,
but Miller balked. In view of the strong feelings attendant upon their
different positions, there would have been little point in trying to

interest someone else in the project. If this was in fact what happened, then the friendship and professional collaboration between Kazan and Miller was probably failing well before Kazan's testimony.

Kazan and Miller were not the only ones who felt Johnson's exposé of the New York waterfront situation could be developed into a good movie. Jack Curtis, Harry Cohn's nephew, had optioned Johnson's account (a fact that would have posed a formidable legal obstacle to Miller's script) and hired Budd Schulberg to prepare a script from the book. The hastily written result made the waterfront conditions a springboard for a rather conventional gangster movie presented from the viewpoint of the victim. The hero of the script, Terry Monahan, is a rebel like Marty. From the outset he is working to defeat the union boss Zero Doyle and bring about an honest shape-up, but he is naïve about the elaborate hierarchy of corruption he is challenging. Doyle is the pawn of the slick gangster Charley Apple, who takes his orders from Leland F. Foley, a smooth businessman described as looking like a respectable senator; he, in turn, is controlled by an even higher up referred to as "J.C." When Terry rejects Apple's mollifying offer of a better position, he gets "bumped off." Thus, halfway through the script, Terry was eliminated. The second half deals with the efforts of his sister, Edie, to carry on his fight. Outraged by the unopposed criminal conduct of the union, she berates Chase, a news reporter freely modelled upon Malcolm Johnson, for not pursuing such an obvious story. She wrongly accusses him of being a weak man. His lame leg, which makes him seem ineffectual and timid, is later revealed to have been a union reprisal for an exposé he wrote years earlier. Now less idealistic and more cautious, he continues to maintain an extensive file on the waterfront criminals. Finally, his love for Edie spurs him to print his findings, which brings the arrest of Terry's two killers and the downfall of Foley.

In personalizing the much publicized waterfront situation, this film was intended to celebrate the heroism of the journalist, Malcolm Johnson, *and* his prize winning report. This would be a *Chicago Deadline* (1949), *Underworld Story* (1950), or *Deadline USA* (1952), with a firm grounding in actual newspaper articles.[12] But Curtis could not get his uncle to finance and distribute the project—perhaps because, by this point, Columbia had already made a tentative commitment to

"The Hook." Amidst the thickening atmosphere of McCarthyism, Schulberg's script, then entitled "Crime on the Waterfront," dared to suggest that the waterfront corruption was not confined to the waterfront. Like Malcolm Johnson, whose book bore the similar title of *Crime on the Labor Front,* Schulberg showed this problem to be the end product of a business-governmental conspiracy that hid its involvement behind a mask of respectability. Still these political liabilities were no greater than glaring defects in the dramatization. "Crime on the Waterfront" was marred by a major division within the plot development. Terry, who was the center of attention in the first half, was replaced by Chase in the second. In effect, Schulberg was shifting the audience's attention and sympathy from one character to another who was radically different. Behind this abrupt shift lay an even more troublesome drawback that had haunted Miller's script as well. The herioism of Miller's and Schulberg's protagonists was improbable and inaccurate. Their foolhardy disregard for insurmountable danger made Marty and Terry unconvincing longshoremen. As Johnson had carefully explained and Schulberg was later to emphasize, the real dockworkers had an instinctive reluctance to become either rebels or martyrs.

Thus by the end of 1951 both "The Hook" and "Crime on the Waterfront" were dead. The following spring, Schulberg met Kazan. As they talked they were undoubtedly surprised to discover that they both had been working on unproduced films about the New York waterfront. They also had another point in common. On May 23, 1951, Budd Schulberg had testified as a "friendly" witness before HUAC, explaining how he, like Kazan, had broken with the Party because of its tyrannical insistence that he conform to its politics and plans. As important as their abandoned waterfront films and their painful testimonies may have been in bringing Kazan and Schulberg together,[13] they benefitted enormously from an intervening turn of events. The same environment of McCarthyism that led to an investigation of Communist influence upon Hollywood turned Congressional attention to the operations of organized crime. In 1951, Estes Kefauver opened hearings and, by 1952, had narrowed his focus to the New York situation. In spotlighting underworld figures like Frank Ryan and Frank Costello, the Kefauver committee publicized the flagrant corruption of the International Longshoremen's Association and spurred the New York State Crime Commission to take action. Corruption on the waterfront was now a well-known fact; a realistic social drama emphasizing this injustice could not be considered an act of subversion. The public attention of the Kefauver investigations, the injustices that testimony uncovered, created an example like the HUAC experiences which drew Kazan and Schulberg together. Moreover, these proceedings furnished a solution to the difficulties that defeated the original waterfront scripts. The Kefauver Committee was hampered by the reluctance of the rank and file to testify against their union bosses. The fear of reprisals was great. Nonetheless, some individuals did. Such testimony had a parallel in Kazan's and Schulberg's before HUAC, but now public sentiment was solidly on the side of the man who dared to reveal what he knew. It exemplified that same refusal to yield to the authoritarian demands that Schulberg and Kazan both cited as the reason for their original break with the Communist Party. Rather than the cowards the HUAC "friendlies" had been branded, these were heroes standing against injustice and oppression, actions befitting "men of individual conscience." The act of testifying also raised the possibility, which audiences would now accept, that one man could defeat a whole union and thereby eliminate the need for a mass insurrection, along with the dangerous Communist implications it raised.

Aided by this perspective from their own ordeals, Kazan and Schulberg saw that only half of the waterfront's drama lay in the workers' struggle against the union—the other half was in their attitude.[14] By the lone act of testifying, Terry could believably hurt those in power, but this demanded that he lay everything on the line. Because "stooling" violated the code of behavior of the men with whom he identified, it carried the risk of alienation and possible death. The burden of decision was *his*. His attack upon the union by his cooperative testimony could certainly not be accused of being Communist inspired. This was emphatically the act of a loner. *How* Terry should go about defeating the union was replaced by a more psychological question of *whether* he should do it. The corrupt waterfront conditions became an infuriating, claustrophobic enclosure pressuring Terry's reluctant evolution from a conventional longshoreman opposed to informing to an angry witness against his colleagues.

The two years that passed between Kazan's initial conversation with Schulberg and the start of filming *On the Waterfront* were a nerve-wracking ordeal for both men, causing the script to be put through eight complete revisions.[15] While many of these resulted from Kazan's close working relationships with Schulberg, others were a direct result of the adverse studio responses that carried the script from RKO to Fox to United Artists and finally to Sam Spiegel, who agreed to produce it with Columbia serving as distributor.

Once Kazan and Schulberg decided to focus their film upon Terry's journey to the courtroom, they set about situating him between opposing sets of more sharply differentiated characters who would make his decision to testify as difficult as possible. Schulberg's revisions preserved some of his original characterizations, but concentrated the corruption within the union local. By turning Terry's brother Charley into Johnny Friendly's pawn, Schulberg reversed the subordination of John O. (Zero) Doyle to Charley Apple and broke the chain that extended upward to the lordly J.C. This decision reduced the earlier script's revelation of widespread corruption and diminished the accuracy of the presentation. It also defused a major objection. Above all, this change paved the way for turning the exposé into a drama of confrontation. Terry now faced superiors he might beat, but who could put considerable pressure on him. Johnny Friendly, the boss, conducts his affairs as a world unto himself. He exploits and intimidates the workers. Because he calls the shots, his defeat is a major victory. Essentially, Johnny Friendly is a sterotypical thug, but Kazan got Lee J. Cobb to embellish his display of swaggering roughness with psychological carry-over from his Eddie Fuseli. The scene in which Friendly explains how he had to fight to get to the top is presented as a lesson for Terry in the way to get ahead. Complaining that he has become a "soft touch," Friendly demonstrates that he cares for Terry. He awards him a cushy job and gives his cheek a tug. But these displays of affection are checked by the smart slap he gives Terry to remind him that he must be tough. Later he beats a disloyal underling to emphasize to Terry the fealty he expects.

According to the logic of this scene, Friendly's ensuing anger at Terry's conduct bespeaks a father's love scorned.

Leland Foley and Charley Apple were consolidated into the dapper Charley, who is now Friendly's subordinate and Terry's brother. Here again, this personalization of Terry's problem demonstrates Kazan's quest for psychological depth. As Kazan got Rod Steiger to play him, Charley is ingratiatingly deferential to his boss and somewhat of a mimic in his outspoken contempt for rank-and-file underlings. In Friendly's presence, Charley adopts an aloof superiority to Terry and tells him flatly what he ought to be doing. When they are alone, he is soft-spoken and conciliatory, expressing a heartfelt concern for Terry's welfare. He is an object lesson in what Friendly expects and a loving brother. Up to his famous taxi ride, Charley is oblivious to any conflict in these divided allegiances. In the course of their disjointed exchange, in which his gift of advice culminates in his pulling a gun, Charley realizes for the first time how Friendly's wishes have always preempted Terry's needs. To Charley's dismay, this effort to help Terry exposes his own unrealized selfishness and duplicity. Charley is destroyed, first figuratively and then literally.

Terry's supporters were likewise fashioned to intensify the pressure weighing upon Terry. Father Barry, who was modeled upon several waterfront priests, especially Father John Corridan, whom Schulberg got to know during a series of research visits to Hoboken following his original script, was developed as a carefully balanced foil to Friendly. Karl Malden's Barry is driven by a *selfless* wish to help others. At the Church gathering and in his address over Dugan's body, he boldly displays an exemplary courage to speak out. He shows himself to be a man of passion and conviction. Yet he pointedly refrains from imposing his will on Terry. In contrast to Friendly's insistence that Terry follow orders, Kazan had Barry have his greatest impact upon Terry—in the scene in which Terry seeks his advice— by refusing to tell Terry what he should do. His hope that Terry will be his own man necessitates that he leave him free to act as one.

Interesting as these characters are in their own right, their primary role is to compound the difficulties of Terry's decision. Terry is Kazan's greatest achievement. The key to Kazan's depiction is found in the contrasting characters who hamstrung Schulberg's original

Eva Marie Saint and Marlon Brando in *On the Waterfront*: Vulnerability, love, and conscience beneath a tough exterior. (The Museum of Modern Art/Film Stills Archive, New York.)

screenplay. Terry was tough and determined. Chase was circumspect and defensive. In collapsing these roles into a single figure, Schulberg presented Kazan with a character who could be played as someone quite different from what he appeared. This Terry does not understand the tangled emotions that impel him and indeed needs direction, as everyone suspects. He is proud *and* vulnerable, vain *and* loving, strong-willed *and* dependent, headstrong *and* confused.

To develop and highlight these divisions in Terry's character, Schulberg endowed him with a background of boxing and a love for his pet pigeons. Terry's ring experience suggests an unflinching response to danger, but it is also a source of distress, which he masks with his toughness. Having thrown a crucial fight at Friendly's orders, he is left with the stigma of a loser. Before Terry can overcome his view of himself as a "bum" and fulfill his potential, he has to realize that the fight he lost really took place outside the ring. Thus his struggle with the union becomes a comeback effort culminating in an actual fist fight between Terry and Johnny Friendly. The pigeon coop, on the other hand, illuminates the essential sensitivity at odds with Terry's rugged appearance and his boxing career, a more believable updating of Joe Bonaparte's violin.*

Kazan was at his best in his presentation of these warring components of Terry's identity. The early scenes show Terry to be a conventional longshoreman. First he joins a line of union henchmen, which visually defines his adherence to union policy. The next morning, at the shape-up, he parades his longshoreman's disposition with his hostile, wise-cracking refusal to cooperate with the federal investigator. To all strangers, including Edie, Terry presents himself as hard, unthinking, and uncaring. Marlon Brando's manner goes with

*The title of one of the later script versions, "Golden Warriors," called attention to this reformulation of *Golden Boy*.

Julie Harris and James Dean in *East of Eden*: A display of the vulnerability and sexuality that Terry Malloy hid. (The Museum of Modern Art/Film Stills Archive, New York.)

191

the worn, raw-boned faces of Terry's fellow workers and the bleak, desolate surroundings; Terry is a product of this environment, well-schooled in the lore for survival. Nonetheless, he is consistently out of step. Significantly, in the opening scenes when Friendly and his followers pile into an awaiting car, Terry continues on past the camera alone. Later, he is obviously upset at the news of the death of Edie's brother Joey, whom he lured to a rooftop, presumably to be beaten for informing. His hang-dog silence around Friendly communicates distinct reservations about union policies. Amidst the milling men at the shape-up, he moves in complete self-absorption. Again and again, he is pictured as a loner—at his coop, at work atop the bags, in the back of the Church. In Brando's portrayal, Terry's behavior around fellow union members, the federal investigator, and even Edie consistently suggests that his feelings do not go with the manner he cultivates. His habit of looking away from people, which suggests disregard for others, is actually an attempt to immunize himself against them. He is, in fact, acutely aware of people and uncomfortably sensitive to the problems they intrude.

This behavioral pattern necessitates revelation of what it hides. Consequently, Terry's barroom meeting with Edie and his taxi ride with Charley are two of the film's most important scenes—and two of the most memorable. These scenes were set up so that in them Terry abandons his toughness and reveals a deeply pained sensitivity. In them Terry discovers his behavior failing to gain him emotional and psychological protection, and he embarks on a crucial movement away from both it and its supporting rationale.

In a prior moment of tenderness at the rooftop pigeon coop Terry has expressed his nascent love for Edie by passing her a pigeon egg, through the fence between them, and asking her to have a drink with him. This hope that this date will deepen their intimacy is shaken at the outset when the bartender makes an offhand reference to his boxing career. Immediately Terry is uneasy. As he tells Edie about his past, he is evasive, obviously avoiding those aspects of his defeat that still bother him. When he goes on to explain his philosophy of "doing it" to the other guy "before he does it to you," Terry's manner takes on the hardness typical of him up to this point. In speaking now like a longshoreman he acts like one, and the message is defensiveness. When Edie, with cautious skepticism, questions, "Isn't every-body a part of everyone else?", Terry attempts to change the mood by encouraging her to drink. Realizing the failure of his attempts at intimacy, he breaks down and pleads, "Help me, if you can—for God's sake." Terry's concern, emphatically recorded with close-ups, establishes that he is not really the person he has been presenting. On the contrary, he is profoundly moved by Edie's questioning and does not care only for himself. Their subsequent dance together, which commemorates their new understanding, is interrupted (rather im-probably), by the subpoena presentation.

Terry shows the effects of this progression when he gets into the cab with Charley. Because he has already made up his mind to testify, he is no longer evasive or closed. At the outset he tells Charley he wants to talk to him. He then addresses Charley and responds to him with a directness notably absent in his behavior up to this point. Now Charley turns away, avoiding what he does not want to hear. Terry's refusal to accept his counsel produces a desperation that climaxes in Charley's resort to his gun. Terry responds first with disbelief and then with a pained admission of all he lost by following Charley's advice. Having brought him out of his earlier position of avoidance, Terry's decision to testify now enables him to express his long denied feelings. Being free of the defensiveness in his thinking, he is free of that same quality in his behavior. After this exchange, buttressed by vengeance for Friendly's ensuing execution of Charley, Terry emerges a man who is strong, assured, even recklessly bold. On the witness stand, he blurts out what he has to say with impatient disre-gard for the questions that are supposed to be eliciting it. Next he throws his hook at Friendly's door and loudly proclaims what his fellow longshoremen are afraid to whisper.

Kazan sets up these crucial scenes by situating Terry in a world of enclosures in which the only hope for escape is ascent, but the pressure is constantly downward toward brutal confrontations. Terry's few moments of solace occur on the roof. Joey, on the other hand, is thrown from the roof and Terry is called down into the dark streets to find his slain brother. Those reckless enough to come to Father Barry's meeting find themselves trapped in a cellar that exits into an enclosed courtyard. Dugan is killed in the hold. For his final bout with Friendly, Terry goes first to the docks and then down the gang-plank to the union's headquarters. Terry's initial conversation with Edie is set in a church park, whose openness and elevation communicates the possibilities this relationship opens up, but the distraught confession to which it leads occurs on the dump below and is viewed by Father Barry through the fence that comments on the impediments to this relationship.* This pattern allowed Kazan plentiful opportunities for the dramatic up-down camera angles he discovered in making *Viva Zapata!*, angles that create a powerful feeling of entrapment.

On the Waterfront distorts the facts of the waterfront situation as *Viva Zapata!* does Mexican history, but it had an effect of truth the earlier film lacks because it so convincingly captures the flavor and spirit of its subject matter. Kazan's graphic depiction of the water-front—the squalor of the docks, the raw wintry chill, the impoverish-ment of the workers' living conditions, the flavor of life indelibly marked by the union's brutality—is a culmination of a realism extend-ing back to *People of the Cumberland*: these are conditions that vividly evoke a sense of deprivation and oppression. Still what makes the film so believable is the character of Terry. As portrayed by Brando, Terry not only looks like a longshoreman, he thinks and acts like one. More-over, his thoughts and actions are related in a credible fashion, and the mounting pressures upon Terry to realize the imperative need for change are masterfully presented. That Kazan linked this realization to the act of testifying reflects his pain over his own HUAC decision. Nonetheless, as he shaped this defensiveness into a key component of Terry's characterization, it became the quality most responsible for his film's power and believability.

Kazan's next film, *East of Eden,* was to be almost as impressive as *On the Waterfront.* Here Kazan was dealing with very different conditions. First, the drama was set in the hot Salinas Valley of Cali-fornia during the year immediately preceding America's entry into World War I. In this respect, the environment was, for Kazan, both

---

*The shooting script called for the preceding encounter between Terry and Father Barry to be actual confession. Instead of having Farther Barry tell Terry to make his "confession" to Edie, Kazan decided the scene would be more dramatic and its meaning less intrusive if it were played out before the same iron fence that served as background to their original conversation.

more alien and more remote. On the other hand, the focus was upon a family, in this case separated parents and two sons. Not only was this the kind of dramatic situation toward which Kazan had always gravitated, but the nature of the interaction was more personal, less concerned with the presentation of oneself to skeptical outsiders. These changes necessitated an important alteration in the spirit of the presentation. As another confused young man whose wish to do what is right is misunderstood and condemned by those he respects, Cal was to evidence some remarkable carry-over from Terry, but the effect was to be quite different. If *On the Waterfront* was an aggressive display of pained defensiveness, *East of Eden* was more an outpouring of the injury and anguish Terry had attempted to hide.

At the outset of this film, Cal learns that his mother, whom he has never known, is the operator of a whorehouse. Because her manifest immorality and hard-headed financial success so sharply contrast with his father Adam's moral rectitude and impractical dedication to doing good, Cal feels divided and confused. This tension is intensified by his envy of his brother's natural accommodation to society and easy success in pleasing his father. The authoritarian manner of Adam's Bible reading drives Cal into rebellion and convinces him that he is cursed to be his mother's son. Still, beneath his defiance lies a desperate longing to win his father's love. Thus, when Adam attempts to update his old-fashioned ice business, Cal dedicates himself to lending all the support he can.

Unfortunately all Cal's noble intentions are jeopardized by his innocent entanglement in dangerous alliances. First, while working for his father, he starts a friendship with his brother's girlfriend Abra. Next, when Adam's ill-conceived venture fails and wipes out all of his savings, Cal hits upon a more sure-fire scheme for recouping his father's five thousand dollar loss. But his plan necessitates that he secure a loan from his tainted mother and capitalize on the opportunity opened up by the expansion of agriculture during the First World War.

The excitement generated by Cal's enterprise carries him to a carnival, where he runs into Abra and treats her to a frolicking tour of the attractions. From atop a stalled ferris wheel he sees his brother Aron trying to protect a much persecuted German immigrant. He scrambles down the wheel to help, only to be blamed by his brother for starting the fight that erupts. Pained, troubled, and drunk, Cal pays a midnight visit to Abra in order to enlist her help in mounting a birthday party for his father at which he plans to present the five thousand dollars he has worked so hard to earn. At the party, Aron, who is without a present, spontaneously announces that he is to marry Abra—thereby pleasing his father and embarrassing the surprised Abra, who has been helping Cal. Amidst the turmoil of Aron's announcement, Cal has difficulty making his presentation, and, when Adam unwraps it, he scorns the five thousand dollars as blood money. Abra rushes to console the distraught Cal. Embittered, even unhinged, by this final rejection, Cal takes Aron to confront the mother he has always believed to have been so virtuous. The brutal encounter created by Cal drives Aron to get drunk and enlist in the Army, which in turn causes Adam to have a stroke. In the final scene, after an appeal by Abra, Adam finally forgives and accepts Cal.

East of Eden brought Kazan back into partnership with John Steinbeck, whose novel was nearing completion when the two worked on *Viva Zapta!* After reading the finished product, Kazan ambitiously pursued control of the film adaptation. The book's jump to the top of the bestseller list in 1952 assured a good audience and already word was spreading that *On the Waterfront* would be a powerhouse. Warners was willing to back the project. Still, there were formidable drawbacks. Widescreen processes were proving so popular that Warners insisted the movie be done in color and CinemaScope; to do what he wanted this time, Kazan would have to make greater concessions to the dictates of the marketplace. Also, Steinbeck's sprawling epic virtually defied reduction to a two-hour film. Steinbeck himself refused to get involved. The revisions of *Viva Zapata!* had exhausted his interest in scriptwriting and he was content to let Kazan adapt his novel as he saw fit.

In the face of Steinbeck's withdrawal and the need to condense this sprawling novel, Kazan arranged for Paul Osborne to prepare the script. Besides his skillful dramatizations of *The Yearling, A Bell for Adano,* and *Point of No Return,* Osborne was a longstanding friend who lived nearby in Connecticut, thus enabling Kazan to monitor closely the script's development. At the outset, Kazan and Osborne decided to dispense with most of Steinbeck's novel and concentrate on the final 100 pages, which treated the breech between Adam Trask's two sons, Cal and Aron. Although this Adam-Cain-Abel triangle established a neat, clearly defined struggle, Kazan and Osborne faced the difficult task of deciding how to present it. In the first place, Steinbeck's narrative style runs counter to normal dramatic structure. The reader gets only a refracted impression of the most significant events. Aron's enlistment, for example, is revealed two days after he's gone; his departure is secret and uneventful. Cal's introduction of Aron to his mother is first registered through the hazy perception of the drugged Kate. Kazan's dramatization of Aron thrusting his head through the window of the railroad car, like the scene of Cal pushing his shocked brother on his mortified mother, conveys the sense of brutal confrontation, guilt, and violence that is uniquely Kazan.

Secondly, Steinbeck concevied his story as that of a family. He presents each member's view of the major events. He is critical of and sympathetic to all four, scrupulously resisting special favor for any of them, though the parents, especially Adam, receive more emphasis. In this respect the novel possessed the potential for being a family drama on the order of the two Miller plays Kazan had directed, but Osborne and Kazan decided that their script would concentrate upon Cal. This decision led to further reductions and modifications. Joe's efforts to blackmail Kate were dropped, as was the major character Lee, Adam's oriental servant. Essentially he was replaced by Sam, the sheriff, whom Kazan and Osborne developed into a paternal figure whose treatment of Cal sharply contrasts with Adam's. No mention is made of Aron's desire to become a minister or of his semester at Stanford. The presentation of Mr. Albrecht, the persecuted German immigrant, is an inflation of a character that Steinbeck passed off in a few sentences. In the novel neither of the sons participates in Adam's ill-fated business fiasco; both are equally hurt by its failure. In the novel, Lee, not Sam, tells Cal about his parents' past; nor does Sam go out of his way to extend Cal special compassion. Lee, not Kate, gives Cal the money to launch his bean-growing project. In addition to tightening the story's structure, these changes significantly altered Steinbeck's characterization. Kate is still the cold, tight-fisted business woman, but her haunting sense of desolation and confusion is barely suggested. Adam is transformed into a stern tyrant; the Steinbeck figure of "kindness and conscience" comes out only in Sam's description of what Adam was like during the early years of his marriage. The film's grim Bible-reading scene is not in the book. In fact, when Steinbeck's Adam learns at one point that Cal has been arrested, he demonstrates a kindly understanding that deepens Cal's love for him. Finally, Steinbeck's Aron is distinguished for his anguish and his independence, quite unlike the abrasive, narrow-minded prude of the film.

If these changes accentuated the objectionable traits in the secondary characters, tilted their balance, and reduced their complexity, they thickened the atmosphere of puritanical repression Kazan wanted[16] and increased the pressures weighing down on Cal. By far the most notable departures from Steinbeck's novel were to be in the film's depiction of the developing affair between Cal and Abra. In the book Abra and Cal have nothing to do with each other until the presentation of the money; they start seeing each other only after Aron has been away in the service for three months. The ice house episode, which establishes a basis for their scandalous relationship, does not come from Steinbeck. Neither does the conversation between Cal and Abra at the railroad siding.[17] During a visit to the Danbury Fair following one of their discussions on the script's development, Kazan and Osborne devised the idea of having Cal run into Abra at a carnival.[18] In Steinbeck's book, Aron does not announce his engagement to Abra on the heels of Cal's rejected gift, nor is there any passionate embrace under the weeping willow. Cal *does* make a nighttime visit to Abra, but its character and meaning are entirely different. In other words, the film's most memorable scenes had little or no foundation in the novel.

Kazan was again returning to the anguish of a figure who is misunderstood and misjudged, the discrediting exposure of cherished beliefs, and the necessary support of a proper but sympathetic woman. In their portrayal of Cal, especially in his affair with Abra, Kazan and Osborne seemed to be drawing as much from *Tea and Sympathy* and *On the Waterfront* as they did from Steinbeck's novel. Cal, like Tom Lee and Terry, ascribes to the standards of the society around him. Similarly, his wish for acceptance is crossed by a waywardness that threatens to reveal hypocrisies. Anguished and defensive, confused and angry, Cal blurts out to his father, "I gotta know who I am." Above all, he, like Tom and Terry, is well-intentioned, but condemned, a figure whose wish to do what is right and good is interpreted by those around him as reprehensible. And once again a woman who embodies many of the ideals of this society steps forth and, in her own act of defiance, reassures him of the legitimacy of the bent that provokes his anguish.

However, Cal's distress manifests itself in a nervous eccentricity that sets him apart from his predecessors. Kazan opens the film with a wordless sequence of shots in which Cal follows Kate home, thus defining his behavior as furtive and compulsive, fraught with hostility and incipient violence. Cal lingers about Kate's house, recklessly calling attention to himself. When he is recognized and challenged, he is unable to account for his behavior. Helpless, he tells the bouncer to inform Kate that he hates her. Because Cal does not understand his feelings, he can neither explain nor control them, and because he cannot reconcile his kinship with Kate with the type of person he is supposed to be, he is twisted, confused, and out of step. Cal is equally drawn to and estranged from his brother and father; he can neither face them nor ignore them. In the ensuing scene, he tells Aron and Abra he will not accompany them to meet Adam, but he follows them in a manner that is both defensive and reminiscent of his pursuit of his mother. Then, at the ice house, he stands in the distance behind a post watching his father, but refusing to join him. He later spies on Aron and Abra from behind the slabs of ice that suggest Cal's alienation and divided emotions just as the iron fence did Terry's in *On the Waterfront*. Kate, Adam, Aron, and Abra provoke, attract, and repel Cal, and there is no satisfactory accommodation for him with any of them. Consequently, the same rage and frustration that impelled him to throw a stone at Kate's house erupts as he savagely hurls ice blocks down the chute.

Kazan cast Jimmy Dean to play Cal. He was the first to recognize the pained intensity that was to rocket Dean to stardom, though Kazan was to suffer enormous frustration in pushing Dean to give him the effects he wanted. "Directing Dean was like directing the faithful Lassie," he has commented. "I either scolded him or I terrified him or I made a fuss over him or I patted him on the shoulder or I kicked him in the butt. He was so driven by instinct and so stupid in so many ways."[19] Trying though they were, such tactics paid off handsomely. Kazan plumbed Dean's ability to transform himself, in chameleon fashion, from a brooding malcontent to a puckish imp, from a mortally wounded victim to a belligerent rebel. By mixing a predominance of long shots with sparing close-ups, coupling Dean's awkward body movements with the pained expressions that would unexpectedly play across his face, Kazan gave audiences another spellbinding performance of vulnerability and defensiveness.

Kazan's presentation of Dean as Cal was uniquely cinematic. The foreground objects Kazan used to reduce the cumbersome dimension of CinemaScope made the camera a prowler. Like Cal, it intrudes upon characters at embarrassing moments, when they are unprepared and unprotected, but its main quarry in this respect is Cal himself. Kazan's askew framing of selected moments was intentionally cued to Dean's contorted body movements to reflect his disturbed emotional-psychological condition. In scenes of acute distress to Cal, which are usually situated within claustrophobic interiors—the Bible reading, his outburst at the ice house, his father's rejection—the camera was tilted so that the resulting image is distorted, not unlike Cal's view of himself and Abra in the funhouse mirrors. By concentrating his camera upon Dean and how he "looked," Kazan crafted a unique picture of intensity and confusion, sexuality and vulnerability. In a revealing comment on the quality he sought from Dean's performance, Kazan observed: "Dean was a cripple, anyway, inside."[20]

Unable to accept his alienation or to ignore the suppressed truth about Kate, Cal finds his self-destructive anguish eased by an exceptional woman who appreciates his needs and even shares them. Like Laura and Edie, she is initially linked with the forces aligned against the protagonist. Abra intuitively fears Cal and is one of the first to condemn his bizarre behavior. She belongs to Aron, readily embracing all his respectability and goodness. Because Aron has won her love with the same ease that he has gained his father's, Abra aggravates Cal's alienation and strengthens his identification with his mother. "She (Kate) ain't no good," Cal concludes. "I ain't no good."

Cal has not only misjudged himself, but Abra as well. The very qualities that Abra finds "scary" in Cal also make him attractive. In her first conversation with Cal at the railroad siding, Abra teases Cal about the loose women with whom he associates. Her questioning of their allure, mixed with coy laughter, reveals her curiosity to be crossed with a nervous attraction to Cal. Teasingly she takes a flower, rakes his face with it, and invites his attention. Later, when the ferris wheel stops, she openly acknowledges her waywardness in a nervous manner that complements Cal's. "I'm not—good enough for Aron," she confesses in words that echo Cal's earlier description of himself. "I know that love is good the way Aron says, but it's more than that. It's got to be. . . . Sometimes I think I'm really bad." Abra's remarks smack of a proposition. She is no longer teasing or playing games. But Cal realizes that her difficult confession is more than a sexual invitation; she is offering the compassion and understanding everyone else has withheld. What appears to be an attraction of opposites turns out to be a shared feeling that enables them to reach first a rapport and finally a compelling love. Abra pulls away from Cal's passionate kiss, but later returns to the more scandalous one under the willow tree in a desperate effort to allay his undeserved rejection by his father. Her initial explanation, at the railroad siding, of how she forgave her father for "not understanding" announces the lesson she subsequently teaches Cal.

In casting Julie Harris as Abra, Kazan fashioned yet another variation upon the plain beauty and wayward propriety that so distinguished his two previous heroines. Like Edie and Laura, Abra is irresistibly drawn to the drama's wounded protagonist, and she gives him direction with a show of "kindness and conscience" so noticeably lacking in his family. Once again a virtuous exterior masks powerful feelings. But Abra's emotion is even more insistently linked to her sexuality. Harris was strikingly different in her combination of wholesomeness and unabashed desire. Cal's meeting with Abra at the railroad siding is reminiscent of Terry's first walk through the park with Edie. Both scenes launch the love affairs that follow; Abra's daisy is as crucial as Edie's glove to dramatizing this key exchange. Likewise, Cal's visit to Abra's bedroom recalls Terry's barroom discussion with Edie—both men break down in these scenes and show a real need for someone else. Yet the sexuality that spans these lovers' temperamental differences is unique. For Abra and Cal, a titillating

attraction verging upon scandal measures their deep feeling for one
another and compensates for the failure of their words.

East of Eden was an impressive film whose greatest strength
lay in Kazan's arresting depiction of Cal's tortured behavior and his
gravitation toward Abra. Once again Kazan was to infuse a proven
formula with a fresh intensity that absorbed a good deal of his own
emotional turbulence. His masterful handling of the issues of conformity and the anguish of rejection drew heavily from the love affair
between Terry and Edie. If *East of Eden* fell short of his previous
achievement, its weakness lay in its failure to create as meaningful a
context for this affair. Kazan's pre–World War I Salinas was not the
bleak environment of hypocrisy and repression of his waterfront. The
colorful backdrops of people in the streets, the war parade, the persecution of Mr. Albrecht, and the tawdry circus contributed very little to
the shifting relationships of the major characters. The polarization of
the stern, demanding Adam with the kindly, sympathetic Sam did not
have the balance of Johnny Friendly and Father Barry. Cal's strained
relationship with Aron lacked the complexity of Terry's with Charley.
Ted McCord's photography was impressive and contributed powerful
effects, but it fell short of Boris Kaufman's. Kazan himself was sufficiently dissatisfied with the results of his initial contact with Cinema-
Scope and color that he returned to black and white for his next
two films.

While Kazan was finishing *East of Eden*, Tennessee Williams
completed a major rewrite of his aborted first play, *Battle of Angels*,
and was hoping that Kazan would again be his director. But, just as
with *The Rose Tattoo*, Kazan had distinct reservations. "The plain
fact," he opened in his letter of response, "is that for the first time in
my life I'm quite exhausted. Out of gas. (petrol) No gissum left. Also
rather discouraged." Indicating that the source of his depression went
somewhat deeper than he was prepared to discuss, he explained that
much of it had to do with the picture he had just completed. He wrote:
"I found myself repeating myself in *East of Eden* which I suppose a
person always does when he does too much too near together. Repeating effects." Indeed Kazan had allowed himself little rest over the
past couple of years. Still he wasn't closing the door. Frankly stating
that his belief that the play "needed work," more than either of them

202

was prepared to invest, he reiterated his words to Audrey Wood that he would "rather wait for one of the new plays, if Tenn wants me to do one of them. . . . I'm jealous of everything [he] write[s]."[21] By this point Williams had sufficiently steeled himself to Kazan's criticisms that he was not devastated as he had been with *The Rose Tattoo*. He also had a new play for a counterproposal.

Kazan immediately recognized that *Cat on a Hot Tin Roof* possessed a combination of humor and conflict that had been lacking in Williams's work since *Streetcar*. Williams had returned to his native south and to an internecine family feud. It was almost as though Williams had reconstructed a modern version of Blanche's Belle Rêve in order to show that prosperity did not eliminate friction, misunderstanding, and misery. Big Daddy is a baronial patriarch who rules "twenty-eight thousand acres of th' richest land this side of the Valley Nile." His pride in his plantation is sustained by his substantial family; it is at once the seat of his kingdom and the assurance of its future. Unfortunately, it is also riddled with weakness and on the brink of a civil war. Like Cal and Aron in *East of Eden*, his two sons are natural born rivals. Gooper is a methodical, weak-willed lawyer, while Brick is a faded football star who possesses the potential to command Big Daddy's respect but who is presently bent on destroying himself with drink. Both have determined wives whose efforts to compensate for their husbands' weaknesses compound these strains. Gooper's wife Mae is as fertile as she is greedy, insistently advancing her five children as a claim upon Big Daddy's favor. Maggie, on the other hand, is battling with equal vigor to stay in his good graces, but she faces an uphill fight. She lacks a child that would compensate for her husband's dereliction, give her respectability, and enable her to fulfill her expected role. Her efforts to hold on to her husband and mend his shattered ego are undermined by the fact that he holds her responsible for the death of his closest friend. Clinging to a belief that Maggie misinterpreted, violated, and destroyed his innocent, intimate friendship with his fellow ball player Skipper, Brick has turned Maggie into a justification for his bitter disillusionment and hostility. As a consequence, Maggie is the cat on a hot tin roof, anxious, aggressive, indomitable.

Maggie's strong will and outspoken independence immediately

liken her to Big Daddy. Both command respect and both face the prospect of imminent defeat. Big Daddy is dying of cancer, but does not know it. The prospective inheritance of Big Daddy's plantation sets off frenetic jockeying for his favor and sparks curiosity as to when he will discover his plight and what its effect will be. Likewise, the audience wonders if Maggie can achieve her objective or if she too is doomed. Can she break down Brick's alcoholically induced isolation or will he eliminate himself and carry her with him?

Williams's dramatization of these possibilities sufficiently excited Kazan to dispell his weariness. But his expressed willingness to mount a Broadway production of *Cat* with financing from the Playwrights' Company, which had backed *Tea and Sympathy,* came with a request for certain revisions in the final act. Williams later explained that Kazan had three very specific reservations:

> one, he felt that Big Daddy was too vivid and important a character to disappear from the play except as an offstage cry after the second act curtain; two, he felt that the character of Brick should undergo some apparent mutation as a result of the virtual vivisection that he undergoes in his interview with his father in Act Two. Three, he felt that the character of Margaret, while he understood that I sympathized with her and liked her myself, should be, if possible, more clearly sympathetic to an audience.

In his post production account of his response to these criticisms, Williams explained: "It was only the third of these suggestions that I embraced wholeheartedly from the outset, because it so happened that Maggie the Cat had become steadily more charming to me as I reworked her characterization." On the other hand, he opposed the reappearance of Big Daddy and the redemption of Brick.[22]

At issue here was an essential conflict in the two men's philosophical outlooks: Kazan believed in character change and improvement while Williams was more pessimistic.[23] Kazan's three previous efforts bolstered his position. In each case, the protagonist's trying ordeal had brought strength and direction, enabling him to surmount the crippling consequences of his struggle. Such, for Kazan, were the

204

makings of success. With these commercially successful, highly acclaimed explorations of an anguish similar to his own, Kazan had triumphed over the criticism, rejection, and failure that followed on the heels of his HUAC testimony. And he was convinced that Williams's play could succeed in the same way.

If the outcome of this debate gave *Cat on a Hot Tin Roof* the imprint of Kazan's styling, it came as a result of an exchange that was both more considered and farther reaching than Williams has suggested. The force of Kazan's influence, which produced such major revisions in the third act, is evident in a small, but significant modification of the second act that Williams made during the course of rehearsals. The long-searching discussion between Brick and Big Daddy was the heart of the play. The meaning of the third act rested upon it. In the preparation of the rehearsal script, Kazan and Williams decided that Brick's revelation of Big Daddy's fatal illness needed better anticipation and greater impact. Initially, they experimented with backgrounds of birthday fireworks and festive songs that climax with this disclosure. These theatrics were dropped in part because they were too much like the third act storm and in part because here it was too obviously compensating for weaknesses in the revelation itself. What was lacking, Kazan and Williams realized, was psychological depth; Brick's announcement was deficient in its motivation. As originally written, the frustrating, disconnected exchange between father and son had converged upon Brick's "glass box" speech, in which he confesses how he drinks to gain the isolation he had when he used to broadcast ball games. Brick then followed this explanation with the announcement that Big Daddy was actually dying, leaving the audience confused as to why Brick has come out with this cruel revelation.[24]

Williams's revision of this exchange built hesitantly but relentlessly to searing charges that draw blood from each. Their heart-to-heart talk is more emphatically a deadly duel that neither wants to fight. Williams reduced Brick's original "glass box" speech and separated it from his announcement. In its new position, this explanation of his behavior calls attention to the evasion at the heart of Brick's drinking and his reliance upon it to sustain his belief that he and Skipper have been innocent victims of Maggie's cruel mistreatment.

Frustrated by the failure of his compassion to bring about Brick's rehabilitation, Big Daddy now resorts to bullying Brick into a reexamination of his assumptions. No longer the befuddled, sympathetic parent of the original version, Big Daddy becomes an angry inquisitor badgering his son to stand on his feet and take responsibility for himself and what has happened. This modification demanded that Burl Ives enlarge his portrayal of the compassionate Sheriff Sam in *East of Eden* so that it comprehended the stern, demanding Adam. This Big Daddy is offended by the weakness of his beloved son. After Brick tells how Maggie strove to break up his friendship with Skipper, Big Daddy charges.

BIG DADDY:	Are *you* satisfied?
BRICK:	With what?
BIG DADDY:	That half-ass story!
BRICK:	What's half-ass about it?
BIG DADDY:	Something's left out of that story. What did you leave out?
BRICK:	Yes!—I left out a long-distance call which I had from Skipper, in which he made a drunken confession to me and on which I hung up!—last time we spoke to each other in our lives. . . .
BIG DADDY:	You hung up?
BRICK:	Hung up. Jesus! Well—
BIG DADDY:	Anyhow now!—we have tracked down the lie with which you're disgusted and which you are drinking to kill your disgust with, Brick. You been passing the buck. This disgust with mendacity is disgust with yourself. *You!*—dug the grave of your friend and kicked him in it!—before you'd face truth with him![25]

Cat on a Hot Tin Roof: Big Daddy (Burl Ives) assails Brick (Ben Gazzara) for his assumed innocence. (Photo by Fred Fehl; reproduced by permission of Hoblitzelle Theatre Arts Library, Humanities Research Center, The University of Texas at Austin.)

With this interpretation, Big Daddy challenges the presumed innocence at the heart of Brick's wounded defensiveness. In effect, Big Daddy charges Brick with a deficient self-understanding and a vain trust that he has been wronged.

Such a wrinkle in the psychological set of Kazan's recent protagonists was a major innovation—up to this point, his suffering, misunderstood heroes were essentially in the right. Ensuing reviews of the play were frequently to complain that in this bruising exchange Williams was pulling his punches because he never let the audience know if Brick was in fact a homosexual. To have given a clear answer to this question would have drained this exchange of its central meaning and warped Brick's characterization. Brick feels confident he has done nothing wrong because he never went to bed with Skipper and probably had no desire to. Maggie, however, has charged that Brick's deep affection for Skipper prevented him from loving her. For Brick to have peremptorily rejected Skipper, because Skipper's feelings may not have been as pure as Brick presumed, constituted a deep violation of trust, an act of betrayal he cannot bring himself to admit. He is guilty of a major mistake.

This charge thrusts Brick into the acutely uncomfortable position of having to justify both his wrongdoing and ensuing misbehavior. Brick counters Big Daddy's assault with the charge that he also is harboring a lie. He proclaims that there may be no more birthday parties for Big Daddy, thereby letting out the suppressed truth about Big Daddy's cancer. Big Daddy is forced to realize that not only is he dying, but he too has been hiding from the facts. Thus the evasions by *both* are simultaneously exposed. This conversation—at once scrambled, searching, and explosive—provided Kazan with the type of confrontation that was his specialty and set up the third act to explore, what, if anything, could be done to mend this rupture.

The shift of Big Daddy's line "CHRIST—DAMN—LYING—SONS—OF—LYING BITCHES" from the end of Act II to the beginning of Act III for the Broadway production seems a curious change. Its conclusion of the middle act created a climax that allowed the next act to begin with a calm and build to the final resolution. Placed at the beginning of the new act, it produces an awkward carryover. This, of course, was exactly the effect Kazan wanted. He and Williams both realized that the issue of "mendacity" was far from over. With her declaration of pregnancy, Maggie assumes responsibility for determining whether the Pollitt family is trapped in an inescapable network of lies or whether she, Brick, and Big Daddy can achieve a redeeming "truth." The fate of Big Daddy's kingdom rests on her shoulders. Big Daddy's reappearance, the first of the three changes Kazan called for, yields the first sign that the play is to end on a positive note. His being on stage enables him to hear Maggie's announcement and to register a profound consolation. However, Big Daddy's contentment is another lie unless she can fulfill her announcement. "Truth is something desperate," Brick says, and whether "she's [Maggie's] got it," as he maintains, depends on her making good on her announcement.

Maggie's bedding of Brick has a familiar ring. Through this act, the drama implies, Maggie will prove herself a warm, giving woman just as Laura does in *Tea and Sympathy*. Likewise Brick will be able to overcome many of the same nagging doubts that torment Tom Lee. However different the temperaments of the characters may be, their problems are to be overcome by a similar type of shared understanding. In response to the revisions Kazan suggested, Williams wrote, "Do you think it contains an echo of 'Tea and Sympathy'? The other, harder ending of it didn't. Here is another case of a woman giving a man back his manhood, while in the original conception, it was about a vital, strong woman dominating a weak man and achieving her will."[26] As Williams and Kazan realized, Maggie's conduct in this scene was crucial, for her actions are a final measure of her integrity. Hanging in the balance is not just her marriage to Brick, her pride, and the scourge of mendacity, but also the whole question of her motives—how much is she dedicated to helping Brick and how much to protecting her own interest? She faces the formidable obstacle of appearing both credible and deserving of the audience's respect. One hesitates to freight any two lines with too much significance, but Williams's original draft contained two that profoundly affected the direction in which Kazan and Williams decided to move. Just after everyone has left and Maggie is alone with Brick she says, "Thank you for—keeping still." After his non-commital response, she adds, "It was gallant of you to save my face!"[27] Pushed by Kazan to make Maggie "more clearly sympathetic to an audience" and to have her efforts produce some positive changes in Brick, Williams drafted four other versions of this last scene for out-of-town performances prior to the Broadway opening. All of these attempted to expand upon these opening comments.

MAGGIE:	Thank you for keepin' still, Brick.
BRICK:	—My keepin' still was th' perfect tribute, Maggie.
MAGGIE:	(Drawing a deep, momentarily exhausted breath) It was gallant of you to save my face.
BRICK:	I was—impressed.
MAGGIE:	—Impressed by what?
BRICK:	You fell on your knees and begged for a piece of his kingdom, you made a strong bid for it, without pretendin' you didn't know he was having to give it up!
MAGGIE:	I didn't, I—!
BRICK:	Yes, you did, Maggie.
MAGGIE:	I—*did*?
BRICK:	—You sure did . . .
MAGGIE:	Was it disgusting? Were you disgusted with me?
BRICK:	No, th' contrary.
MAGGIE:	—What?
BRICK:	—Respectful, Maggie.
MAGGIE:	Respectful of what?
BRICK:	Your honesty!
MAGGIE:	Oh, but I lied, I—
BRICK:	Yeah, but you had—*Ev'ry Intention!*—of makin' the lie come true. (Pause)
MAGGIE:	How?! (Pause) I tried and I FAILED!—to rape you.
BRICK:	You're not the type that stops tryin', are you Maggie?[28]

Kazan was hoping to use this exchange to wind down the dramatic tempo and resolve the problem that surfaced at the end of Act II. These fragments of dialogue were intended to provide Maggie and Brick a breathing space, a pause, in which to reexamine their relationship and grope toward a reconciliation. But, Kazan and Williams realized that the little these words said was far too much. Brick's denial that Maggie has demeaned herself was an improbable departure from his characterization up to this point. Even more troubling, though, was the very self-abasement of Maggie's comments. In performance, Kazan and Williams saw that this disparagement betrayed the strong-willed determination that distinguished Maggie. Consequently they scratched Williams's original apology and all the expansion upon it. The Broadway ending condensed the conversation between Brick and Maggie to a few halting remarks that left much of the meaning to the stage actions and atmosphere to convey. If the suggestive silences, tentative gestures, and final bedding increased rather than diminished the resemblance between *Cat*'s ending and that of *Tea and Sympathy* they also allowed Maggie to appear *both* strong and successful, as Kazan and Williams wanted.

Brick's reluctance to talk, which Kazan and Williams preserved in their compromise conclusion, was familiar enough, but it compelled Kazan to develop unusual staging for other sections of the play, using a large number of direct addresses to the audience. In his persistent effort to avoid conversation and abstract himself from his immediate situation, Brick constantly frustrates the give-and-take of conventional dialogue. Characters wind up talking at him rather than with him. Since most of the first act has him on stage alone with Maggie and more than half of the second alone with Big Daddy, the staging of their interaction posed a real problem. For his solution Kazan turned to the operative rationale of the confrontation. He saw that Big Daddy's and Maggie's assaults upon Brick carried a large measure of self-defense. By having Maggie and Big Daddy direct their remarks as much to the viewers as to Brick, Kazan gave the drama the flavor of a courtroom trial. The audience, like a jury, had to judge both the case and those making the charges. Kazan had Jo Mielziner design the stage so that it slanted noticeably toward the audience, forming what one reviewer called "a pedestal for the actors," and even had Big Daddy move to the forward edge to deliver his lines.[29] The positioning of a large double bed in the center of the stage insisted upon its ever increasing relevance to the outcome.

Kazan's selection of Barbara Bel Geddes for the lead was consistent with his wish that Maggie be fiery, clawing, captivating—

The ending of *On the Waterfront*: The vindication of a fierce determination to continue working. (The Museum of Modern Art/Film Stills Archive, New York.)

and sympathetic. Kazan was particularly anxious that Maggie's abuse of Brick express outrage and personal offense, but be understood to come from a deep concern for his welfare. Bel Geddes, of course, had attained stardom overnight under Kazan's direction, and he was once prompted to observe, "But if Barbara Bel Geddes had not become a star in *Deep Are the Roots,* she might really have grown. But this very talented girl's going nuts now because she's asked to do the same thing over and over: the blinky-eyed ingenue."[30] While Kazan was perceptive enough to see that Bel Geddes had the talent to convey Maggie's tempestuous independence, he selected her for the part because he knew the fervent, well-intentioned virtue she so strongly projected would affirm Maggie's main objective to be helping Brick and proving herself a devoted wife. In fact, Kazan so strongly associated these qualities with Bel Geddes that he had approached her to play Laura in *Tea and Sympathy.*[31] Bel Geddes's display of independence and commitment, her defiance and dedication, her sexuality devoid of promiscuity, resulted in a memorable Maggie who nonetheless possessed the familiar earmarks of a Kazan heroine. Ben Gazzara was then given the job of suggesting the seething emotions behind Brick's affected cool. His refusal to articulate his confused feelings established his kinship to Kazan's two previous male leads; his crutch and hobbling gait graphically insisted upon the crippled state of mind they all possessed. The finished product won both the Pultizer Prize and the New York Drama Critics' Circle award for best drama of the year and went on to play 694 performances, making it and *Tea and Sympathy* the two longest running productions ever fielded by the Playwrights' Company.

The final shooting script for *On the Waterfront* called for Terry to get beaten to death for his attack upon Johnny Friendly.[32] The actual ending—the one in which Father Barry and Edie help the beaten Terry to his feet so he could lead his fellow longshoremen back to work— was a last minute change Kazan himself developed. As much as the longshoremen's fearful, hesitant observation of Terry was a variation upon similar scenes of alienation in *Boomerang, Gentleman's Agreement, Pinky,* and *Panic in the Streets,* Terry's bloody staggering walk was an insistent parade of anguish that commented on the state of mind of the man who staged it. It was almost as though, deeply injured by the consequences of his decision to testify, Kazan was calling attention to both his wounds and his own refusal to be defeated. Having channeled so much of his own defensiveness into his brilliant depiction of Terry, Kazan was unwilling to allow his hero to be sacrificed as his Zapata had been. The longshoremen's emphasized hesitation to come to Terry's defense dramatized the lack of support for Kazan's own testimony.* By the same token, Terry's agonized determination to return to work communicated the spirit in which this film and its three complementary productions had been mounted.[33] All were to be brilliantly dramatized portraits of pain, alienation, and straining for approval. The misunderstood Tom Lee driven to the brink of suicide, the defensive Terry who secretly longs to proclaim the injustice done him, the rejected Cal clambering to Abra's rooftop bedroom to beg for help, and the crippled Brick who drinks to keep his innocence intact comprehended feelings Kazan understood. If each of these four undertakings were deeply personal statements, it was the innovative skill with which Kazan shaped and varied them that made them into the uniquely compelling dramas that they were. Taken together, these four productions constituted the high-water mark of Kazan's career, but, they left him, like Terry at the end of *On the Waterfront,* with the looming unanswered question of where to go from his remarkable achievement.

*This ending evidences an attempt to avoid the Communist implications that haunted *Zapata* and the early scripts of *On the Waterfront.* There was no way the longshoremen's begrudging acceptance of Terry as their leader could be interpreted as a Communist act of insurrection. Rather than, a celebration of worker solidarity such as the ending of *Waiting for Lefty,* this conclusion displays a contempt for the common people. This conclusion was to be harshly condemned by the British critic Lindsay Anderson as a "Fascistic" indictment of liberalism. See Lindsay Anderson, "The Last Sequence of 'On the Waterfront,'" *Sight and Sound* 24 (Jan.–March, 1955): 127–30. More accurately, it reflects Kazan's bitter disillusionment over the possibility of a spontaneous, democratic outpouring of support such as was shown in the ending to *Viva Zapata!* and hoped for in the conclusion of his address at Harvard.

EIGHT

Quest for Self-Expression

Kazan's achievements had cost him dearly. His forty-six-year-old face was lined and worn. The man who had long been known as the bright, energetic young director was aging fast. As he admitted to Williams just before he took on *Cat on a Hot Tin Roof,* he felt exhausted and depressed. He needed rest. He also needed a new objective. Into his last four efforts, Kazan had channeled a large measure of the pain and defensiveness caused by his preceding setbacks. This transference not only served to ease the pressure of his distress, but also made him exceptionally effective in the presentation of his psychological dramas. Having won an outpouring of audience support for his tortured protagonists and reclaimed his professional prominence, he now had to move on and find different material that would be similarly engaging. The inevitable difficulty of such a readjustment was to be even more complicated for Kazan, given the yet unrealized impact of these successes upon his relationship to his audience.

Ever since World War II, Kazan had been attracting the public to ingeniously varied conflicts between an older generation and the one upcoming—between fathers and sons. What had made these dramas so meaningful—especially for Kazan—was their critical commentary upon contemporary American social conditions. He had made Blanche DuBois and Willy Loman memorable to postwar audiences, which keenly felt that the idealistic war effort had robbed them of the best years of their lives. Yet, in granting Blanche and Willy the compassion they deserved, Kazan had also presented them as members of an older generation who were damaged and deranged by their failure to accommodate their old-fashioned values to change. He sympathized with the critical antagonisms of the younger characters Stanley and Biff and understood their frustrated yearning for respect. For this reason when Kazan later sought vehicles for his own distress, he chose young men. As they took over the leads in his dramas and older figures were relegated to supporting roles, these young men harbored the same longing for acceptance, but with dwindling hope.

Kazan's whole career was premised upon the role of this outsider and his wish for accommodation. With his last four productions, this wish had settled into a posture of alienation that generated enormous emotional power—and frustration. Kazan's audience never fully understood a rebel who was so unable to communicate the source of his distress. Kazan had used these characters to reflect upon very personal concerns, but, in cuing their rebellion to the dominant culture's heightened sensitivity to the problems of its restless youth, Kazan's personal concerns went unnoticed. Both he and his rebel were truly misunderstood.

The misunderstanding grew with time. After the demise of McCarthyism, social criticism became less dangerous, and, for the mass audience, less interesting as well. Despite his continued skill and resourcefulness, Kazan's undertakings after *Waterfront* also evidence waning commitment. Increasingly he gravitated to dramas set in the past that either occasion nostalgia or license frenzy. Critics began to fault his styling and to attack him as an embodiment of the establishment. Though stung by these charges, Kazan did little to dispute them.

Now, again in a position to do as he pleased—after years of pushing for such power—Kazan grew uncertain and directionless. Even more troubling, he derived little of his former satisfaction from directing. Something had gone wrong, but what? For an answer, Kazan turned to his past, and, in familiar fashion, into himself. Out of this introspection came new purpose, uncertain at first yet finally as strong as any before: he would confront that identity which had always been latent in his work. He would finally do his own writing and his writing would explore who he was.

One of Kazan's first moves following his spectacular comeback was the establishment of his own filmmaking company—Newtown

216

Productions. This was conceived to give him the artistic independence which he had long been seeking. In turning to Tennessee Williams and Budd Schulberg for filmscripts, Kazan was consciously teaming up with the writers responsible for his recent successes. The resounding commercial failure to come from these collaborations were to be painful lessons in the dangers of pushing for greater responsibility while relying on someone else's material.

Newtown's first offering was *Baby Doll* (1956)—a black comedy of perversity and depravity that became embroiled in controversy for its "carnal suggestiveness."[1] *Baby Doll* was the fruit of Williams's agreement to prepare an original filmscript for Kazan. In line with the terms of their December 1951 decision regarding *Camino Real* and after various experiments and discussions,[2] Kazan and Williams decided to make *21 Wagons of Cotton* the basis for their filmscript and then to bolster it with an insertion of *The Unsatisfactory Supper* just prior to the conclusion. This "anthology movie," as Kazan conceived of it,[3] required extensive reworking and smoothing in order to sustain interest and character consistency. But, the thorniest problem, it turned out, lay in agreeing upon the spirit of the presentation.

The heart of the drama is the struggle between Archie Lee and Vacarro over Baby Doll, whose fully developed body and childish mind inflames both men's twisted desires. As with *Cat on a Hot Tin Roof,* Williams and Kazan were to disagree over how this clash should be resolved. In deference to Warner's request that there be some retribution for Vacarro's brutal persecution of Archie Lee's wife, Williams prepared an ending in which Archie Lee gets Vacarro to join a frog-hunting gig and then kills him with a spear. When Kazan requested yet another ending, Williams wrote back, "The ending of the script, as it now stands, is by far the most distinguished and best part of it. I say that to you sincerely. I can make variations on that ending, but I can't turn these people or this comedy into 'heavies' and 'tragedy' without kissing my sense of truthful theatre goodbye."[4] Extensive negotiations were unable to resolve this disagreement and Kazan had to draft his own ending.

Kazan's attraction to Williams's black humor had always been attended by certain reservations. Quite rightly he was leery of handling a "comedy" in which Vaccaro taunted Baby Doll to the point of frenzy, ravished her, and wound up getting sadistically killed. However funny the unfolding circumstances might be, the events contained too many serious implications. Consequently, as Williams suspected, Kazan's ending was to take on "tragic" overtones, and they were to reverberate through all the events leading up to it.

Kazan approached Williams's script as a series of mood sequences. *Baby Doll* holds its viewer by the sheer virtuosity of cutting, camera movement, and almost surrealistic behavior. The film deflects attention away from motive and meaning, but Kazan strove to block out the action so that it had a well-structured progression. Kazan systematically reduced the comic tone of the opening so that it shaded toward his more accustomed atmosphere of anxiety and looming confrontation. By the point at which Archie Lee speeds off into the night to burn Vacarro's gin, the movie's tone is as dark as this shot.

The following scenes dwell ominously on the hostility of the townspeople toward Vacarro and the mayhem of the fire in order to set up his vengeful resolution. In the long ensuing scene with Baby Doll, Vacarro is as relentlessly purposeful as the courtroom lawyers of Kazan's earlier films. Before sentence can be passed, Vacarro must prove the crime. In the process of confirming Archie Lee's guilt, Vacarro also establishes the irresponsible naïveté and taunting sexuality of Baby Doll that drove Archie Lee to commit his crime. The audience laughs at Baby Doll's behavior but uneasily senses the malevolent intent being masked by Vacarro's gentlemanly manner. His excitement of Baby Doll with his whip and his gleeful romp on the hobby horse to the background music of "Shame on You" were planned and paced by Kazan so they led to the attic scene in which Baby Doll is brutally stripped of her foolish innocence.

Kazan's masterful orchestration of this evolution from daydream to nightmare left him in an awkward position. Logically, Vacarro should have pocketed Baby Doll's signed confession of Archie Lee's crime and then blundered onto her husband's spear. Different though their reasons were, neither Kazan nor Williams were willing to accept the menacing blackness of this progression. Williams stomped off and Kazan engineered a thoroughly unconvincing clean-up campaign. In an abrupt reversal following the attic scene, Vacarro turns gallant and generous. Baby Doll's sexual invitation at this point is as improbable as the implication that he did not accept it. Equally unbelievable is Vacarro's offer of accommodation for the unwanted Aunt Rose. Kazan's attempts to keep the mood ominous and eerie were forced and the film limped to its contrived conclusion. Kazan's ending wrings a calm from the preceding storm, but he does this with a hollow flourish of styling that dodges all the major issues.

Kazan's next Newtown film was to be another overzealous miscarriage of his usual styling. With *A Face in the Crowd* (1957), which he developed for Kazan from a short story written in 1955, Schulberg launched an attack upon the television industry reminiscent of his *What Makes Sammy Run*'s indictment of the movies. Likewise, his Lonesome Rhodes was modeled upon Arthur Godfrey as Sammy had been on Jerry Wald. Though Rhodes is a hillbilly, he possesses Sammy's ruthless drive to get to the top and the same cynical understanding of how entertainment operates. "'A Face in the Crowd' is a sharp warning," Kazan was to write in a newspaper article prepared for the film's release. "There is power in television. It can be perverted."[5] On the surface Kazan and Schulberg were responding to the tremendous expansion of television that continued to lure viewers away from the movies, but their reflection upon the kind of person who succeeds best in TV unleashed such venom that they were to lose control over their character and their presentation. Like their protagonist, they insulted the audience they presumed to be enlightening.

For Kazan and Schulberg, Rhodes was essentially a vehicle for exposing the duplicity of the television industry and its conspiratorial abuse of power. With his broad smile and folksy manner, Rhodes cultivates the image of the common man speaking to the common man and for the common man. While the ruthless selfishness of Rhodes's off-screen conduct was supposed to emphasize the falsehood of this guise, the exaggerated manner in which it is presented indicts the public that so gullibly accepts it. Moreover, it was not enough that Rhodes be a consummate phoney; he was also endowed with a twisted psyche that compels him to abuse his girlfriend, drown himself in drink, and damn the people who adulate him. As presented, this neurosis is hard to understand and even harder to take. Does this behavior derive from a peculiar knot in Rhodes's soul? Or is it the result of an inability to live with success? Is the final outburst that brings Rhodes's downfall a product of guilt? Or the ever greater strains of his duplicitous life? Or is it an overwhelming disgust at the public's ready acceptance of everything he says and does? Whatever the case, the character strains the bounds of credibility and Kazan's overblown styling compounds the problem. As one reviewer observed, "Rage is Kazan's undoing. He hacks and haws with such ill-considered fury that the patient soon becomes a mere victim and the satire falls to pieces."[6]

The poor box-office returns on *Baby Doll* and *A Face in the Crowd* doomed Newtown and meant that Kazan would have to enlist studio support for future films. Meanwhile he could return to Broadway. However, the stature that made him welcome discouraged venturesomeness. In a 1957 article on the current Broadway scene for the *Saturday Review*, Arnold Maremont revealed that the combination of narrowing tastes and escalating costs had created a situation whereby, outside of a narrow circle of heavyweights, a prospective backer faced a strong likelihood that he would lose all his investment.[7] Set against this backdrop, Kazan's next Broadway undertakings had the character of capitalizing on his record of success. Although he now chose his assignments with particular caution for their commercial prospects, each still had its risks. Yet Kazan approached them in the spirit of a challenge to his well-developed skills. Kazan's achievement would lie in an imaginative application of what he had already learned rather than in promoting a fresh idea or saying something new.

Kazan's decision to handle William Inge's *The Dark at the Top of the Stairs*, which opened in December 1957, had the earmarks of a grand marriage of convenience. With each one surpassing the long run of its predecessor, Inge's three plays, *Come Back Little Sheba* (1949), *Picnic* (1952), and *Bus Stop* (1955) had won him a reputation of being immune to failure. He possessed box-office strength equal to Kazan's. Yet, with his Kansas background, his concentration upon atmosphere, and his opposition to message plays, Inge was hardly a kindred spirit. Also his vivid portrayal of frustration and small-mindedness in his rural midwestern towns was accompanied by a distinct affection for their communal spirit and individuality. Typically, Inge's plays were laced with strands of nostalgia, in part because they were based on people Inge had known years earlier and in part because they were drafted long before they were performed. *The Dark at the Top of the Stairs* was not only to be Inge's most autobiographical play, but one he began back in 1945 and had been rewriting for the previous six years.

The Dark at the Top of the Stairs used the setting of a small Oklahoma town during the 1920s in order to examine the reverberations set off by a faltering marriage. Inge's play is essentially a depiction of averted confrontation. The Flood family—Cora, Rubin, and their two children, Reenie and Sonny—is emotionally withering from their inability to cope with loneliness and rejection. All suffer from a commonplace yearning to be respected and loved. Things happen, the mood varies, but there is no fundamental change and no resolution. Back in 1950, Inge was inclined to disparage this effort. "I realize now," he observed "that the play had none of the action or plot interest that are minimum essentials in any Boradway production."[8] In the course of his revisions, Inge changed many lines and individual scenes. He concentrated the mood of each section and gave his characters greater psychological depth. But the dramatic action—what little there was—remained essentially the same. The only significant changes were the elimination of scenes between Rubin and his mistress and a radical alteration in the characterization of Reenie's date from a polite, nondescript visitor from Denver to the exceptionally mature Sammy Goldenbaum, who is acutely mindful of the local prejudice against him. Refusing either to hide his Jewishness or to relinquish his cheerful, outgoing manner, he counsels Sonny on how to cope with rejection. When he leaves, only Cora's brother suspects that he may not be as confident and happy as he appears. Later, in a revision Inge added to the third act, it is announced that Sammy has committed suicide after being publicly castigated by the hostess of a dance.

"Sammy Goldenbaum, son of a broken home who is kept at a military school by his irresponsible mother," John Gassner wrote in his appraisal of the production, "was responsible for the most unforgettable scene of the production when he calls on the daughter to take her to a dance."[9] More recently, Gerald Weales has written, "There is something a little old-fashioned in Sammy's presence on the stage in 1957."[10] Sammy was as out of place in the play's Oklahoma

221

The Dark at the Top of the Stairs: Sammy Goldenbaum (Timmy Everett) is an eventful intrusion upon the commonplace frustrations of the Flood family. Here Judith Robinson plays Reenie. (Photo by Fred Fehl; reproduced by permission of Hoblitzelle Theatre Arts Library, Humanities Research Center, The University of Texas at Austin.)

small-town setting as he was in Inge's usual cast of characters. Kazan, of course, was a trailblazer for such victims of racial prejudice. Sammy was not simply an excuse to turn *The Dark at the Top of the Stairs* into a message play. He was a catalyst fashioned to disrupt the hopeless continuum of the Flood family's existence. The announcement of his suicide, set against his earlier defiance of adversity, intrudes a realization of how personal preoccupations have blinded each character to his needs. When Rubin enters after this announcement, he does so to apologize for his fears and to take his wife to bed. Like the ray of light Kazan cast upon Rubin's naked feet at the play's conclusion, the force of Sammy's influence gave the play a decidedly upbeat note.

If Kazan was not in fact behind these changes, he certainly played an important role in generating the effects they were designed to produce. "Over the placid lake of this play," Robert Brustein was to write in his unflattering appraisal of *Dark,* "Elia Kazan hurled thunderbolts. His production was in a state of carefully controlled frenzy. . . . Inge proposes calm and lassitude, Kazan imposes theatrical hi-jinks. What with all the nut-cracking, chicken-eating, behind-patting, jewelry-fingering, shoe-shining, sewing, crying, stuttering and yawning that went on, his characters were rarely empty-handed or empty-mouthed—and in a play almost devoid of climaxes we are served up a climax every five minutes."[11] This criticism was harsh and at odds with the estimates of most reviewers who tended to praise both the play and Kazan's direction. Yet, beneath the vitriol of Brustein's comments lay a legitimate point. Kazan had evoked eventfulness from a play striking for its lack of it. He absorbed audiences in the desperation of these ordinary people and gave it poignancy. He paced the flow of the commonplace occurrences so that they became as important to viewers as they were to the characters. He created a sense of change and progression without eliminating the play's underlying stasis. For Kazan, no less than for Inge, *The Dark at the Top of the Stairs* represented an updating of earlier efforts and their collaboration necessitated a difficult reconciliation of their differences. The long, prosperous run of *Dark* proved that their efforts had not miscarried.

Brustein's criticism stung Kazan, and for good reason. In addition to claiming that he had altered the play's mood, he charged that Kazan's styling was inappropriate and self-serving. This was ominous. "One day, after his latest success, *The Dark at the Top of the Stairs,* had opened," Boris Aronson, the set designer for several Kazan productions, once recalled, "I ran into him [Kazan] in the street and I said: 'Look—for the rest of your life you can do that type of show. And it's very well done, well written, well acted, well designed, well lit, well directed. But you have to do something which is much less safe, but much more satisfying. Something which also has a very good chance of failing.' "[12]

Kazan apparently took this advice to heart, for several weeks later he agreed to direct *J.B.* Certainly this was not a sure bet. Drawing his inspiration from the book of Job, the poet Archibald MacLeish had written a modern verse play that converted the Biblical man of sorrows into a business executive whose prosperity, familial happiness, and philosophic assurance are shaken by a series of setbacks suggestive of the social conditions that had evolved since World War II. Because of Broadway's longstanding aversion for Biblical adaptations and verse plays, MacLeish had been unable to get anyone to produce his original creation, and so he opted to go ahead with publication. Reviewers quickly proclaimed MacLeish's book a major literary landmark. An ensuing production at Yale attracted Brooks Atkinson, and moved him to open an ensuing reflection with the assertion, "In form as well as content MacLeish's *J.B.* ranks with the finest work in American drama."[13] Such praise from the drama critic of the *New York Times* made a Broadway production inevitable. The challenge posed by *J.B.*'s combination of potential and risk was too tempting for Kazan to pass up the invitation extended him to serve as director.

"The thing I like so much about your play," Kazan wrote in a letter to MacLeish shortly after accepting the directorship, "is that it is about our state of soul and feeling, our Fates as presently felt by us all, our Future. In other words, it is not a play about Job; it is a play about the mid-century American and mid-century America."[14] After marking how the quality of the work was above question, he followed with some ten pages of suggested revisions.[15] As one would expect, Kazan's proposals were cued to the theatrical presentation. He was thinking of what might be done to enrich the drama of MacLeish's play. He was also nudging the play into the ken of his experience.

One of Kazan's first concerns was the characterization of Zuss and Nickles, the two failed actors-turned-circus-vendors who mount the play and observe what happens to Job. Kazan proposed that they be converted from middle-aged figures into a cantankerous beatnik and a conservative old actor.[16] Behind this change, of course, stood the oppositions of Joe Keller-Chris, Willie-Biff, Johnny Friendly-Terry, Adam-Aron, and Big Daddy-Brick. This change was not intended to convert the Zuss-Nickles relationship into an Oedipal struggle or to gain more complex characters. On the contrary, making the pair old and young, father and son, was aimed at accentuating their philosophic opposition, associating it with familiar differences of opinion, and producing comic jousting. As Kazan would write in his notebook, "There should be a lot of humor in this performance."[17]

Brooks Atkinson's original review of the Yale production had noted *J.B.*'s resemblance to *The Skin of Our Teeth*.[18] "Though Atkinson was referring to the play's imaginative consideration of man's desperate plight, from his earlier direction of *The Skin of Our Teeth*, Kazan could see Zuss and Nickles functioned like Sabina in cuing and controlling the audience's reaction. Since *J.B.*'s situation was fundamentally as absurd as the Antrobuses, the humorous outbursts of derision and incredulity voiced by Zuss and Nickles, like those of Sabina, raised audience consciousness of the point and allayed potential incredulity. As they were moved by *J.B.*'s travail, so too was the audience. "The marvelous thing about your play to me is that *initially* Zuss and Nickles become emotionally involved in what's happening and become partisan," Kazan wrote in his first letter to MacLeish by way of a suggestion that the effect be strengthened.[19]

For Kazan, *J.B.* was a play about psychological breakdown, but it was not a psychological drama. *J.B.* was no less a familiar stereotype than Zuss and Nickles. By situating *J.B.* between them, as he did in the stage design and stage movements, Kazan played him off against their evaluations. *J.B.* was as oblivious to their ideas as he was to them as characters. The disasters that finally cause him to think, painful and personal though they are, finally lead to a collapse of the logic and morality emanating from God's presumed authority. Once this

225

breaks down, J.B. has to reach into himself and find the answer, and that answer is the play's message.

Behind its free verse, its philosophical speculations, and its unusual frame, Kazan could see that *J.B.* was agit-prop drama. Focusing upon the play's ritualistic pattern,[20] he pushed MacLeish to strengthen this quality and then sought to embellish the results with as much theatrical flair as possible. In the original version, there was considerable variation in the space and emphasis MacLeish devoted to the relentless series of setbacks—the death of J.B.'s son just after the armistice, the car wreck killing another son and daughter, the rape and murder of his daughter, the atomic destruction of his bank, and finally abandonment by his wife. Kazan had him prune and work these announcements so that they followed like even blows of a hammer. He carefully worked up the vignettes introducing these scenes— the V-J celebration, the police sirens, the spectacular A-bomb explosion, to create excitement and eventfulness. In this way, the first act became a neatly arranged sequence of devastating setbacks. Nowhere in this agit-prop quality more apparent than in the revised first act conclusion in which a group of miserable, impoverished outcasts gather around the broken J.B. to give him warmth and consolation. Stripped of all his capitalistic contentments, J.B. is about to be realigned with "the people." From a group huddle recalling Kazan's first directing assignments, J.B. rises up and ends the act with his cry, "Show me my guilt, O God!"[21]

Having effectively agitated on behalf of the problem, the way was now cleared for the solution. But unlike the reforms trumpeted at the conclusions of typical agit-prop plays, *J.B.* had no remedy— the second act was as systematic as the first in J.B.'s rejection of proffered help. In other words, *J.B.* followed the progression of agit-prop in order to signal the contrasting outlook of its conclusion. By dismissing Eliphaz (the psychiatrist), Zopha (the cleric), Bildad (the communist), and a variety of specious philosophical consolations without abandoning his trust in a higher power, J.B. rises to the level of a modern Job. There is no logic, no justice, and no explanation for the afflictions that have befallen him, only the vast, immutable power of the universe—and love. Having set up this second act departure with his first act streamlining, Kazan pushed MacLeish to give it more dramatic impact through a sharp reduction in the amount of philosophical disquisition and a concentration of J.B.'s final reunion with his wife into a wordless tableau reminiscent of *Tea and Sympathy*'s conclusion.

For Kazan, *J.B.* was an impressive achievement. He had taken on a formidable challenge and produced another commercial and critical success that was to bring MacLeish a third Pulitzer Prize. On the other hand, *J.B.* was not the innovative departure it appeared. All script modifications and ingenious stage business bespoke the hand of the master director creatively drawing upon his accumulated experience. In this respect Kazan was doing pretty much the same thing that he had done with *The Dark at the Top of the Stairs*. This approach, concentrating upon the promise of the immediate production and lacking the personal commitment of his earlier work, left Kazan in the position of living off his past. Such assured reliance on his well-developed talents carried the danger that his choices would become familiar, that his efforts would call attention to themselves, and that the results would appear mannered. When Brustein first leveled this charge against *Dark*, he was a lonely dissenter, but Kazan's next effort brought a crowd to his side.

Kazan was able to take on *J.B.* only because of a last-minute postponement of an earlier commitment that originally had been made with high hopes, but that brought him both frustration and embarrassment instead. The last-minute decision to push back the opening of Tennessee Williams's *Sweet Bird of Youth* was one of many delays that plagued that production. Williams originally drafted the play between stints on *Baby Doll*, and, in April 1956, decided to give it an experimental production with the Studio M Playhouse in Coral Gables, Florida.[22] The audience was taken aback by the featured affair between an over-the-hill Hollywood star and her aging gigolo. Their efforts to stave off time's erosion of their beauty and promise with heavy doses of drugs and sex went well beyond any of Williams's previous studies of human depravity. Despite general agreement that the play needed more work, MGM was confident enough of its upcoming film of *Cat on a Hot Tin Roof* that it was willing to commit a half million dollars to the project in return for the film rights.[23]

When he agreed to participate in this planning, Kazan believed that Williams had rich material and some powerful scenes. He was also aware of Williams's escalating use of alcohol and drugs and uneasy over his waning ability to fulfill the promise of his conceptions. The residual carry-over from his previous work was also growing more noticeable. *Sweet Bird* was to be faulted for its resemblances to *Cat*—the familiar centerstage bed, the male with his doubts and unfulfilled potential, the mercurial, determined female, and a bigoted Southern politician who conducted himself very much like Big Daddy. Kazan himself was much more concerned with the dramatic flatness of the second act. Over the next two years, his suggestions and Williams's revisions accomplished little improvement, and there was diminishing likelihood that any more would come. Convinced that the first act was a brilliant *tour de force,* and reassured by the production's solid funding and promising cast, Kazan decided to push ahead and hope for the best.

Although *Sweet Bird* had a rocky out-of-town run, it was a success before it ever got to New York. By opening night it already had booked forty-four group parties, thirty-five for the whole house, which came to a whopping $390,000 of advance ticket sales.[24] Like the fading movie queen who receives another plum role at the play's end, *Sweet Bird* was destined for the limelight despite all fears to the contrary. Reviewers for the major newspapers responded favorably to what they saw. There was, however, little enthusiasm in this approval. The magazine reviews that followed were more critical, often quite hostile. "The staging, by Elia Kazan," proclaimed the *New Yorker,* "is operatic and hysterical; so is the writing; and both seem somehow unreplenished, as if they had long been out of touch with observable reality . . . none of Mr. Williams' other plays has contained so much rot."[25] "And indeed, Elia Kazan's staging, which makes an unsavory story acceptable to impact-hungry audiences by its constant injections of cosmic-sized force," the *Saturday Review* asserted, "increases the disjointed quality of the play's events. . . . Mr. Kazan's direction and his persuasion of the playwright to alter his play to suit it is deplorable."[26] In his more analytic approach, Harold Clurman's assessment for the *Nation* was perhaps the most damning of all. He charged that instead of moving the audience or raising its understanding, Williams had only capitalized on the luridness of his characters' debase-

228

ment. His sensationalization of their miseries was an exploitation of the heritage of social drama.[27] The success of *Sweet Bird* left both Kazan and Williams little to be proud of.

For several years now, Kazan's films and stage work had been lacking in that drive for self expression that lay at the heart of his finest work. Hesitantly, but inexorably, he was realizing that in order to get back in touch with his source of inspiration he was going to have to decide what he wanted to say and then speak for himself. *Wild River* (1960) was to mark an important step in this direction, though its net effect was to corroborate Kazan's fears that this new objective would be difficult to achieve. As with his last four films, Kazan started work on *Wild River* with the script's preparation, but in this case he did the writing. After three different drafts, his critical judgment told him that he was still a long way from a viable film. Frustrated and discouraged, he decided to seek help. By the time he finally got an acceptable result, he had gone through three writers and six more drafts. Consequently, Kazan invested as much effort on this film as any to date, but once again the script credit went to someone else.

Compelled now to seek studio backing, Kazan found his script generated little interest. Rather than give up, he settled for an arrangement whereby Fox accepted *Wild River* in place of the three films called for by his contract, which had been in limbo since Zanuck's decision to drop *Waterfront*. A later screening of the finished product simply confirmed the executive staff's original belief that the project would be a write-off. *Wild River* was given a quiet release and quickly withdrawn. Few noticed it and fewer bothered to see it.

Failure though it was, *Wild River* signaled a turn in Kazan's thinking as important as his attempt to become a scriptwriter. Up to this point Kazan had been preoccupied with what was going on in the American society in which he was living. Although *Viva Zapata!* and *East of Eden* had been set in the past, they were conceived as commentaries on social conditions at the time these films were made. *Wild River,* on the other hand, represented an effort on Kazan's part to turn backward and reassess the history he had lived, the battles he had won and lost.

With *Wild River* Kazan returned to the material of his first film,

Wild River: A wistful re-examination of battles Kazan fought at the outset of his career. (The Museum of Modern Art/Film Stills Archive, New York.)

People of the Cumberland. When Kazan originally made that documentary with Ralph Steiner, he had been a young left-wing idealist from New York who believed that the problems of Appalachia could be solved by education, organization, and governmental leadership. His celebration of the beliefs of the Cumberland school and unionization concluded with a shot of a dam just as *Wild River* does. What is striking about *Wild River* is how differently Kazan now came to view this symbol of hope for a better way of life. Looking at the Depression from the far side, Kazan had mixed feelings about the spirit of progress and improvement that he had so enthusiastically promulgated in his documentary.

Chuck Glover, the lead character, is a young representative of the TVA who is given the job of evicting a matriarch on an island so that a dam can be built. He discovers himself in the awkward position of implementing a governmental policy that sacrifices individuals to the cause of a greater good. From his first encounter with his adversary Ella Garth through his involvement with her daughter and battle against local bigotry, Glover's dramatic rationale seems to be to brood over the disruptive consequences of his actions.

The movie's opening use of footage from Pare Lorenz's *The River,* one of the best-known documentaries of the 1930s, calls attention to Kazan's intent to reassess assumptions of the Depression years. In recounting the benefits to be gained by harnessing the river's energy, the documentary's narrator trumpets the benefits of the TVA and criticizes the unenlightened locals who resist its efforts. At this point, the old black and white film fades into Technicolor. Silence replaces the narrator's stern voice and the camera quietly savors the unspoiled beauty of the river. The mood is nostalgic; the theme— inevitable change and irrecoverable loss. *Wild River* returns to the conditions of human need from which Kazan's original commitment to social realism was forged in order to show a breakdown in the crusading spirit and to question the merits of its goals.

Kazan originally planned Glover to be Jewish,[28] which would have likened him to the outsiders and pariahs of his previous work. However, Paul Osborne, his final choice for scriptwriter, convinced him that the same effect could be achieved by a wholesome, all-American protagonist with whom audiences could more readily identify. Since the film was set in the South, it would be more logical to have prejudice directed at blacks, but rather than turn the TVA representative into a black so that he could become a proponent of equality and suffer accordingly, Kazan and Osborne had their white Glover favor the employment of blacks according to the same pragmatic, rational thinking exemplified by the proposed dam. This decision alienates him from those who support his cause. In sharp contrast to the emergent spirit of civic cooperation in *The People of the Cumberland,* the townspeople of *Wild River* favor outside intervention only to the extent that it fattens their pocketbooks and causes no change in the existing social order.

These bigots make Glover's job difficult and provoke his questioning of what he hopes to accomplish. In the process, Ella Garth becomes something of an endangered species. She is an unyielding opponent to everything he represents, from his promotion of governmental dependency to his tongue-tied uncertainty. She is an iron-willed reactionary, set in her ways and unwilling to compromise. Although she embodies the river's unharnessed power to do damage, she staunchly upholds noble values imperiled by the spirit of progress—individualism, conviction, and family solidarity. As a stalwart opponent to the kind of youth aggrandized in his films only five years earlier, she elicits a measure of sympathy from Kazan that was never granted Johnny Friendly, Adam, or Big Daddy.

Unfortunately, Kazan was reluctant to give up his overworked romance formula. Given Kazan's final decision to entrust his script to the script writer who had prepared *East of Eden,* it is hardly surprising that Glover's difficulties are both compounded and eased by his affair with Carol. One simply cannot watch the awkward, halting exchange between Montgomery Clift and Lee Remick without sensing a carry-over from the relationship between James Dean and Julie Harris. By the same token, the beating that tests Glover's commitment strongly recalls the one Terry receives in *On the Waterfront.* Nevertheless, *Wild River* sounded a new note. Kazan's dramatic presentation stresses Glover's pronounced aversion for confrontation. After years of turning scripts into concentrations of charged moments, he purposely avoids his familiar abrupt swings from calm to storm, from lyric tenderness to violence. Consequently, his *Wild River* is downright sluggish. Movement is slow, almost without direction. People wander through the landscape or drift lazily on the water, either surveying the scene or studying people; each appears silent, observant, unapproachable. Reserve is the keynote. The camera spends an exceptional amount of time savoring the context and causing the film to drag. *Wild River's* studious departure from the vigorous styling that had recently incurred such heavy criticism both failed and left the impression that Kazan had grown pensive and skeptical about the social causes he had so insistently pushed in the past.

The failure of *Wild River* made Kazan more cautious and more determined with his next film, *Splendor in the Grass*. Delegating all writing responsibilities—this time to William Inge—while closely attending to the script's development as he had done so many times before, Kazan directed his efforts at the burgeoning numbers of teenage filmgoers. The result was another commercial success on the order of *Sweet Bird of Youth*, and equally tarnishing to his reputation. Like *Wild River*, *Splendor in the Grass* was another return to the past, presented this time with all the turbulence and anguish viewers had come to expect from Kazan. There was to be nothing nostalgic about this revisit to the years of Kazan's youth. In this case, the past was more like justification for the oppression Kazan attacked in so many of his dramas.

Splendor in the Grass shows the rural Oklahoma of thirty years earlier to be a bastion of puritanism. As teenagers living at the time of the stock market crash, Bud Stamper and Deanie Loomis are in love, but their feelings are crossed by sharp family differences and the era's squeamishness about sex. The adults of the film are a collection of authority figures—mom and dad, school teacher and minister, doctor and dean—who tell the younger generation how to behave while exhibiting the consequential hang-ups, which discredit their advice. For all the importance the film accords the crash of the stock market, economics has little to do with what happens. Basically the crash is license for a whole series of inadequately motivated breakdowns. At the New Year's Eve party, which ushers in 1929, Bud's sister runs amok and sets off a chain reaction. Bud falls sick, Deanie goes insane, and finally his father jumps out of a window. Against this background of collapse, cause ceases to be a crucial factor. Deranged behavior seems to be the norm, and the viewer is overwhelmed with lurid scenes of hysteria and violence. Ginnie gets gang-raped and a big fight ensues. Deanie pulls Bud on top of her, and, with desperation rather than passion, pleads that he make love to her. However impressive the bathroom interrogation of Deanie is at communicating her mother's insensitivity and warped morality, the resulting flight of the naked daughter strains for the audience's attention.

Splendor in the Grass reaped strong box office returns, but it took a pounding from the critics. "A Martian who saw this film," wrote Stanley Kauffmann, "might infer that all adolescents deprived of sexual intercourse go crazy."[29] Brendan Gill fulminated, " 'Splendor in the Grass' is as phony a picture as I can remember seeing. Not only that, it's phony in a particularly disgusting way . . . what it amounts to is a prolonged act of voyeurism."[30] *Time* would dismiss the film as "jargoned-up and chaptered out till it sounds like an angry psycho-sociological monograph describing the sexual mores in the heartless heartland."[31]

Several months before he bagan filming *Splendor in the Grass,* Kazan announced that he would not direct Williams's upcoming play, *Period of Adjustment.*[32] Word quickly spread that his decision represented a final split. "Kazan has suddenly gotten the crazy idea that he is not good for my work," Williams told a correspondent from the *New York Times.* "I think that Kazan has been upset by the people who accuse him of looking for popular successes, people who snipe at his so-called melodramatic interpretation of my plays."[33] Indeed, Kazan was bothered by the strains of *Sweet Bird,* but this break was symptomatic of a distress that ran much deeper. Too many outspoken young critics were hunting his head. In a follow-up discussion of Kazan's direction of *Sweet Bird* and *J.B.,* Kenneth Tynan had proclaimed that "Mr. Kazan has grown harsher, and at the same time more sentimental," and concluded, "It would be helpful if a committee could be formed to prohibit the warlike use of Kazan and to restrict him to peaceful purposes; for if his present tendency continues unchecked, it may mean the end of theatrical civilization as we know it."[34] Moreover, the conditions of Broadway production were becoming a high-risk gamble for dwindling stakes. The "hit" mentality had taken over; shows either closed quickly or enjoyed long lucrative runs. Of the 25 percent of the offerings that were profitable, half of them came from abroad.[35] Expenses were so high that Kazan publicly decried the less than twenty days of rehearsals for his well-financed productions of *J.B.* and *Sweet Bird of Youth*.[36] Kazan was not just breaking with Williams—he was fed up with Broadway and wanted to get away from these intolerable conditions.

Nonetheless, Kazan had few choices. His reputation was so closely linked to Broadway that for him to go elsewhere would smack of a Broadway invasion. Ironically, this reputation opened an exit. The current ambitious planning for the Lincoln Center included a Repertory Theatre and, when the organizers began to search for a figure with enough stature to serve as its director, Kazan's name was at the top of their list. In April 1961, approximately one year after his split with Williams, the *New York Times* announced that Kazan had agreed to serve as co-director of the Repertory Theatre with Robert Whitehead.[37] With guaranteed funding for a drama school and for an undecided slate of plays to be presented three years in the future, Kazan told reporters, "I've had Broadway. I'm not even reading scripts any more for Broadway production. The whole Broadway set-up is inimical to the theatre. It's almost impossible to do daring work because of the current economy of Broadway. Costs have become so absurd, producers are actually abandoning plays they know are worthwhile, because of the high cost of running them."[38]

Not only had Kazan escaped Broadway, but he had realized a dream he had been entertaining ever since the collapse of Group Theatre. Nonetheless, there was something ominously familiar and vague about Kazan's confident pronouncements. Had he not expressed a similar disgust for Hollywood conditions when he set up Newtown Productions? What were these "worthwhile" plays that producers were abandoning? As head of the projected showcase of American theatre, did Kazan have a clear vision of what sort of plays the Repertory Theatre should mount? Or did he intend to throw his weight behind individual selections as he had done so disastrously with Newtown?

After a year of discussions, Kazan wrote a promotional article for the Center's theatrical program which opened with yet another attack on Broadway. What followed suggested that the dominant concern and major innovation of his Repertory program would be its

1,100 seat theatre and its adaptable forward thrust stage. Its program of offerings was vaguely defined as a combination of "best new plays," modern American classics, and traditional masterpieces. When a skeptic challenged these plans with the charge "You can't be everything to everybody," Kazan wrote that he and Whitehead were moved to respond "Why not?" Such was their logic. Compromises were not to be made; they were to be transcended.[39]

It did not take long for Kazan's grand scheme to develop worrisome cracks. As head of the Actors Studio, Lee Strasberg charged that its acclaim entitled it to participate in the schooling. Kazan countered that his training program had to be independent. He resigned from the Studio and spurred Strasberg to convert the Studio into a rival production company. From Off Broadway came complaints that with Kazan and Whitehead at the helm, the Repertory Theatre was no more than a subsidized Broadway outpost and that its claims of newness were just a smoke screen for more of the same. "One may wonder why," Robert Brustein asked in an article for *Harper's*, "when it is commercialism that is debasing our theatre—the Lincoln Center project was handed over to two men who have hitherto shown no great interest in any other system?"[40]

Finally in April 1963, the rampant speculation on the Repertory's program was checked with an announcement that the opening production would be a new play by Arthur Miller. Miller's return from nine years of silence and his reunion with Kazan after their much publicized HUAC split had the makings of the "event" the Repertory wanted for its opening.

After the Fall was *Death of a Salesman* carried to the level of abstraction. The main character, Quentin, was a Willie Loman wrestling with time's alteration of his expectations and a convenient vehicle for Miller to explore the major concerns of his own life—the parents who reared him, the stock market crash that warped their lives, the McCarthy era that altered his, and especially the women who dominated his thoughts. In this "trial of a man by his own conscience, his own values, and his own deeds,"[41] Kazan could see that Miller was creating an autobiographical drama on the order of O'Neill's *Long Day's Journey into Night*. It also accorded with his hope that this first offering would present audiences with something they would find both familiar and innovative.

Unfortunately, at the time of this announcement Miller's play was still far from completion. When rehearsals began a year and a half later, Miller was still working on the second act. He then had to be sent off for ten days to redo the play's conclusion. Next, extraneous events so disrupted rehearsals that Kazan found himself living Quentin's confusion more than directing it. Barbara Loden, who had appeared in Kazan's past two films and would later become his wife, needed constant reassurances that she was up to the demanding role of Maggie. Jason Robards, who was playing Quentin, went off on a bender that brought rehearsals to a standstill. The day he returned President Kennedy was assassinated. Then two weeks later, Molly Kazan had a massive stroke and died. A journalist who attended these rehearsals was later to write that during them "Gadg Kazan waited, watched, relished. He seemed to let Arthur have his full say without interfering except occasionally to agree heartily with Arthur or even to embellish Arthur's comments. I don't ever remember hearing Gadg take a stand or express a point of view contrary to Arthur's."[42]

Since the opening of *After the Fall* launched the Repertory Theatre, reviewers felt obliged to praise the achievement it represented, but ensuing evaluations of the play itself ran from those praising it as a "tour de force" and "overpowering" to detractors who judged it "cerebral pornography," "an act of exhibitionism," and "an internal bull session." If *After the Fall* was not an acclaimed masterpiece and Kazan's direction went largely unnoticed, the result generated enough interest to draw audiences. However, Kazan's next two undertakings, *But for Whom Charlie* and *The Changeling*, were unqualified disasters. *The Changeling* was the first traditional play Kazan ever attempted, and the reviews were scathing. This avalanche of hostile criticism was perhaps best summarized by *Newsweek*'s assertion: "When an audience literally cringes in embarrassment, when it can scarcely muster even the conventional rounds of applause, when it laughs at a play whose implacable terror is unmatched in all dramatic literature—then we are in the presence of a cultural disaster."[43]

This setback could not have come at a worse time. Season subscription ticket sales for the Repertory Theatre had dropped from $46,000 to $30,000. Instead of stemming this decline, *The Changeling* sent it into a dive. Amidst rising administrative frenzy, Kazan resigned. Weeks later, the Repertory Theatre was dead—before its first birthday and before the delayed construction of the Vivian Beaumont theatre had been completed.

"I'm going to work for Lincoln Center," Kazan once remarked to an interviewer, "as long as I can do what I want to do. When I can't do that, I'll quit."[44] As with Newtown Productions, Kazan participated in the Lincoln Center assuming that the results would bear his imprint, yet once again his efforts notably lacked the informing purpose and drive for recognition of his recent work. Part of the problem was that Kazan was simply unable to function as an institution. Such a position robbed him of the opposition he needed. By background, temperament, and ingrained posture, he was an outsider. Having lost interest in Broadway, he found Lincoln Center was no renewal. His efforts to reconcile all the competing hopes for the Center pleased no one, least of all himself. Instead of firing his determination, the haggling and disputing only wearied him.

There was also another side to this dilemma. For years, Kazan had drawn his inspiration from the work of others. In their words, he discovered what he wanted to say. Yet, since he began working on his script for *Wild River*, he had been longing to speak for himself. What he learned from his frustrating involvement with Lincoln Center was that the indirection of directing would never develop the identity he was now pursuing. Moreover, that identity was no longer a reputation, a list of credits, a Terry Malloy whose plight gripped filmgoers' attention, but rather the end result of his accumulated experience, something he himself had created.

Back in his April 1961 announcement that he was quitting Broadway, Kazan indicated that his filmmaking was also headed in a new direction. He was going abroad to complete his first original screenplay and would say nothing more about it other than it was a "personal idea." He would not even reveal what country he was visiting lest it "give away part of the movie idea."[45] Actually this was a project that had been on Kazan's mind for years. In 1955 Kazan had been inspired by a vacation trip to Turkey to do a movie about his family's

238

emigration. In late 1956, while he was shooting *Baby Doll*, he told Frederic Morton, "I want to do a picture about immigration which has never really been done before. I want to do a picture on my people, the Greeks. I'm getting impatient. Maybe because I've got more confidence, maybe because there's less time every day."[46] From the outset Kazan planned to base his film upon the experience of his uncle, who later financed his parents' immigration. Kazan's own father, however, finally provided the impetus. Kazan was able to do little with all the family history he had been amassing until his father died in September 1960. Following the funeral, Kazan shackled himself to a regimen and four months later completed the first draft of a screenplay.

Strong as these family influences were, psychotherapy was to play an equally important role. With a mass of notes, and fragmented scenes, and the accumulated frustration of his effort on his *Wild River* script, Kazan changed psychiatrists, enlisting a tougher one to push him to overcome the blockage that defeated his efforts to write. Concluding that the psychiatrist he had been with for years was trying to adjust him to society, he sought one who would get him to do what he really wanted to do.[47] Out of this came *America America*, which for Kazan was to be a fictionalized inquiry into his origins. This filmscript, first published as a novel and later made into a film* was family history delving into his innermost feelings. As in so many of his directing successes, Kazan was once again using the experience of others to probe his own psyche, but now he called attention to himself and his personal background as never before. The finished film opens with a dark screen and Kazan is heard saying "My name is Elia Kazan. I am a Greek by blood, a Turk by birth, and an American because my uncle made a journey." "What kind of a man are you

---

*By August of 1961, Kazan had a complete, revised script, but none of the studios was interested. With a shoestring budget, he began shooting in the summer of 1962, only to have censorship by the Turkish government kill the project. The strong boxoffice returns of *Splendor in the Grass* finally made Warners willing to put up enough financing for filming to be completed the following summer. By the end of 1962, completion of the film was so doubtful Kazan published a novelized version of the script. Shortly after the novel appeared, Kazan finally raised enough funding to complete the film, which was released in December 1963.

anyway?" everyone keeps pressing his protagonist Stavros. Not unsurprisingly, his character and experiences reflect qualities central to Kazan's own career. Stavros is a dreamer moved by the majesty of distant snowcapped peaks and pained by the humiliation of subjugation in his native Anatolia. He is the wayward son who cannot abide his father's capitulation to a system that exploits him and the naïve idealist who must learn to be a fighter. Along the way, he is told that he is "nothing," a "sheep," a "whore," a "hamal," which spurs him to disprove his accusers. His initial efforts to reform the existing social system turn out to be dangerous and doomed. He learns that the religious beliefs of his friend Abdul and the comfortable middle-class contentment of the Sinyosoglou family are a trap. He concentrates upon survival first, but without ever relinquishing hope for achieving *his* goal, and decides that honor is personal and private, something best kept within himself. Ironically, he is victimized by the very intensity that enables him to succeed. In a systematic fashion, he loses or rejects all those for whom he truly cares. "Don't trust me," he confesses. By the end, Stavros is alone. "So he's left with his obsession," Kazan once observed.[48] The glaring contrast between the vague inspirational idea of America stirred up within Stavros's mind and the torturous, disillusioning struggle to get there resonated with meaning for Kazan. Although *America America* is about a young man's trip to America, it is filled with the nostalgia of a battle-scarred director reflecting on his own fight for acceptance into American culture.

America America was also a return to the sort of materials and styling Kazan handled best. He had never been comfortable dealing with an open stage set or Technicolor. His protagonists were most convincing in a gloomy, desperate atmosphere of oppression. They needed the threat of tight rooms, clustered buildings, or forbidding landscape; beauty was an unlikely alternative and to be presented only as such. These conditions forced people to face whatever they were hiding from—a person, an unwanted realization, a denied feeling. Much of the frenzy and hysteria faulted in Kazan's more recent efforts had come from straining for effects that required theatrics to compensate for the waning interest in dramatized depictions of social injustice. For all the exoticism in Kazan's fictional return to Turkey at the turn of the century, one cannot help sensing that he was getting back to an environment in which these conditions existed. They virtually demanded his use of black-and-white documentary styling, which was an almost obsolete brand of moviemaking in 1964. The carefully observed faces and background boldly attest to location shooting, even if many scenes were actually done in New York. Individual close-ups savor the character that hardship and deprivation have given the local populace. Artfully arranged groups communicate a collective will, a formidable barrier of suspicion and hostility. This backdrop of adversity, exploitation, and social abuse is peopled with fathers and brothers—imposing figures of authority who demand too much of Stavros and loyal companions who offer help but cannot be relied upon. Stavros's relationship with Thomna presents another example of lovers divided by a chasm of conflicting goals. As in so many previous Kazan productions, the main scene in the lovers' relationship takes place around a bed that occasions uncomfortable intimacy and leads to a painful confession.

In its very personal statement, *America America* was not saying anything Kazan had not already said, but with his unusual subject matter he achieved an eloquence and virtuosity that had been lacking in his recent films. Though the film itself is uneven and overlong, individual sections, such as the death dance, Stavros's dealings with the Kebabians, and especially the opening montage, carry the imprint of a master moviemaker. When contemporary audiences rejected *America America* as an overblown piece of self-indulgence, they missed the accomplishment that retrospective screenings have revealed.

Due to a nightmare of production difficulties, *America America* (1964) was released less than a month before the opening night of *After the Fall* and soon proved a commercial disaster. Consequently, when Kazan quit Lincoln Center, he could only return to moviemaking on terms dictated by the studios. Another Broadway foray for Kazan would, at best, have been only a much diminished version of his past achievements. Where was he to go? "You know the truth?" Stavros had asked at the end of his movie-long journey. "The thing I'd like most is to start this journey over. That's the truth. Just to start it over." For Kazan, the writing of *America America* had been a crucial start in this direction. Only then he was still striving to be a film-

241

maker. With *The Arrangement*, his next effort, Kazan resolved to shuck the career that had brought him fame and power and write a novel about a man who did likewise. With his portrayal of Eddie Anderson's mad quest to liberate himself from all the intolerable compromises of his life by burning the decaying home of his parents, Kazan put a torch to his directing career and became the writer he had long wanted to be.

In tracing the radical transformation of a prosperous, middle-aged executive, *The Arrangement* openly proclaimed itself to be fictionalized autobiography. Eddie Anderson, the creative force behind the advertising firm of Williams and MacElroy, possesses a quick ingenuity for effective solutions to perplexing problems. He has it all—professional success and a perfect marriage. But beneath his serene surface of contentment festers a malaise that an office secretary unlocks. Gwen is not just another girlfriend; she is the one goal left for him to conquer. Her devastating effect on Eddie lies in her opposition, her refusal to be impressed, and her challenge to his well-ordered existence. She tempts him to explore the confusing psychological terrain of doubt, frustration, and anger that he has been scrupulously avoiding.

Within weeks Eddie goes from a portrait of respectability to a rebellious drop-out. He throws up his job, smashes his marriage, and embarks on a course of willful self-destruction. One of the keys to Eddie's collapse is his tripartite personality. In his heart he is Evangelous Armes, the insecure youth who fought hard to show his father and the world that he was not a failure. At work he is Eddie Anderson, the boy wonder who skillfully markets his products and masks their defects. In his spare time, he is Evans Arness, the author who exposes sham and duplicity. Although he has always held up the truth as his ideal, he compulsively seeks deceptions and consequently never integrates these different identities. They are part of the network of arrangements he is driven to destroy. Finally, Eddie's rampage snowballs out of control and he winds up in a straightjacket. But this liberation of his buried angst enables him to leave the sanitarium for an impoverished, undistinguished life doing whatever he pleases.

Behind Eddie, Evans, and Evangelous was, of course, Elia. Eddie was an ideal surrogate that allowed Kazan to appear as he might imagine and to reshape the ingredients of his life as he chose. Eddie's parents and his early life are similar to Kazan's own—Kazan's interviews even used many of the same phrasings in describing them. Eddie's narrative—so disarmingly frank in its open acknowledgment of his eccentricities, frustrations and failings—invites his audience to make sense of his behavior. Eddie himself does not understand it. Without quite realizing it, the reader is thrust into the position of an analyst. "What helped me most," Kazan once observed in discussing this novel, "was my psychoanalysis, because I'd been psychoanalyzed into articulation, into wishing to speak. It was the most helpful thing that ever happened; the whole thing of just *talking*.[49] Psychoanalysis had propelled Kazan through the drama of *America America*. With *The Arrangement*, it helped him develop a fresh, engaging style. Eddie's story is an unburdening confession, shaped from obvious elements of Kazan's life, that, in typical fashion, reveals personal feelings rather than specifics of his private life. His rampage alleviated Kazan's accumulated frustration. Though it was not great literature, it was a fictionalized self-revelation, like his best plays and films, which called attention to both him and his creativity.

Having passed a year imagining himself to be a forgotten man freed from all the falsehoods of his previous work, Kazan returned to New York, solicited the advice of his editor, and undertook a host of revisions. The result was given a splashy send-off and suddenly he was the best-selling novelist.

Eddie's tale of dropping out topped the best seller list through most of 1967 and brought Kazan a handsome contract and complete responsibility for a big-budget film adaptation. Unfortunately for Kazan, *The Arrangement* had one more irony left in store. Kazan's happy reunion with the big-business mentality attacked by his book was fatal. *The Arrangement* was one of Kazan's worst films and a box-office disaster. Eddie himself is a victim of the film's allegiance to proven formulae for success. Eddie the executive is a stereotype. The wayward Eddie is sophomoric. The Eddie who drops out is dull. Deprived of the voice Kazan had discovered, Eddie is reduced to a spent version of Kazan's other inarticulate heroes.

After the failure of *The Arrangement*, Kazan resolved to concentrate upon his writing. He would no longer strain to get the attention of an audience, and he would avoid the fights for which he used to spoil. He would be a spectator more interested in the game than the victory. His novels since *The Arrangement*—*The Assassins, The Understudy, Acts of Love*—have been diverse reflections upon a world without direction, without meaning, and beyond redemption. All battles to improve it are doomed. Even self-understanding is hopeless. Kazan's use of a broad range of personal-impersonal styles evidences uncertain experimentation. In none of these novels has he come up with a story equal to the one Eddie told, though his recently published *The Anatolian* is his strongest effort since. Part of this stems from the fact that Kazan's best work has typically been very personal and intent upon commenting on existing social conditions. This later work, on the other hand, is speculative, curious, detached. His strong commitment to writing, attested to by his steady stream of novels, seems directed only to opening new perspectives on life. There is little drive for conclusions; the once all-important outcome has lost its significance. He is interested in his subject matter, but not involved in it.

Since his disastrous film version of *The Arrangement*, Kazan has directed only one film—*The Last Tycoon* (1976). Having owned the film rights to this Fitzgerald novel for years, Sam Spiegel saw the torrent of publicity for the 1974 remake of *The Great Gatsby* as an opportunity for salvaging his investment. With funding now available, Harold Pinter was hired to prepare the script. Robert De Niro, Jack Nicholson, Robert Mitchum, and Tony Curtis were recruited to give the film an impressive cast. Kazan was then persuaded to serve as director. He, of course, had been responsible for making Spiegel's earlier production of *On the Waterfront* the success that it was. Still, Kazan was an odd choice for this assignment. Typically, Kazan's films avoided people who were powerful, famous, and wealthy, along with their glittering lifestyles; his films were practically an assault upon the extravagant romances that Fitzgerald was inclined to write.

However, in this portrait of Hollywood during the heyday of studio production which Fitzgerald loosely based upon the career of Irving Thalberg, Kazan could find much of personal interest. Having himself risen to power in Hollywood at a young age, Kazan brought

Deborah Kerr and Kirk Douglas in *The Arrangement*: A personal inquiry into the dissolution of an unacceptable identity. (The Museum of Modern Art/Film Stills Archive, New York.)

special insight to the enigmatic character of Monroe Stahr. Stahr, like Kazan, is a practical idealist. He is the only one capable of handling all the difficult people on whom his films depend—the emotional performers, the haughty writer, the narrow-minded executives. All the while he entertains a vision of possibilities that transcend these harsh realities. He wants to make a quality film, not simply a profitable one. Movies are his life because they challenge him to create his own reality.

With De Niro—coming off his success in *Mean Streets* and *Godfather II*—cast to play Stahr, Kazan might well have developed Stahr's ghetto background into an important facet of his characterization. But Kazan's Stahr makes little of this potential. As Stahr, De Niro is impeccably groomed, aloof, and bemused—nothing like the forceful, energetic young "Gadg." People are constantly appealing to this Stahr for the sort of solutions Eddie Anderson was supposed to provide, but he is persistently serene, unruffled, strangely untouchable. The audience sees that he is troubled. He takes pills; his girl-friend grows exasperated at his unfulfilled, undefined expectations. But this core of dissatisfaction causes few cracks in his polished reserve.

This puzzling characterization drained the film of dramatic intensity, which led to mixed reviews and lackluster box office returns. Stahr appears so abstracted from all that happens that critics found him an unconvincing studio head. Still, Kazan's disappointing depiction of Stahr communicates an important point about his thinking. No less than Stahr, Kazan had become weary of the profession that brought him fame. His directing in this film was perfunctory and uninspired. Having previously turned his back on directing in order to become a novelist, Kazan was unable to channel much of himself into this effort, or to mold the diverse elements of his presentation into an effectively realized vision; like Stahr, he seemed to feel that movies no longer express what he wanted to say.

In his recent public appearances, usually made in promotion of one of his novels, Kazan is routinely questioned about the well-known plays or films he had directed. Kazan generally responds that he would prefer to talk about his current rather than his past work. Presently the famous director considers himself a writer who moves to satisfy the yearning for self-expression formerly channeled into his directing. This does not prevent the rumor mill from reporting Kazan's plans for directing another play or film. Nor does it rule out the possibility that Kazan will actually do so. Nonetheless, all Kazan cares to say as director has been said.

The Last Tycoon might be viewed as offering a final comment upon the change in attitude that has attended this shift. Because Fitzgerald's novel was never completed, Kazan needed an ending, as so often in the past. His solution was to show De Niro walking on a studio back lot. As he comes to the entrance of a huge, cavernous warehouse, the camera closes on the back of his head and frames it with the darkness of the building's interior. Visually Kazan is showing Stahr in the same situation that Terry was in at the end of *On the Waterfront*. However Stahr is leading no one and going nowhere. Gone is the anguished soul-searching that infused his characterization of Terry, as well as the fierce drive to attract audiences to his depiction of waterfront injustice. Gone too is that kind of drama and the market conditions that made it possible. In Hollywood and on Broadway, it is a memory, a dated example of different times, different audiences, and different values. With a pensive calm, not unlike Kazan's in several of his novels, Stahr surveys the vast darkness, drawing no conclusions and offering no judgments. Yet in Stahr's calm one feels a haunting awareness that somehow a major change has taken place.

Notes

Introduction

1. Quoted in Margaret Brenman-Gibson, *Clifford Odets, American Playwright, the Years from 1906 to 1940* (New York: Atheneum, 1981), p. 510.
2. Maurice Zolotow, "Viewing the Kinetic Mr. Kazan," *New York Times*, March 9, 1952, II, 3.
3. Ibid.
4. Arthur Miller, "The Salesman Has a Birthday," in *The Theatre Essays of Arthur Miller*, ed. Robert A. Martin (New York: Viking Press, 1978), p. 13.
5. Elia Kazan, "Notebook for *A Streetcar Named Desire*," in *Directing the Play*, ed. Toby Cole and Helen Krich Chinoy (New York: Bobbs Merrill Co., 1953), p. 296.
6. Quoted in Robin Bean, "The Life and Times of Elia Kazan," *Films and Filming*, 10 (May 1964): 41.
7. Michael Delahaye, "A Natural Phenomenon: Interview with Elia Kazan," *Cahiers du Cinéma in English*, 9 (March 1967): 29.

Heritage of the Outsider

1. Thomas B. Morgan, "Elia Kazan's Great Expectations," *Harper's* 225 (Sept. 1962): 72.
2. Michel Ciment, *Kazan on Kazan* (New York: Viking Press, 1974), p. 10.
3. Ibid., p. 12.
4. Elia Kazan, "Pursuit of the Usey-less," *Williams Alumni Bulletin* 57 (Nov. 1964): 4.
5. Elia Kazan, *The Arrangement* (New York: Stein & Day, 1967), p. 197.
6. "Long, Long Ago," *Theatre Arts* 34 (Sept. 1950): 39.
7. Morgan, "Great Expectations," p. 72.
8. Elia Kazan, "The Common Element in the Drama" (unpublished ms., Williams College, June 1930), pp. 7 and 9.

9. Elia Kazan to George Pierce Baker, April 21, 1930, Yale School of Drama, New Haven, Connecticut. Cited in Frederick Ricci, "An Analysis of the Directing Techniques of Elia Kazan in Theatre and Film as Illustrated in *A Streetcar Named Desire*" (Ph.D. diss., Columbia University, 1974), p. 9.

10. A. H. Licklider to George Pierce Baker, May 15, 1930, Yale School of Drama.

11. Lewis Gillenson, "Man of the Theatre," *Harper's Bazaar*, Nov. 1951, p. 206. See also Murray Schumach, "A Director Named 'Gadge,'" *New York Times Magazine*, Nov. 9, 1947, p. 55.

12. Elia Kazan to George Pierce Baker, April 21, 1930.

13. Morton Eustis, "Theatre Building and Ownership," *Theatre Arts* 18 (Sept. 1934): 665–67.

14. Mordecai Gorelik, "Theatre Is a Weapon," *Theatre Arts* 18 (June 1934): 421.

15. Quoted in John Gassner, *Dramatic Soundings: Evaluations and Retractions Culled from Thirty Years of Dramatic Criticism* (New York: Crown Publishers, 1968), p. 431. See also p. 473.

16. James Poling, "Handy 'Gadget,'" *Collier's* 129 (May 31, 1952): 60.

17. Ibid.

18. Kazan, *The Arrangement*, p. 14.

19. In this capacity he may have developed what was to become a regular practice for both the Group and for himself; the thirty-seven volumes of clippings the Group has donated to Lincoln Center's theatre library is almost rivaled by the eighteen plus personal scrapbooks Kazan has deposited at Olin Library, Wesleyan University, Middletown, Connecticut.

20. Ciment, *Kazan on Kazan*, p. 122.

21. Harold Clurman, *On Directing* (New York: Macmillan, 1972), pp. 148–49.

22. Kazan, "Look, There's the American Theatre," *Tulane Drama Review* 9 (Winter 1964): 72.

23. *New Theatre* 1 (Jan. 1934): 10–11.

24. Jay Williams, *Stage Left* (New York: Scribner's, 1974), p. 98.

25. Ibid., p. 89. Morgan Yale Himmelstein says the goal of presenting more realistic plays was one of the main reasons the WLT changed its name to New Theatre or Theater of Action in early 1935. *Drama Was a Weapon: The Left-Wing Theatre in New York, 1929–41* (New Brunswick: Rutgers University Press, 1963), p. 17.

26. Ciment, *Kazan on Kazan*, p. 199.

27. Elia Kazan and Art Smith, "Dimitroff," *New Theatre* 1 (July/Aug. 1934): 20.

28. "Pastoral 44th Street," *New York Times*, May 20, 1934, IX, 2.

29. Ciment, *Kazan on Kazan*, pp. 18–19.

250

Strength and Sensitivity

1. *New York Herald Tribune,* June 30, 1935, V, 4.
2. Morgan Yale Himmelstein, *Drama Was a Weapon: The Left-Wing Theatre in New York, 1929–41* (New Brunswick: Rutgers University Press, 1963), p. 17. See also Malcolm Goldstein, *The Political Stage: American Drama and Theatre of the Great Depression* (New York: Oxford University Press, 1974), p. 48.
3. Jay Williams, *Stage Left* (New York: Scribner's, 1974) p. 165.
4. Ibid.
5. While Kazan was making *Pie in the Sky,* his wife wrote an illuminating article on improvisation. See Molly Day Thacher, "Why Improvise?" *New Theatre* 1 (March 1935): 14–15.
6. Program for premiere of *Pie in the Sky,* May 25, 1935, "Nykino" File, Lincoln Center Theatre Collection, New York.
7. Leo Hurwitz, "The Revolutionary Film—Next Step," *New Theatre* 1 (May 1934): 23.
8. Ralph Steiner and Leo Hurwitz, "A New Approach to Film Making," *New Theatre* I (Sept. 1935): 22–23.
9. Some of Frontier's first efforts were described as being liberalized versions of the *March of Time.* See *Variety,* April 21, 1937, p. 5. See also Peter Ellis, "Sights and Sounds," *New Masses* 23 (May 11, 1937): 29.
10. Program for *Pie in the Sky.*
11. Steiner and Hurwitz, "A New Approach to Film Making," pp. 22–23.
12. *Variety,* April 21, 1937, p. 4.
13. Mark Van Doren, "The Double Edge," *Nation* 146 (May 21, 1938): 596.
14. Harold Clurman, *The Fervent Years: The Story of the Group Theatre and the Thirties* (New York: Hill and Wang, 1957), p. 181.
15. *New York Times,* Jan. 17, 1937, X, 1.
16. *New York Times,* April 13, 1937, p. 31.
17. *New York Herald Tribune,* Feb. 16, 1936, V, 1. *New York Post,* April 17, 1936, p. 16. See also Norman Stevens, "The Case of Group Theatre," *New Theatre* 1 (July 1936): 5.
18. *Thirty Years of Treason: Excerpts from Hearings before the House Committee on Un-American Activities 1938–1968,* ed. Eric Bentley (New York: Viking Press, 1971), p. 489.
19. In his HUAC testimony, Kazan stated that he was a Communist from "the summer of 1934 until the late winter or early spring of 1936." Since *The Crime,* which Kazan directed for the Theater of Action opened March 1, 1936, Kazan's defection most probably occurred shortly thereafter. The Theater of Action had strong Communist Party ties. Although his involvement

with *People of the Cumberland,* which was sponsored by the left-wing Frontier Films and photographed over the summer of 1937, might suggest that his break with the Party was not as abrupt as he said, Kazan explained: "About 1936, I began a connection with an outfit called Frontier Films, but the Party had nothing to do with my making this connection. The organization consisted of four or five men, of whom I remember Paul Strand, Leo Hurwitz, and Ralph Steiner. From long friendship with Steiner, I believe him to be a strong anti-Communist. I do not know the party affiliation of the others. They were trying to raise money to make documentary films. They put me on their board, but I attended few meetings." *Thirty Years of Treason,* pp. 486, 488.

20. Clurman, *The Fervent Years,* p. 134.

21. John Gassner, *Dramatic Soundings: Evaluations and Retractions Culled from Thirty Years of Dramatic Criticism* (New York: Crown Publishers, 1968), p. 431.

22. Clurman, *The Fervent Years,* p. 185.

23. Morton Eustis, "The Director Takes Command, III," *Theatre Arts* 20 (April 1936): 279–80.

24. Interview with Harold Clurman by Thomas H. Pauly, May 20, 1979.

25. *New York Times,* Nov. 5, 1937, p. 18.

26. Thomas B. Morgan, "Elia Kazan's Great Expectations," *Harper's* 225 (Sept. 1962): 72.

27. Schumach, "A Director Named 'Gadge,'" *New York Times Magazine,* Nov. 9, 1947, pp. 55.

28. *New York Times,* Feb. 23, 1940, p. 18.

29. Maurice Zolotow, "Viewing the Kinetic Mr. Kazan," *New York Times,* March 9, 1952, II, 3.

The Conquest of Broadway

1. Harold Clurman, *The Fervent Years: The Story of the Group Theatre and the Thirties* (New York: Hill and Wang, 1957), pp. 37, 86, and 244.

2. Unpublished letter from Harold Clurman to Elia Kazan, October 23, 1941, Olin Library, Wesleyan College, Middletown, Connecticut.

3. *Theatre Arts* 26 (April 1942): 220–21.

4. With his profits from *Blues in the Night,* Kazan would purchase his country retreat—Sandy Hook, Connecticut, which he still owns and uses.

5. Richard H. Goldstone, *Thornton Wilder: An Intimate Portrait* (New York: Saturday Review Press, 1975), pp. 164–65.

6. *Nation* 155 (Dec. 5, 1942): 629.

7. James Poling, "Handy 'Gadget,'" *Collier's* 129 (May 31, 1952): 60.

8. Murray Schumach, "A Director Named 'Gadge,'" *New York Times Magazine,* Nov. 9. 1947, p. 18.

9. Quoted in *New York Herald Tribune,* Dec. 6, 1942, VI, 1.

10. Hermine Rich Isaacs, "First Rehearsals," *Theatre Arts* 28 (March 1944): 144.

11. Ibid.

12. Michel Ciment, *Kazan on Kazan* (New York: Viking Press, 1979), p. 46.

13. "Elia Kazan," *Current Biography 1948* (New York: H. W. Wilson, 1949), p. 337.

14. Ciment, *Kazan on Kazan,* p. 33.

15. Elia Kazan, "Audience Tomorrow: Preview in New Guinea," *Theatre Arts* 29 (Oct. 1945): 577.

16. Arnaud D'Usseau and James Gow, "Manufacturing a Problem Play," *New York Times,* Oct. 14, 1945, II, 1.

17. S. N. Behrman to Robert Sherwood and Playwrights' Company, May 5, 1945, Playwrights' Company Papers, Wisconsin Historical Society, Madison, Wisconsin.

18. Maxwell Anderson to Robert Sherwood, Dec. 22, 1945, Playwrights' Company Papers.

19. Harold Clurman and Elia Kazan, "To the Theatre Going Public," *New York Times,* March 1, 1946, p. 17, and Maxwell Anderson, "To the Theatre Public," *New York Herald Tribune,* March 4, 1946, p. 10. See also *New York Times,* March 5, 1946, p. 20, and March 7, 1946, p. 31.

20. *Home of the Brave,* which also concerned problems of postwar adjustment and immediately preceeded *Truckline Café* at the Belasco Theatre, had received generally favorable reviews, but was only able to run sixty-nine performances and lost its backers $60,000.

21. *New York Herald Tribune,* Oct. 8, 1946, p. 19.

22. *Variety,* July 11, 1945, p. 11.

23. Schumach, "A Director Named 'Gadge,' " p. 18.

24. Brooks Atkinson was to write, "If you want to know what Mr. Miller personally thinks about life you will more likely find it in the dialogue and actions of young Chris Keller who represents the moral standards of the play than in Joe Keller whose loose thinking the play repudiates." *New York Times,* Sept. 7, 1947, II, 1.

25. Arthur Miller, "Sign of the Archer," Humanities Research Center, University of Texas, Austin, Texas (hereafter cited as HRC). The title page of this manuscript reads "property of Harold Clurman," who originally purchased it. It is the version on which Kazan's acceptance of the directorship would have been based.

26. *New York Theatre Critics' Reviews: 1947,* p. 476.

27. Ibid., p. 475.

28. *New York Times,* April 22, 1947, p. 33.

29. *Nation* 164 (Feb. 15, 1947): 193.

30. *New York Times*, Sept. 7, 1947, II, 1. Atkinson's insistent support of *All My Sons* was a prime determinant in gaining it the New York Critics' Award for Play of the Year.

31. Arthur Miller used this phrase in 1947 to describe Kazan's purpose in Schumach, "A Director Named 'Gadge,'" p. 18, and Kazan himself was to repeat it again and again over the next ten years.

32. Kazan, "Audience Tomorrow," p. 577.

33. Ciment, *Kazan on Kazan*, p. 32.

34. R. C. Lewis, "A Playwright Named Tennessee," New York Times, Dec. 7, 1947, VI, 19, 67.

35. Tennessee Williams to Audrey Wood, April 21, 1947, HRC.

36. Tennessee Williams to Elia Kazan, April 19, 1947, Olin Library, Wesleyan University, Middletown, Connecticut.

37. Elia Kazan, "Notebook for *A Streetcar Named Desire*," in *Directing the Play*, ed. Toby Cole and Helen Krich Chinoy (New York: Bobbs Merrill Co., 1953), pp. 296–98.

38. Ibid., pp. 296–97.

39. Ibid., pp. 299–300.

40. Ibid., p. 299.

41. Kazan would come to see Brando's portrayal of Stanley as his main contribution. See Ciment, *Kazan on Kazan*, p. 71.

42. Harold Clurman, *Lies Like Truth* (New York: MacMillan, 1958), pp. 75–78.

43. Quoted in David William Weiss, "Jo Mielziner's Contribution to the American Theatre" (Ph.D. diss., University of Indiana, 1965), p. 141.

44. *New York Times*, Nov. 9, 1947, II, 3.

The Fox Way

1. Michel Ciment, *Kazan on Kazan* (New York: Viking Press), p. 49.

2. Mel Gussow, *Don't Say Yes Until I Finish Talking: A Biography of Darryl F. Zanuck* (Garden City, N.Y.: Doubleday & Co., 1971), p. 75.

3. Col. Darryl F. Zanuck, "Do Writers Know Hollywood?: The Message Cannot Overwhelm the Technique," *Saturday Review* 26 (Oct. 30, 1943): 12.

4. *Variety*, Dec. 9, 1946, p. 9.

5. Ciment, *Kazan on Kazan*, p. 49.

6. Ibid., p. 52.

7. Ibid., p. 51.

8. Ibid., p. 86.

9. See Elia Kazan, "Writers and Motion Pictures," *Atlantic Monthly* 199 (April 1957): 67.

10. An account of all the location difficulties *Boomerang* posed for

Kazan can be found in Murray Schumach, "White Plains Invaded by Movies," *New York Times*, Nov. 2, 1946, p. 17.

11. *House on 92nd Street* cost one million dollars to make and took in $2.5 million in domestic receipts, *13 Rue Madeleine* cost $2 million and grossed $2.75 million at home and $1.2 million abroad.

12. Anthony Abbot, "The Perfect Case," *Reader's Digest* 47 (Dec. 1945): 23.

13. "Laura Hobson," *Current Biography 1947* (New York: H. W. Wilson, 1948), p. 313. In another somewhat similar promotional stunt that same summer (July 19, 1947), Kazan accompanied Peck and McGuire to Darien, where they performed for the local residents a scene from their upcoming film.

14. Ciment, *Kazan on Kazan*, p. 57. Stuart Byron and Rubin Martin, "Elia Kazan" (Interview), *Movie* 19 (Winter 1971–72): 3.

15. Elliot E. Cohen, "Mr. Zanuck's 'Gentleman's Agreement': Reflections on Hollywood's Second Film about Anti-Semitism," *Commentary* 5 (Jan. 1948): 51.

16. *Variety*, Aug. 18, 1948, p. 3.

17. Ciment, *Kazan on Kazan*, p. 60.

18. *Commonweal* 51 (Oct. 14, 1949): 15.

19. *Dramatics*, Dec. 1949, p. 18.

20. Gussow, *Don't Say Yes*, p. 148.

21. Schumach, "A Director Named 'Gadge,'" *New York Times Magazine*, Nov. 9, 1947, p. 56.

Taking Charge

1. Virginia Stevens, "Elia Kazan," *Theatre Arts* 31 (Dec. 1947): 21.

2. Before the play opened, Wolfe Kaufman, the Studio's publicity agent, announced that this play "was felt to be unlikely fodder for the commercial Broadway machine." "Actors Studio Makes Its Bow on Broadway," *New York Times*, Sept. 5, 1948, II, I.

3. Michael Delahaye, "A Natural Phenomenon: Interview with Elia Kazan," *Cahiers du Cinéma in English* 9 (March 1967): 10–11.

4. Michel Ciment, *Kazan on Kazan* (New York: Viking Press, 1974), p. 32.

5. Kenneth Thorpe Rowe, *A Theatre in Your Head* (New York: Funk & Wagnalls, 1960), p. 50.

6. Ibid., p. 44.

7. Ibid., p. 51.

8. Ibid., p. 49.

9. Ibid., p. 45–46.

10. Ibid., p. 47.

11. Ibid., p. 49.
12. Ibid.
13. Ibid., p. 48.
14. Ward Morehouse, "Keeping up with Kazan," *Theatre Arts* 41 (June 1957): 22.
15. John Gassner, "Death of a Salesman: First Impressions, 1949," in *The Theatre in Our Times* (New York: Crown Publishers, 1954), pp. 364, 366.
16. Richard Murphy to Thomas H. Pauly, July 2, 1978. See also *Variety*, April 21, 1948, p. 3. Kazan would return to this material years later in his novel *Acts of Love*.
17. Kazan describes the nature of this collaboration in Bernard R. Kantor, Irving R. Blacker, and Anne Kramer, *Directors at Work: Interviews with American Filmmakers* (New York: Funk and Wagnalls, 1970), p. 154.
18. Richard Murphy to Thomas H. Pauly, July 2, 1978.
19. Ciment, *Kazan on Kazan*, p. 65.
20. *Commonweal* 52 (Aug. 18, 1950): 460.
21. Frederick Ricci, "An Analysis of the Directing Techniques of Elia Kazan in Theatre and Film as Illustrated in *A Streetcar Named Desire*" (Ph.D. diss., Columbia University, 1974), p. 112.
22. Murray Schumach, *The Face on the Cutting Room Floor: The Story of Movie and Television Censorship* (New York: William Morrow, 1964), p. 73.
23. Ibid., p. 74.
24. Ibid., p. 75.
25. During the first week of filming, this controversy was still unresolved, but Brando told the *New York Times* that during the rape scene he would not be allowed to pick up Blanche. *New York Times*, Aug. 27, 1950, II, 5.
26. Quoted in Ricci, "Directing Techniques," pp. 116–17.
27. Ibid., p. 117. This revision was Kazan's idea. Williams suggested a quite different one that was finally rejected. "In the Script: *A Streetcar Named Desire*," *Sight and Sound*, 21 (April–June 1952): 173–75.
28. Elia Kazan, "Pressure Problems," *New York Times*, Oct. 21, 1951, II, 5.
29. Schumach, *The Face on the Cutting Room Floor*, p. 71.
30. Ibid., p. 79.

"Man of Individual Conscience"

1. Cobbett Steinberg, *Reel Facts: The Movie Book of Records* (New York: Random House, 1978), p. 371.
2. For a fuller discussion of this resurgence of the Biblical epic and the nature of its middle-class appeal, see Thomas H. Pauly, "The Way to

Salvation: The Hollywood Blockbuster of the 1950s," *Prospects* 5 (1980): 467–87.

3. Quoted in Walter Goodman, *The Committee: The Extraordinary Career of the House Committee on Un-American Activities* (New York: Farrar, Straus, Giroux, 1964), p. 172.

4. John Cogley, Table 15 in *Report on Blacklisting I: Movies* (New York: Fund for the Republic, 1956), pp. 282, 284.

5. Kenneth L. Geist, *Pictures Will Talk: The Life and Films of Joseph L. Mankiewicz* (New York: Scribner's, 1978), pp. 173–206.

6. Ibid., p. 191.

7. David Caute, *The Great Fear: The Anti-Communist Purge under Truman and Eisenhower* (New York: Simon and Schuster, 1977), p. 499.

8. In his testimony before HUAC on April 10, 1952, Kazan acknowledged that he supported the position of the Hollywood Ten at the time of the 1947 hearings and had donated $500 to fund their defense. To a charge his name was listed as supporting a radio program for the Ten in late August, 1950, he replied, "I am surprised at the date. It is possible that I was approached and gave permission to use my name as late as this, but it seems to me more likely that my name was reused without asking me, since I had allowed its use earlier." *Thirty Years of Treason: Excerpts from Hearings before the House Committee on Un-American Activities, 1938–1968,* ed. Eric Bentley (New York: Viking Press, 1971), p. 491.

9. Harold Clurman, *All People Are Famous* (New York: Harcourt Brace, Jovanovich, 1974), p. 139.

10. Paul J. Vanderwood, "An American Cold Warrior: *Viva Zapata!* in *American History/American Film: Interpreting the Hollywood Image,* ed. by John E. O'Connor and Martin A. Jackson (New York: Frederick Unger, 1979), pp. 185–87. See also Robert E. Morsberger, "Steinbeck's Screenplays and Productions" in John Steinbeck, *Viva Zapata!: The Original Screenplay,* ed. Robert E. Morsberger (New York: Viking Press, 1975), pp. 133–34.

11. *Saturday Review* 35 (April 5, 1952): 22.

12. Ibid.

13. This was a major point of agreement among Kazan, Steinbeck, and Zanuck when the project was first launched. For a discussion of the pressure Darryl Zanuck put on Kazan and Steinbeck to develop the "entertainment" aspects of the film in the later drafts. See Vanderwood, "An American Cold Warrior: *Viva Zapata!*" pp. 191–93.

14. *New York Times,* June 17, 1951, II, 5.

15. *Saturday Review* 35 (April 5, 1952): 22.

16. These scripts are to be found in the archives of Twentieth Century–Fox, Los Angeles, California, except for the manuscript follow-up to the first draft continuity, which is held by the Humanities Research Center, University of Texas, Austin, Texas (hereafter cited as HRC).

17. *Saturday Review* 35 (April 5, 1952): 22.

18. John Steinbeck, "Zapata," undated ms., without page numbers, HRC.

19. Steinbeck and Kazan experimented with several interim endings. In the first, young students in a school named after Zapata are heard singing that he is not dead—an ending strongly reminiscent of that of *Pinky*. The other aborted endings are variations of this idea of Zapata being an indestructible spirit.

20. *New York Times*, April 12, 1952, p. 7.

21. Bentley, *Thirty Years of Treason*, pp. 493–94.

22. This statement, which appeared in *New York Times*, April 12, 1952, p. 7, is reproduced in Bentley, *Thirty Years of Treason*, pp. 482–84.

23. *Harvard Crimson*, May 15, 1952, pp. 1–2. See also *New York Times*, May 15, 1952, p. 39.

24. Thomas Fensh, *Steinbeck and Covici: The Story of a Friendship* (Middlebury, Vermont: Paul S. Eriksson, 1979), pp. 181–82.

25. Elia Kazan, "Where I Stand," *Reader's Digest* 61 (July 1952): 45–46.

26. Michel Ciment, *Kazan on Kazan* (New York: Viking Press, 1974), p. 108. In his sympathetic, philosophical condemnation of Kazan—and all the other members of the entertainment world who named names for the HUAC investigators—Victor Nevasky presents a somewhat different, more critical picture of Kazan's defensiveness in *Naming Names* (New York: Viking Press, 1980), pp. 199–223.

27. *Harvard Crimson*, May 15, 1952, p. 2.

28. Interview with Harold Clurman, by Thomas H. Pauly, May 20, 1979.

29. Caute, *The Great Fear*, pp. 508–509.

30. "Kazan Talks," *Time* 59 (April 21, 1952): 106.

31. *Nation* 174 (April 26, 1952): 394.

32. *Steinbeck: A Life in Letters*, ed. Elaine Steinbeck and Robert Wallsten (New York: Viking Press, 1975), p. 450.

33. *Nation* 174 (April 26, 1952): 394.

34. *Thirty Years of Treason*, p. 486.

35. *Harvard Crimson*, May 15, 1952, p. 2.

36. Thomas B. Morgan, "Elia Kazan's Great Expectations," *Harper's* 225 (Sept. 1962): 74.

37. Lewis Gillenson, "Man of the Theatre," *Harper's Bazaar*, Nov. 1951, p. 134.

38. George Tabori, "An Age of Wanderers," *New York Herald Tribune*, March 9, 1952, IV, 1.

39. Quoted in Aline B. Louchheim, "Tabori's Flight into Reality," *New York Times*, March 9, 1952, VI, 18.

40. *Variety*, April 23, 1952, p. 51.

41. *New York Times*, March 30, 1952, II, 1.

42. Twentieth Century–Fox production file for "Man on a Tightrope," Twentieth Century–Fox, Los Angeles, California, and *Variety,* March 12, 1952, p. 4.

43. *New York Herald Tribune,* May 31, 1953, IV, 1, 3.

44. Williams describes his view of Kilroy in an unpublished introduction to the play written back in 1946, HRC.

45. *Saturday Review* 36 (March 28, 1953): 25.

46. *New York Times,* March 15, 1953, II, 1.

47. Unpublished letter from Elia Kazan to Tennessee Williams, Nov. 17, 1952, HRC.

48. Tennessee Williams, "Afterword," *Camino Real* (New York: Dramatists Play Service, 1953), p. 8.

49. Unpublished letter from Molly Kazan to Tennessee Williams, Dec. 9, 1952, HRC.

50. *New York Times,* March 15, 1953, II, 1.

51. *Saturday Review* 36 (March 28, 1953): 26.

52. *Variety,* May 23, 1953, p. 69.

53. Memo from Darryl F. Zanuck to Philip Dunne, March 12, 1953, Philip Dunne Collection, Library, University of Southern California, Los Angeles, California.

54. Memo from Darryl F. Zanuck to Philip Dunne, May 7, 1953, Philip Dunne Collection.

Comeback

1. Unpublished letter from Elia Kazan to Robert Anderson, Playwrights' Company Papers, Wisconsin State Historical Society, Madison, Wisconsin.

2. Unpublished letter from Elia Kazan to Barbara Bel Geddes, Aug. 7, 1953, Playwrights' Company Papers.

3. Press release for *Tea and Sympathy,* Theatre Library, Lincoln Center for the Performing Arts, New York City.

4. *New Republic* 129 (Oct. 19, 1953): 21.

5. Michel Ciment, *Kazan on Kazan* (New York: Viking Press, 1974), p. 35.

6. *New York Herald Tribune,* Oct. 11, 1953, IV, 1. See also the original review by Walter Kerr for the *New York Herald Tribune* and Brooks Atkinson for the *New York Times* in *New York Theatre Critics' Reviews: 1953,* pp. 267 and 269. The reviews of the pre-Broadway run in Washington particularly stressed the delicacy of Kazan's staging.

7. Ciment, *Kazan on Kazan,* p. 105.

8. Arthur Miller, "Notebook for 'The Hook,'" p. 1, Humanities Research Center, University of Texas, Austin, Texas (hereafter cited as HRC).

9. Arthur Miller, "The Hook," unpublished screenplay, p. 65, HRC.

10. Miller, "The Hook," Cover, HRC.

11. Ciment, *Kazan on Kazan*, pp. 102–3.

12. At the same time that Schulberg wrote this script, RKO made tentative commitments to "The Hook" and a film adaptation of *The Harder They Fall* as part of an ambitious production slate based on "the city desk idea." Six months later, as the industry scrambled to fight the competition of T.V., these plans were scrapped in favor of an all color program.

13. In an article prepared for the premiere of *On the Waterfront*, Schulberg wrote that he and Kazan originally planned to collaborate on a film that had something to do with "the strange ways of justice in a town I knew." Budd Schulberg, "Waterfront: From Docks to Film," *New York Times*, July 11, 1954, II, 5. Roger Tailleur is often cited for having observed how the experiences of Kazan and Schulberg with HUAC influenced *On the Waterfront*'s glorification of a stool pigeon. Actually Tailleur derived his point from Eric Bentley. See "On the Waterfront" in *What Is Theatre?* (London: Dennis Dobson, 1957), pp. 98–102.

14. Schulberg's evolving view of his material is reflected in an article he wrote for the *New York Times* while he was revising his script. In this he opened: "Here's the forgotten fact: it is this basic insecurity—breeding fear, dependence, shiftlessness, demoralization—that feeds the power of this mob." In stressing how the corrupt leadership had falsely labeled the efforts at reform as the work of Communists, Schulberg characterized the longshoremen as "loyal, God-fearing Americans" who have "nothing to do with ideologies." Budd Schulberg, "Joe Docks, Forgotten Man of the Waterfront," *New York Times*, Dec. 28, 1953, VI, 3 and 30.

15. Schulberg, "Waterfront: From Docks to Film," p. 5.

16. Ciment, *Kazan on Kazan*, p. 121, and Delahaye "A Natural Phenomenon: Interview with Elia Kazan," *Cahiers du Cinéma in English* 9 (March, 1967): 31.

17. Kazan and Osborne developed this scene from a reference in one of the few conversations Steinbeck allows Cal and Abra. See John Steinbeck, *East of Eden* (New York: Viking Press, 1952), p. 500.

18. Interview with Paul Osborne, by Thomas H. Pauly, May 7, 1978.

19. Michel Ciment and Roger Tailleur, "Entretien avec Elia Kazan" *Positif* 79 (Oct. 1966): 14.

20. Stuart Byron and Martin Rubin, "Elia Kazan," *Movie* 19 (Winter 1971–72): 8.

21. Unpublished letter from Elia Kazan to Tennessee Williams, Aug. 1954, HRC.

22. Tennessee Williams, "Note of Explanation" in *Cat on a Hot Tin Roof* (New York: New Directions, 1955), pp. 151–52.

23. Ciment, *Kazan on Kazan*, p. 40.

24. Tennessee Williams, "Cat on a Hot Tin Roof," original manuscript, HRC, pp. 95–105. Tennessee Williams, "Cat on a Hot Tin Roof," in the

Robert Downing Collection, HRC, Act II, pp. 38–47A (Downing was stage manager for the Broadway production).

Tennessee Williams, "Cat on a Hot Tin Roof," Playwrights' Company Papers, Act II, pp. 38–43. In order to establish more clearly that Brick was guilty not of a homosexual inclination but an excessive idealization of his friendship with Skipper, Williams modified Maggie's earlier account of Brick's relationship with Skipper.

25. Tennessee Williams, *Cat on a Hot Tin Roof* (New York: New Directions, 1955), pp. 91–92.

26. Unpublished letter from Tennessee Williams to Elia Kazan, Nov. 23, 1954, HRC.

27. Williams, "Cat on a Hot Tin Roof," original ms., HRC, p. 135.

28. These are all held by HRC. One page of the manuscript is written on stationery from the St. James Hotel in Philadelphia, where *Cat* opened its out-of-town run.

29. *Saturday Review* 38 (April 9, 1955): 32.

30. Elia Kazan, "Look, There's the American Theatre," *Tulane Drama Review* 9 (Winter 1964): 69.

31. See unpublished letter from Elia Kazan to Barbara Bel Geddes, Aug. 7, 1953, Playwrights' Company Papers.

32. *Waterfront*, no. 8, Budd Schulberg Papers, Firestone Library, Princeton University, New Jersey. With this script there are loose-leaf pages of two alternative endings that were never used. When Budd Schulberg wrote his novelization of *Waterfront*, he retained his original ending.

33. Kazan has said, "Terry Malloy felt as I did." Ciment, *Kazan on Kazan*, p. 110.

Quest for Self-Expression

1. Quoted from the Catholic Legion of Decency's condemnation. See the *New York Times*, Nov. 28, 1956, p. 32.

2. These preliminary versions are contained in the Williams Papers at the Humanities Research Center, University of Texas, Austin, Texas.

3. Michel Ciment, *Kazan on Kazan* (New York: Viking Press, 1974), p. 74. Kazan once told a French interviewer, "He [Williams] did not even write *Baby Doll*. It was I who assembled the script from previously written pieces, added a detail here and there and gave it form." Jean Domarchi and André S. Labarthe, "Entretien avec Elia Kazan," *Cahiers du Cinéma* 130 (April 1962), p. 10.

4. Unpublished letter from Tennessee Williams to Elia Kazan, July 23, 1955, HRC.

5. Elia Kazan, "Paean of Praise for *A Face in the Crowd*," *New York Times*, May 26, 1957, II, 5.

6. *Time* 68 (Dec. 24, 1956): 61.

7. Arnold Maremont, "Why Men Become Angels: Investment in the Theatre: Business or Philanthropy?" *Saturday Review* 40 (Feb. 23, 1957): 11–14.

8. Phyllis Anderson, "Diary of a Production," *Theatre Arts* 34 (Nov. 1950): 58.

9. John Gassner, *Theatre at the Crossroads: Plays and Playwrights of the Mid-Century American Stage* (New York: Holt, Rinehart and Winston, 1960), p. 172.

10. Gerald Weales, *American Drama since World War II* (New York: Harcourt, Brace and World, 1962), p. 42.

11. Robert Brustein, "The Men-Taming Women of William Inge," *Harper's* 217 (Nov. 1958): 52–53.

12. "Boris Aronson," *Working with Kazan* (Middletown, Conn.: Wesleyan University Press, 1973), no page given.

13. *New York Times*, May 4, 1958, II, 1.

14. "The Staging of a Play," *Esquire* 51 (May 1959): 146.

15. Five pages of Kazan's detailed suggestions were not printed, but a comparison of the original *J.B.* with the Broadway version published in the Feb. 1960 issue of *Theatre Arts* (pp. 33–64) suggests what they would have been.

16. "The Staging of a Play," pp. 146, 148.

17. Ibid., p. 150.

18. *New York Times*, April 24, 1958, p. 37.

19. "The Staging of a Play," p. 144.

20. Ibid., p. 150.

21. The original *J.B.* is composed of eleven scenes. Kazan proposed that the play be split into two acts with completely continuous action in each. "The Staging of a Play," p. 144.

22. *New York Times*, April 17, 1956, p. 27. See also *Theatre Arts*, 40 (Aug. 1956): 66–67.

23. Unpublished letter from Tennessee Williams to Audrey Wood, July 23, 1956, HRC. See also *New York Times*, March 12, 1959, p. 26.

24. *New York Times*, March 12, 1959, p. 26.

25. *New Yorker* 35 (March 21, 1959): 98–100.

26. *Saturday Review* 42 (March 28, 1959): 26.

27. *Nation* 188 (March 28, 1959): 281–8.

28. *Kazan on Kazan*, p. 131.

29. *New Republic* 145 (Oct. 16, 1961): 21.

30. *New Yorker* 37 (Oct. 14, 1961): 177.

31. *Time* 78 (Oct. 13, 1961): 95.

32. *New York Times*, April 28, 1960, p. 29.

33. *New York Times*, Oct. 8, 1961, p. 53.

34. Kenneth Tynan, "Dilemma of the Theatre," *Holiday* 26 (Oct. 1959): 176.

35. *Best Plays of 1961–62*, ed. Henry Hewes (New York: Dodd, Mead and Co., 1962), p. 3.

36. *New York Times*, April 7, 1961, p. 26.

37. Ibid.

38. Ibid.

39. Elia Kazan, "Theatre: New Stages, New Plays, New Actors," *New York Times*, Sept. 23, 1962, 6:2, p. 18.

40. Robert Brustein, "Repertory Fever," *Harper's* 221 (Dec. 1960): 51.

41. Arthur Miller, "Foreword to *After the Fall*" in *The Theatre Essays of Arthur Miller*, ed. Robert A. Martin (New York: Viking Press, 1978), p. 257.

42. William Goyen, "After the Fall of a Dream," *Show* 4 (Sept. 1964): 45.

43. *Newsweek* 64 (Nov. 9, 1964): 92.

44. Frederic Morton, "Gadg," *Esquire* 47 (Feb. 1957): 123.

45. *New York Times*, April 7, 1961, p. 26.

46. Morton, "Gadg," p. 123.

47. Ciment, *Kazan on Kazan*, p. 129.

48. Stuart Byron and Martin Rubin, "Elia Kazan," *Movie* 19 (Winter 1971–72): 12.

49. Ciment, p. 155.

Bibliography

Performances

Stage

Chrysalis by Rose Albert Porter. (Louis.) Martin Beck Theatre, Nov. 15, 1932 (23 performances).

Men in White by Sidney Kingsley. (Orderly.) Broadhurst Theatre, Sept. 26, 1933 (311).

Gold Eagle Guy by Melvin Levy. (Polyzoides.) Morosco Theatre, Nov. 28, 1934 (65).

Waiting for Lefty by Clifford Odets. (Clancy.) Civic Repertory Theatre, Jan. 5, 1935 (3).

Waiting for Lefty by Clifford Odets. (Agate.) And *Till the Day I Die* by Clifford Odets. (Baum.) Longacre Theatre, March 26, 1935 (96).

Paradise Lost by Clifford Odets. (Kewpie.) Longacre Theatre, Dec. 9, 1935 (73).

Johnny Johnson by Paul Green. (Private Kearns.) 44th Street Theatre, Nov. 19, 1936 (68).

Golden Boy by Clifford Odets. (Eddie Fuseli.) Belasco Theatre, Nov. 4, 1937 (250). (Also Joe Bonaparte in 1938–39 tour.)

The Gentle People by Irvin Shaw. (Eli Lieber.) Belasco Theatre, Jan. 5, 1939 (141).

Night Music by Clifford Odets. (State Takis.) Broadhurst Theatre, Feb. 22, 1940 (20).

Liliom by Ferenc Molnar. (Ficzur—"The Sparrow.") 44th Street Theatre, March 25, 1940 (56).

Five Alarm Waltz by Lucille Prumbs. (Adam Boguris.) Playhouse Theatre, March 13, 1941 (4).

Film

Café Universal. Nykino, unreleased and possibly never assembled.

Pie in the Sky. (Tramp.) Nykino, May 1935.

City for Conquest. (Googie.) Warner Bros., Sept. 1940.

Blues in the Night. (Nickie Harayon.) Warner Bros., Dec. 1941.

265

Productions Directed

Stage

The Second Man by S. N. Behrman. Toy Theatre, Atlantic City, 1931.

Dimitroff by Elia Kazan and Art Smith. (Co-directed by Art Smith.) Civic Repertory Theatre, June 1, 1934.

The Young Go First by Peter Martin, Charles Scudder, and Charles Friedman. (Co-directed by Alfred Saxe.) Park Theatre, May 28, 1935 (23).

The Crime by Michael Blankfort. (Co-directed by Alfred Saxe.) Civic Repertory Theatre, March 1, 1936 (3).

Casey Jones by Robert Ardrey. Fulton Theatre, Feb. 19, 1938 (25).

Quiet City by Irwin Shaw. Belasco Theatre, April 16, 1939 (2).

Thunder Rock by Robert Ardrey. Mansfield Theatre, Nov. 14, 1939 (23).

It's Up to You by Arthur Arendt. Traveling production sponsored by Department of Agriculture, 1941.

Café Crown by Hy S. Kraft. Cort Theatre, Jan. 23, 1942 (141).

The Strings, My Lord, Are False by Paul Vincent Carroll. Royale Theatre, May 19, 1942 (15).

The Skin of Our Teeth by Thornton Wilder. Plymouth Theatre, Nov. 18, 1942 (359).

Harriet by Florence Ryerson and Colin Clements. Henry Miller Theatre, March 3, 1943 (377).

One Touch of Venus by S. J. Perelman and Ogden Nash. Imperial Theatre, Oct. 7, 1943 (295).

Jacobowsky and the Colonel by S. N. Behrman. Martin Beck Theatre, March 14, 1944 (417).

Sing Out, Sweet Land by Jean Kerr and Walter Kerr. International Theatre, Dec. 27, 1944 (102).

Deep Are the Roots by Arnaud D'Usseau and James Gow. Fulton Theatre, Sept. 26, 1945 (477).

Dunnigan's Daughter by S. N. Behrman. Golden Theatre, Dec. 26, 1945 (38).

Truckline Café by Maxwell Anderson. (Only producer.) Belasco Theatre, Feb. 27, 1946 (13).

All My Sons by Arthur Miller. (Also co-producer.) Coronet Theatre, Jan. 29, 1947 (328).

A Streetcar Named Desire by Tennessee Williams. Ethel Barrymore Theatre, Dec. 3, 1947 (855).

Sundown Beach by Bessie Breuer. Belasco Theatre, Sept. 7, 1948 (7).

Love Life by Alan Jay Lerner. 46th Street Theatre, Oct. 6, 1948 (252).

Death of a Salesman by Arthur Miller. Morosco Theatre, Feb. 10, 1949 (742).

Flight into Egypt by George Tabori. Music Box Theatre, March 18, 1952 (46).

Camino Real by Tennessee Williams. National Theatre, March 19, 1953 (60).

Bibliography

Tea and Sympathy by Robert Anderson. Ethel Barrymore Theatre, Sept. 30, 1953 (712).

Cat on a Hot Tin Roof by Tennessee Williams. Morosco Theatre, March 24, 1955 (694).

The Dark at the Top of the Stairs by William Inge. (Also co-producer.) Music Box Theatre, Dec. 5, 1957 (468).

J.B. by Archibald MacLeish. ANTA Theatre, Dec. 11, 1958 (364).

Sweet Bird of Youth by Tennessee Williams. Martin Beck Theatre, March 10, 1959 (375).

After the Fall by Arthur Miller. ANTA Theatre, Jan. 23, 1964 (208).

But for Whom Charlie by S. N. Behrman. ANTA Theatre, March 12, 1964 (47).

The Changeling by Thomas Middleton and William Rowley. ANTA Theatre, Oct. 29, 1964 (32).

Film

People of the Cumberland. Co-directed with Robert Stebbins, Eugene Hill, and William Watts, Pioneer Films, 1937.

A Tree Grows in Brooklyn. Twentieth Century–Fox, Feb. 1945.

Sea of Grass. MGM, March 1947.

Boomerang. Twentieth Century–Fox, March 1947.

Gentleman's Agreement. Twentieth Century–Fox, Nov. 1947.

Pinky. Twentieth Century–Fox, Oct. 1949.

Panic in the Streets. Twentieth Century–Fox, Aug. 1950.

A Streetcar Named Desire. Twentieth Century–Fox. Sept. 1951.

Viva Zapata! Twentieth Century–Fox, Feb. 1952.

Man on a Tightrope. Twentieth Century–Fox. May 1953.

On the Waterfront. Horizon Films, July 1954.

East of Eden. Warner Bros., March 1955.

Baby Doll. Newtown Productions, Dec. 1956.

A Face in the Crowd. Newtown Productions, June 1957.

Wild River. Twentieth Century–Fox, June 1960.

Splendor in the Grass. Newtown Productions, Oct. 1961.

America America. Warner Bros., Dec. 1963.

The Arrangement. Athena Enterprises, Nov. 1969.

The Visitors. Chris Kazan–Nick Proferes Productions, Feb. 1972.

The Last Tycoon. Paramount, Dec. 1976.

Publications

Novels

America America. New York: Stein and Day, 1962.

The Arrangement. New York: Stein and Day, 1967.

The Assassins. New York: Stein and Day, 1971.
The Understudy. New York: Stein and Day, 1974.
Acts of Love. New York: Alfred Knopf, 1978.
The Anatolian. New York: Alfred Knopf, 1982.

Articles (in chronological order)
"The Common Element in the Drama." Unpublished thesis, Williams College, June 1930.
Kazan, Elia, and Art Smith. "Dimitroff." *New Theatre* 1 (July/Aug. 1934): 20–24.
"The Director's Playbill." *New York Herald Tribune*, Sept. 12, 1943, 5–6: 1, 3.
"Audience Tomorrow: Preview in New Guinea." *Theatre Arts* 29 (Oct. 1945): 568–77.
Kazan, Elia, and Harold Clurman. "To the Theatre Going Public." *New York Herald Tribune*, March 1, 1947, p. 17.
"Notebook for *A Streetcar Named Desire*." In *Directing the Play*, edited by Toby Cole and Helen Krich Chinoy. New York: Bobbs Merrill Co., 1953, pp. 296–310.
"About Broadway and the Herring Catch." *New York Times*, Oct. 16, 1949, p. 23.
"Entr'acte" (letter to Editor). *Theatre Arts* 31 (June 6, 1947): 10–11.
"Long, Long Ago." *Theatre Arts* 34 (Sept. 1950): 39.
Excerpts from Elia Kazan's "Notebooks for *Death of a Salesman*." In Kenneth Thorpe Rowe, *A Theatre in Your Head*. New York: Funk and Wagnalls, 1960, pp. 44–59.
"Pressure Problem." *New York Times*, Oct. 1951, II, 5.
Letter (on *Viva Zapata!*). *Saturday Review* 35 (April 5, 1952): 22.
"Testimony before House Committee on Un-American Activities." In *Thirty Years of Treason: Excerpts from Hearings before the House Committee on Un-American Activities 1938–68*, edited by Eric Bentley, pp. 484–95. New York: Viking Press, 1971.
"A Statement." *New York Times*, April 12, 1952, p. 7. Reprinted in *Thirty Years of Treason*, pp. 482–84.
"Where I Stand." *Reader's Digest* 61 (July 1952): 45–46.
"Movie That Had To Be Made." *New York Herald Tribune*, May 31, 1953, IV, 1, 3.
"Writers and Motion Pictures." *Atlantic Monthly* 199 (April 1957): 67–70.
"The Staging of a Play." *Esquire* 51 (May 1959): 144–57. (Reprints Kazan's letters to MacLeish on *J.B.*)
"Paean of Praise for A Face above the Crowd." *New York Times*, May 26, 1957, II, 5.
"Ten Best for a Repertory Theatre." *New York Times Magazine*, Nov. 9, 1958, pp. 74–75.

Bibliography

Preface to *Seen Any Good Films Lately?* by William K. Zinsser, pp. 11–14. New York: Doubleday, 1958.

"Theatre: New Stages, New Play, New Actors." *New York Times*, Sept. 23, 1962, 6:2, 18.

"In Quest of the Dream." *New York Times*, Dec. 15, 1963, II, 9.

"Pursuit of the Usey-less." *Williams Alumni Bulletin* 57 (Nov. 1964): 4.

"Process Development of Repertory, or a Team Needs Patience and Years." *World Theatre* 14 (Jan. 1965): 85.

On What Makes a Director, pp. 6–22. Los Angeles: Directors Guild of America, 1973.

"All You Need to Know, Kids." *Action* 9, no. 1, (Jan.–Feb. 1974): 4–11.

"Inside a Turkish Prison." *New York Times Magazine*, Feb. 4, 1979, pp. 33–35, 48–51. Also letter to *New York Times Magazine*, March 11, 1979, pp. 122.

Interviews

"A Quiz for Kazan." *Theatre Arts* 40 (Nov. 1956): 30–32, 89.

"An Interview: Elia Kazan." *Equity* 42 (Dec. 1957): 10–13.

Kazan, Elia. "What Makes a Woman Interesting?" *Vogue* 140 (Jan. 1962): 27–28.

"Candid Conversation with Elia Kazan." *Show Business Illustrated* 2, no. 2 (Feb. 1962): 26–27.

Domarchi, Jean, and Andre S. Labarthe. "Entretien avec Elia Kazan." *Cashiers du Cinema* 130 (April 1962): 1–18.

Kazan, Elia. "Look, There's the American Theatre." *Tulane Drama Review* 9 (Winter 1964): 61–83.

"Elia Kazan Ad-Libs on *The Changeling* and Its Critics: A Show Soliloquy." *Show* 5 (Jan. 1965): 39–41.

Ciment, Michel, and Roger Tailleur. "Entretien avec Elia Kazan." *Positif* 79 (Oct. 1966): 1–17.

Delahaye, Michael. "A Natural Phenomenon: Interview with Elia Kazan." *Cahiers du Cinema in English* 9 (March 1967): 12–39.

Tavernier, Claudine. "Entretien avec Elia Kazan." *Cinema* 70 (Nov. 1970).

Byron, Stuart, and Rubin Martin. "Elia Kazan," *Movie* 19 (Winter 1971–72): 1–13.

"Elia Kazan." In *Directors at Work: Interviews with American Filmmakers*, edited by Bernard R. Kenton, Irwin R. Blacker, and Anne Kramer, pp. 150–73. New York: Funk and Wagnalls, 1970.

O'Brien, Glenn. "Interview with Elia Kazan." *Inter/View* 20 (March 1972): 10–13, 44.

Ciment, Michael. "Entretien avec Elia Kazan. Sur 'The Visitors.'" *Positif* 138 (May 1972): 29–37.

Silver, Charles, and Joel Zucker. "Visiting Kazan: An Interview," *Film Comment* 8 (Summer 1972): 15–19.
Leroux, A. "Elia Kazan et les multiples visages de l'Amerique." *Cinema Que* 2, no. 4 (Dec.–Jan. 1972–73): 27–33.
Ciment, Michael. *Kazan on Kazan.* New York: Viking Press, 1974.
"Dialogue on Film: Elia Kazan." *American Film* 1, no. 5 (March 1976): 33–48.

Selected Works Relevant to Kazan's Life and Career

Anderson, Lindsay. "The Last Sequence of *On the Waterfront.*" *Sight and Sound* 24 (Jan.–March 1955): 127–30.
Anderson, Robert. "Walk a Ways with Me." *Theatre Arts* 38 (Jan. 1954): 30–31.
Archer, Eugene. "Elia Kazan—The Genesis of a Style." *Film Culture* 2, no. 2 (1956): 5–7, 21–24.
———. "Genesis of a Genius." *Films and Filming* 3, no. 3 (Dec. 1956): 7–9.
———. "The Theatre Goes to Hollywood." *Films and Filming* 4, no. 1 (Jan. 1957): 13–14.
Ardrey, Robert. "Writing for the Group." *New York Times,* Nov. 19, 1939, X, 3.
Basin, Andre. "A l'est d'Eden." *Avant-Scene* 163 (Nov. 1975): 3–26, 43–63.
Bean, Robin. "Elia Kazan on 'The Young Agony.'" *Films and Filming* 8, no. 3 (March 1962): 26–27, 43.
———. "The Life and Times of Elia Kazan." *Films and Filming* 10 (May 1964): 35–41.
Bentley, Eric. "On the Waterfront." In *What Is Theatre?* pp. 98–102. London: Dennis Dobson, 1957.
Biskind, Peter. "The Politics of Power in *On The Waterfront.*" *Film Quarterly* 29 (Fall 1975): 25–38.
Brustein, Robert. "America's New Culture Hero: Feelings without Words." *Commentary* 25 (Fall 1958): 123–29.
———. "The Men-Taming Women of William Inge." *Harper's* 217 (Nov. 1958): 52–57.
Callahan, J. F. "The Unfinished Business of *The Last Tycoon.*" *Literature/Film Quarterly* 4, no. 3 (Summer 1978): 204–13.
Campbell, R. "The Ideology of the Social Consciousness Movie: Three Films of Darryl F. Zanuck." *Quarterly Review of Film Studies* 3 (Winter 1978): 49–71.
Changas, E. "Elia Kazan's America." *Film Comment* 8 (Summer 1972): 8–14.
Clurman, Harold. *The Fervent Years: The Story of the Group Theatre and the Thirties.* New York: Hill and Wang, 1957.

Bibliography

Cohen, Elliott E. "Mr. Zanuck's *Gentleman's Agreement*: Reflections on Hollywood's Second Film about Anti-Semitism," *Commentary* 5 (Jan. 1948): 51–56.

Collins, Gary. "Kazan in the Fifties." *The Velvet Light Trap* 11 (Winter 1974): 41–45.

Corliss, Richard. "The Legion of Decency." *Film Comment* 4, no. 4 (Summer 1968): 25–61.

Cowie, Peter. "Elia Kazan." In *50 Major Film Makers*, pp. 132–37. South Brunswick, N.J.: A. S. Barnes, 1975.

Ditsky, John. "Words and Deeds in *Viva Zapata!*" *Dalhousie Review* 56 (1976): 125–31.

Dundy, Elaine. "How to Succeed in the Theatre without Really Being Successful." *Esquire* 13 (May 1965): 88–91, 153–58.

Dunne, Philip. "An Approach to Racism." *New York Times*, May 1, 1949, II, 5.

Eustis, Morton. "The Director Takes Command, II." *Theatre Arts* 20 (April 1936): 277–80.

Frankel, H. "Son of the Oven Maker." *Saturday Review* 50 (March 4, 1967): 26.

Gassner, John. *Dramatic Soundings: Evaluations and Retractions Culled from Thirty Years of Dramatic Criticism.* New York: Crown Publishers, 1968.

Giannetti, Louis. "*America America*: The Cinema of Elia Kazan." In *Masters of the American Cinema*, pp. 333–53. Englewood Cliffs, N.J.: Prentice-Hall, 1981.

Gillenson, Lewis. "Man of the Theatre." *Harper's Bazaar* (Nov. 1951): 134, 205–10.

Goldstein, Malcolm. *The Political Stage: American Drama and Theatre of the Great Depression.* New York: Oxford University Press, 1974.

Hamilton, William. "On the Waterfront." *Film Music* 14 (Sept.–Oct. 1954): 3–15.

Hey, Kenneth. "Ambivalence as a Theme in *On the Waterfront* (1954): An Interdisciplinary Approach to Film Study," *American Quarterly* 31, no. 5 (Winter 1979): 666–96.

————. "On the Waterfront: Another Look." *Film and History* 9, no. 4 (Dec. 1979): 82–86.

Himmelstein, Morgan Yale. *Drama Was a Weapon: The Left-Wing Theatre in New York, 1929–41.* New Brunswick, N.J.: Rutgers University Press, 1963.

Hughes, Robert. "*On the Waterfront*: A Defence and Some Letters." *Sight and Sound* 24, no. 4 (Spring 1955): 214–16.

"In the Script: *A Streetcar Named Desire*." *Sight and Sound* 21 (April–June 1952): 173–75.

Isaacs, Hermine Rich. "First Rehearsals—Elia Kazan Directs a Modern Legend." *Theatre Arts* 28 (March 1944): 143–50.

271

Bibliography

Johnson, Malcolm. *Crime on the Waterfront*. New York: McGraw-Hill, 1950.

"Kazan, Elia." *Current Biography, 1948*. New York: H. H. Wilson, 1949, pp. 336–38.

"Kazan, Elia." *Current Biography, 1972*. New York: H. H. Wilson, 1973, pp. 249–52.

"Kazan, Elia." *Contemporary Authors*. Detroit: Gale Research Co., 1969, vol. 21–24: 471–73.

Kitses, Jim. "Elia Kazan: A Structural Analysis." *Cinema* 7, no. 3 (Winter 1972–73): 25–36.

Kracauer, Siegfried. "Those Movies with a Message." *Harper's* 196 (June 1948): 567–72.

Meyer, Nancy, and Richard Meyer. "*After the Fall*: A View from the Director's Notebook." In *Theatre, Annual of the Repertory Theatre of Lincoln Center*, edited by Barry Hyams. New York: Hill and Wang, 1965.

Miller, Arthur. "Arthur Miller Ad-Libs on Elia Kazan," *Show* 4 (Jan. 1964): 55–56, 97.

———. "The Year It Came Apart," *New York* 8 (Dec. 30, 1974–Jan. 6, 1975): 30–44.

Morehouse, Ward. "Keeping Up with Kazan." *Theatre Arts* 41 (June 1957): 90–91.

Morgan, Thomas B. "Elia Kazan's Great Expectations." Harper's 225 (Sept. 1962): 66–68, 71–75.

Morton, Frederic. "Gadg!" *Esquire* 47 (Feb. 1957): 49, 118–22.

Movie 19 (Winter 1971–72). Whole issue devoted to Kazan.

Pettit, Arthur. "*Viva Zapata!* A Tribute to Steinbeck, Kazan, and Brando." *Film and History* 7 (May 1977): 25–45.

Poling, James. "Handy 'Gadget.'" *Collier's* 129 (May 31, 1952): 56–60.

Sarris, Andrew. "Less Than Meets the Eye: Elia Kazan." In *Directors and Directions 1929–1968*, pp. 158–59. New York: E. P. Dutton, 1968.

Schechner, Richard. "New York: Sentimentalist Kazan." *Tulane Drama Review* 9 (Spring 1965): 194–98.

Schulberg, Budd. "*Waterfront*: From Docks to Film." *New York Times*, July 11, 1954, II, 5.

———. Afterword to *On the Waterfront: A Screen Play*, pp. 141–53. Carbondale, Ill.: Southern Illinois University Press, 1980.

———. "Why Write It When You Can't Sell It to the Pictures?" *Saturday Review* 38 (Sept. 3, 1955): 5–6, 27.

Schumach, Murray. "A Director Named 'Gadge.'" *New York Times Magazine*, Nov. 9, 1947, pp. 18, 54–56.

———. *The Face on the Cutting Room Floor: The Story of Movie and Television Censorship*. New York: William Morrow, 1964.

Steinbeck, John. *Viva Zapata!: The Original Screenplay*. Edited by Robert E. Morsberger. New York: Viking Press, 1975.

Stevens, Virginia. "Actor and Director of Stage and Screen." *Theatre Arts* 31 (Dec. 1947): 18–22.

Tailleur, Roger. "Elia Kazan and the House Un-American Activities Committee." *Film Comment* 4, no. 1 (Fall 1966): 43–58.

Thacher, Molly Day. "Why Improvise?" *New Theatre* I (March 1935): 14–15.

"Three Directors in Danger." *Cinema* 1, no. 6 (Nov.–Dec. 1963): 4–9.

Tynan, Kenneth. "American Blues: The Plays of Arthur Miller and Tennessee Williams." *Encounter* 2 (May 1954): 13–19.

Williams, Jay. *Stage Left.* New York: Charles Scribners, 1974.

Williams, Tennessee. "Note of Explanation" in *Cat on a Hot Tin Roof,* pp. 151–52. New York: New Directions, 1955.

Working with Kazan. Edited by Jeanine Basinger, John Frazer, and Joseph W. Reed, Jr. Middletown, Conn.: Wesleyan Film Program, 1973.

Vanderwood, Paul J. "An American Cold Warrior: *Viva Zapata!*" In *American History/American Film: Interpreting the Hollywood Image,* edited by John E. O'Connor and Martin A. Jackson, pp. 183–201. New York: Frederick Unger, 1979.

Yacowar, Maurice. *Tennessee Williams and Film.* New York: Frederick Unger, 1977.

Zolotow, Maurice. "Viewing the Kinetic Mr. Kazan." *New York Times,* March 9, 1952, pp. 1, 3.

Dissertations on Kazan

Clark, Leroy Watson. "The Directing Practices and Principles of Elia Kazan." Kent State University, 1976.

Lee, Carolyn Ann. "An Analysis of the Cinematic Elements in Selected Films of Elia Kazan, 1952–1962." University of Michigan, 1976.

Ricci, Frederick. "An Analysis of the Directing Techniques of Elia Kazan in Theatre and Film as Illustrated in *A Streetcar Named Desire.*" Columbia University, 1974.

Schueneman, Warren Walter. "Elia Kazan: Director." University of Minnesota, 1974.

Todras, Arthur. "The Liberal Paradox: Clifford Odets, Elia Kazan, and Arthur Miller." University of Indiana, 1980.

Index

Index